CITA

by EDWARD SANDERS

Poem from Jail (1963)

Peace Eye (1966)

The Family: The Manson Group and Aftermath (1971, New Edition 1990)

Egyptian Hieroglyphics (1973)

Tales of Beatnik Glory, Volume 1 (1975)

Investigative Poetry (1976)

20,000 A.D. (1976)

Fame & Love in New York (1980)

The Z-D Generation (1981)

The Cutting Prow (1983)

Hymn to Maple Syrup & Other Poems (1985)

Thirsting for Peace in a Raging Century: Selected Poems 1961–1985 (1987)

Poems for Robin (1987)

Tales of Beatnik Glory, Volumes 1 & 2 (1990)

Hymn to the Rebel Cafe (1993)

Chekhov (1995)

1968: A History in Verse (1997)

America: A History in Verse: Volume 1, 1900–1939 (2000)

EDWARD SANDERS

AMERICA
A HISTORY IN VERSE

VOLUME I 1900–1939

BLACK SPARROW PRESS · SANTA ROSA · 2000

ACKNOWLEDGMENTS

Parts of this book appeared in the *Woodstock Journal* and in the pamphlet *Arise, o Wobblies* published by Boog Literature. The Introduction was published as a letterpress broadside by Kavyayantra Press in Boulder, Colorado.

Thanks to Annette Roberts for the considerable help in research, to Austin Metze for scanning the images, to Eric Goldman for the loan of Franklin Roosevelt's papers, to Susanne Toth for the information on Einstein, to Gary Snyder for the gift of Cadillac Desert, to Justin Veach for the help with Cuba and Germany, and to Miriam Sanders for the insight that research is an every-living-moment activity.

Black Sparrow Press books are printed on acid-free paper.

LIBRARY OF CONGRESS CATALOGING-IN-PUBLICATION DATA

Sanders, Edward
   America: A History in Verse, Volume 1, 1900–1939 / Edward Sanders
     p.   cm.
   1-57423-117-0 (paperback)
   1-57423-118-9 (cloth trade)
   1-57423-119-7 (signed cloth)
Library of Congress Catalog Card Number: 00-130490

4/8/2001

Table of Contents

Seething Nation! Vast & Flowing!
Day & Night & Dawn!

I know the story of America
is a million stranded fabric
        woven by billions of hands & minds

On any little aspect of America
You could write a 1,000-page book
It's such a data-retentive time

There's one history of America
        in a nearby library
                in 24 volumes!

So I apologize for anything
a reader might find completely important
                that I have left
                        from my trembling weave.

I love the way my nation seethes
I love its creativity
& the flow of its wild needs
                to build itself
                on a tiny place
                in a spiral galaxy
                        called the Milky Way.

I love my nation's music
the 43-note scale of Harry Partch
the genius of Charlie Mingus & Lenny Bernstein
the mumbling square-backed guitar of Bo Diddley
the bebop sax of Bird
Gershwin, Dylan, Phil Ochs, Bonnie Raitt
Stephen Foster, Charles Ives, Phil Glass
Joan Baez, Janis Joplin, Jimi
      & others too many
          to list in this opening chant.

I love the poets of my song-soul'd Land
& I love its unsung geniuses
        resting in the sod
I love all the good things so many millions have done
          to make a Better World.

I dwell especially
      by your creeks & forests O America
I revel in your glens & dells
your cliffs & deserts

I love all your species O America
        flaws & claws.

I know of course
      I have to trace the
        violence of my nation
& that unsettles me

"*Arma virumque cano,* that's the story of America,"
Miriam said
      when I told her I was writing this book

It's true that arms & bloodshed
        too often tint the time-track
but it's also true
      the Nation shakes aside the violence
         & shines.

And who am I, someone could ask, to write
a history of America?
I am a bard
      trained with my every breath
         for 41 years

to chant & sing, whisper, shout, keen, dance with joy
                              & try to trace with grace

what the Fates & Human Mammals have wrought
                              in the Time-Track of America

& now my time arrives
          to grasp my sunflower walking stick
                              to speak my nation

Seething Nation! Vast & Flowing
Day & Night & Storm!

AMERICA *a history in verse*

VOLUME 1
1900–1939

The century began
        with the war against Spain
and the grabbing of the Philippines
                in '98 & '99

for the issues & secret whispers of destiny
                        there arrayed
remained with the nation
        the next one hundred years.

The gore of th' Civil War
was thirty-five years in the past
& some in America
        were shoving for markets and might

The navy in particular was eager to get more ships
        surge through sea lanes
                patrol more harbors

William McKinley was president since '96
and his forty-year-old
        assistant secretary of the navy
                one Teddy Roosevelt
had already published a four-volume
                Winning of the West

Roosevelt had the high metabolism of a hamster
                and part of him always
                tried to shove the nation to battle

In '97 he confided to a pal:
        "I should welcome almost any war
        for I think this country needs one."

(It was a clear synecdoche of Roosevelt's serial aggression:
that is, confusing his own
                impulsivity to violence
                        with the nation's)

Whatever he was
  he set a good part of the tone
                of the first 20 years.

The nation was already attuned to conquering.

On the Great Plains
        'tween '60 & '10
the Indian villages were decimated
by the U.S. Army
      so that the railroads,
                then the farmers
      could grab the best of the land

The Indians were beaten now &
          the continent solely seized—
Go West could now be *Go to the World*
So many had come to America
          from so many lands
dissenters, rebellious sons,
          stomped-down daughters
             yearning for yes
that maybe it was time to assemble
          beneath the
to sail forth more or less unified
to the seas of their progenitors

      The USA was filled with debate
      Some wanted imperialist expansion
      Others opposed foreign colonies
      while some just wanted Open Borders
          in other nations
      so as to grab up resources
          and sell stuff back & forth
            in a trade-batty frenzy

    what Howard Zinn calls
    the "peaceful development of free trade"
          —a gourd of words with razors inside

    for some in power just cannot live
          without a little war
    to tinge the trade

    Didn't everybody do it?
    Look at the unseemly invasions of Africa
          by the seething nations of Europe
          or the graceless droolings of the same
            to section ancient China
              as if she were a quarter of beef

It was a spectacle
        to make a *nouveau riche* nation
                tremble with envy:
England, France, Germany, Denmark, the Netherlands
shoving their way
        through the streets
           of pliant nations

A War in Cuba

Cuba was discovered by Columbus on his first voyage
Velazquez conquered the isle in 1511
& the Spanish had owned it ever since

In '95 a rebellion began
        against a cruel & ruthless, multi-century
                Spanish colonial system
                and a hated network
                of "Friars" that
                      treated the Cubans like dirt.

Some in the US
thought that the Cuban revolt against Spain
        had Holy Freedom aspects of 1776

but other empire-empirical types
such as the young Winston Churchill
wanted Spain to keep control

He'd written an article in the *New Republic*
that since ⅖ of the Cuban insurgents were black
the result, shudder shudder,
        could be "another black republic"

—referring of course to Cuba joining Haiti
the first nation run by blacks in the New World.

Hundreds of thousands of Cubans
        from the rural areas
        were forced into concentration camps
by a general named Valeriano Weyler.
        The Hearst & Pulitzer papers
           began to shriek at the
                Spaniards in Cuba as evil

A new, more liberal regime in Spain came to power in '97
It promised autonomy to the Island
                    (with Spain still having the ultimate say)

The American consul general in Havana, Fitzhugh Lee,
                              a promoter of intervention
urged sending the battleship *Maine* to Havana
          to lurk in the harbor
                    as a banner of national power
or to aid in the safety of Americans
          in case of chaos
                    if the rebels should toss out the Spanish

          Meanwhile America had things to sell
          "War is a bloody good biz"
          said th' steel magnates of Pa.
               (ships & cannons)
          said the lumber kings
               (big forests in Cuba to grab)
          th' gunmakers
               (rifles, cannons, stabbing devices)
          and Massachusetts cloth
               (uniforms, bandages!)

Why not stomp the mean-souled men of Spain
                              out of Cuba?

So, when on February 15, '98 the *Maine* blew up and sank
                              with 268 dead
the US public was inflamed and assumed Spain had done it

There were two competing reports:
one from Spain that said the cause was an
                    internal flaw in the *Maine*
                         (unstable gunpowder stored next to coal bunkers)
but the US told its people the attack
                    was a subsurface mine.

Terror has its silence
& so the case is open
                    a hundred years later
                              over who did what

(In 1976 US Admiral Hyman Rickover
published a study
    that the ship had most likely been sunk
                    from a fire in a coal bunker

that caused five tons of powder nearby to explode
taking out the forward third of the ship)

──────────────── **Yellow Journalism** ────────────────

They say it was a war brought on in part
                by Yellow Journalism—
You know how the NY City television stations
                 focus on slaughter & murd?

      That's how the newspapers focused
                    at century's turn

      America has such excitable people
      maybe it's in the genes
           of those who'd strayed here
                  from so many worried lands

      Yellow J works like an
                amphetamine of aggression
      to rile up the masses
         REMEMBER THE MAINE, TO HELL WITH SPAIN!
                    was a rhyme of the time.

      "Surely the people is grass," the prophet Isaiah sang
      ("because the spirit of the Lord bloweth upon it")

      whereas the mine owner says
                "the Masses are Asses"
      & Yellow J knows that hoi polloi ὁι πολλοί
           can be coaxed
                pretty quickly
                    to torches and pitchforks.

      It was the era that showed
                how the sharp serifs of journalism
                    make nations bleed

On February 18
William Randolph Hearst's
   New York American
published an extra edition

with the headline   **WHOLE COUNTRY THRILLS**
               WITH THE WAR FEVER YET THE
               PRESIDENT SAYS 'IT WAS AN ACCIDENT'

Yellow J was perceived
          as riling public hatred
    against McKinley
          for not declaring war
till the Republicans were worried
the Democrats would use it
          to pound the drums of the masses

———————————— **The Antique Empire of Spain** ————————————

Meanwhile 7,000 miles away in the Philippines
          insurgents there were also fighting Spain
led by a guerrilla leader named Emilio Aguinaldo.

On his own the
    Assistant Secretary of the Navy
told Captain George Dewey
commander of the Eastern fleet in Hong Kong
that if war were declared
    he was to steam to Manila
          to tear down the Spanish fleet.

Meanwhile a Senator from Vermont
          named Redfield Proctor
had visited Cuba
    & issued a report on conditions

He said more than 400,000 were still in concentration camps
with much starvation

        The skulls of evil were stretching single file
        from the camps of Cuba
          all the way to the
          paste-up rooms of the Hearst & Pulitzer papers

The Senator gave a speech
            on March 17

        A war was needed, he said, to protect American property
        & prevent them dang
                    leftist rebels
                            from taking over!

April 11
        McKinley sent a message to Congress asking for war:

        He said the USA was "a Christian, peace-loving people"
                    but that
        "In the name of humanity, in the name of civilization,
        in behalf of endangered American interests
        which give us the right and duty
                    to speak and to act, the war in Cuba must stop"

April 19
        US Congress recognized Cuban independence
        and called on the Spanish to leave

        (the US tended to snub
                    the Cuban rebels
                never treated them as equals
                            or talked to them at all)

April 20
        Congress in a joint resolution gave McKinley
                            "the power to intervene"

        The Senate added the Teller Amendment to the resolution:
"That the United States hereby disclaims any disposition to exercise
sovereignty, jurisdiction, or control over said island, except for the
pacification thereof, and asserts its determination when that is
accomplished to leave the government and control of the island to its
people."

                Teller was a Senator from Colorado
                His Amendment to the
                            intervention resolution
                was a good tactic to calm American liberals
                        and anti-imperialists

Songs are sometimes the prolegomenon to bloodshed
as in the House of Representatives
        the night they voted
                the war-smitten shout-sang "Dixie" and
                        the "Battle Hymn of the Republic"

——————————— **The Anti-Imperialist League** ———————————

The year of the Spanish War
        the Anti-Imperialist League was formed
—a peculiar American mix of intellectuals, trade unionists, writers,
prominent biz types (including Andrew Carnegie)
        scholars such as Charles Eliot Norton of Harvard,
                plus "antilabor aristocrats" and thousands of liberals

who shook their head in disgust at the
                maim-minded shoving for markets,
                        & the mangled borders of nations

The novelist William Dean Howells, for instance
opposed the war
        spoke out
                became pres of th'
                Anti-Imperialist League

He called himself a socialist
as he aged
        instead of toryizing (the more usual path).

Just as Hardy returned to verse in his old age
in Howells it brought out his radical vision.

The cold, genius eye of Mark Twain too
                took in the
                restless moans
                        of the Border Bashers
the laughable groveling for money
        & the religion-spouting murderous fists
                        of mercantile misery—

Though at first he supported
        the stomping of Spain from Cuba

Twain later became a vice president
                              of the A-I League

                              •

On 4-22
T. Roosevelt resigned as Secretary of the Navy,
                    to lead a volunteer cavalry called the "Rough Riders"

            He ordered himself a Lieutenant-Colonel's uniform from
            Brooks Brothers
            the color o' blue, and
                        no yellow on the collar, please—

            perhaps he didn't want the the hue of flee
                                        to tinge his glee.

            Americans of many kinds
            miners, cowboys, cops, college students *et alia multa*
            held up their hands
                        to join the Rough Rider regiment

───────────────────── **A Picnic War** ─────────────────────

On the first of May
the US Navy under Captain Dewey
                    attacked the Spanish ships in Manila harbor
                                        the Philippines

His steam ships puffed
                back and forth
                        sinking and destroying

till the Spanish surrendered
with only 6 Americans hurt, none seriously
            though 381 Spanish troops were "killed and wounded"

The yellow press and many Americans swooned in a kind of
            wargasm
as the troops went ashore
            and took Manila August 13

—————————————— **Then Cuba** ——————————

The 9th & 10th Cavalry were
                black units known for their kill-skills
                                in the Indian Wars
The 9th & 10th were taken to a staging ground in Tampa
                                to get ready for Cuba

where even though they were the best of soldiers
                stood trapped in the whim webs of dribble-headed crackers

as when in Tampa a rumor
that drunken white sailors had used a black child
                                for target practice

triggered a riot for several days
                with 27 blacks and 3 whites hurt.

Meanwhile June 10 came
& the Americans invaded at Guantánamo Bay
                        but their horses never arrived

Nor did they arrive by June 24
the first land battle at Las Guásimas in Cuba
                        near the harbor of Santiago.

Just about the first ashore
        were the Rough Riders
                and the 9th & 10th black cavalry

        There were scads of reporters
                        including Stephen Crane

        The horseless Rough Riders
                sang a ditty
                        as they charged ashore:

                Rough, rough, we're the stuff
                We want to fight, & can't get enough!
                        Whoopee!

        It wasn't a Pope-level couplet
                        but Pope isn't needed to stir a risk-taking vim.

22

The Spanish soon fled their positions
& the Rough Riders & their horseless cavalry
reached the hilltop
            & the Battle of Las Guásimas
                        shouted shut.

Sixteen Americans were dead
            in the first fight of th' picnic war

July 2
——————— **The Battle of San Juan Hill** ———————

A few days later the Americans
arrived at the rings of guns
            around Santiago itself

Late that morn
it was very, very warm
in the thick-grown jungle

        as 5,000 Americans
                    began to sharpshoot
the Spanish strongpoint on San Juan Hill

Rapid-fire Gatling-guns
                were brought to the sharpshoot
                in the afternoon

so that the Rough Riders & the black cavalry
could stealth-stalk
            through high grass
                    clump by clump
                            in the Gatling distractions

up to the hilltop
till, darkness surrounding,
            the Americans won the ground.

July 3
Battle of Santiago Bay

The Spaniards retreated to Santiago itself
and on July 17
       24,000 surrendered

& on the 24th
the Spanish gov't asked for peace
       and the picnic war was over

It was something the nation seemed always ready to tolerate—
a war where the deaths were few
       In Cuba just 379
       & the grief therefore contained
       in a huge nation's disparate pockets

& most of the more than 274,000 American troops
surged home in joy and youthful triumph

The Grabbing of Hawaii

In the midst of the war
in July o' '98
       the "issue" of Hawaii came up

The Hawaiian Isles
       known as the Sandwich Islands
          had been a target of Christian missionaries
some of whom had become big time pineapple farmers
          & in effect ran the Islands

One Sanford Dole
       (you know, Dole Pineapple)
          was the President of Hawaii at the time

Some were anxious that the Germans
       who were looking for Pacific islands
          might seize Mr. Dole's hegemony zone.

The imperialists
       wanted to grab it

such as the Senate Foreign Relations Committee
which recommended
                    seizing the Sandwiches posthaste

Others wanted America
            to stay within her borders
                        true to her nonmalignant destiny–

It was a big debate
and one that would not really be resolved
                        for the next 100 years

                    •

        In late September
        there was a huge celebration
        & a parade up 5th Avenue

        The Rough Riders
        gave TR the Frederic Remington bronze
                        named *The Bronco Buster*

        To his credit he publicly thanked the black troops for their bravery
        yet the heroes he praised
                    could not get served
                        in the restaurants of the south
                                    upon their return

        while the white troops
        feasted free of chit

————————————— **The War Hero Moves Forward** —————————

The NY Republican machine
chose Teddy to run for governor that fall

He was on everyone's mind
                    and swept the race.

And then in December
the Treaty of Paris was signed with Spain

McKinley couldn't grab Cuba
                    because of Teller

but he insisted on Puerto Rico, Guam & the Philippines

Cuba was to be occupied
      by an American force
            till such time the nation okayed
            a compliant "independent" gov't

The US gave Spain $20 million
                    to ease the pain.

The war was now just a thing of ink and pride
& tough American big biz types
began taking the Cuban railroads, mines and sugar plantations

      United Fruit went into sugar
            bought 1.9m acres for 20¢ an acre
                  and Bethlehem Steel grabbed up most of Cuba's minerals

It became in effect a vassal state of
              the USA

Meanwhile the Treat of P
            had to be ratified by ⅔ of the US Senate

There was fierce opposition
till finally the populist Democrat William Jennings Bryan

urged passage
      in order to put the war in the past

so that, slimly, the Treaty was passed
               on February 6, '99.

      (Bryan later ran for president
      with part of his platform
            to give the Filipinos their freedom)

——————— **The War Against the Philippines** ———————

The Filipino insurrectos
      did not want one 400-year set of slavers
      replaced by another

so in February of '99
        rose up against the American conquistadores

Emilio Aguinaldo was still their leader

He proposed a Filipino independence within a US protectorate
but the US refused.

There was a big debate in the Congress
        over the seizing of the Philippines

                a glut of harumphing on Destiny
                                and Civ'
                greed-driven chitchat about
                                scads of cash
                and how we good Protestants
                        have to imbue the savages
                                with our mores, stories & stores

The mercantile interests were mumbling the
                4/4 Sousa of sell sell sell sell:

first stuff to Philippines
        then stuff to China

hemp, tobacco, coffee, sugar, coconuts, rice:
        the booty of the Philippines
                plus make them
                        worship a Protestant Christ

There were sputtery tsk-tsks on the ways of "orientals."
McKinley
        wanted to "Christianize" the Filipinos
                who mostly were Catholics
(Some in the self-proud American Protestant power structure
        felt Catholics were not really Christians
                        as weird as that may seem)

Their Cosmos was this:
The Reformation alone held the candles of God
                        & those who won the Civil War
                                owned the wax

The decision to go to war in Manila

might not have occurred
had not William Jennings Bryan
voted okay at the last minute

The US fired first
to set off a 1,000 days of blood & blot

──────────────── **The Anti-Imperialist League** ────────────

Against this paternal/imperial chant
the well-placed group of Americans
known as the Anti-Imperialist League
tried its best
to educate the people
on the threat imperialism posed to the nation

William James was one of the prominent intellectuals
associated with the League

They published
the real story of the Philippine slaughter
the torture & evil blood
throughout the nation.
Of course—publishing
and stopping a war
are often unequal
for
ink & blood
forge a tarrying font

──────────────────── **Racism** ────────────────────

It took till '02 to stomp down the Filipinos
with 70,000 US troops
& thousands of battle deaths
with My Lai–level slaughter

One American general told a major that
the age limit for killing was "Everything over ten."

Gen Arthur MacArthur
(father of Douglas)

28

led the US troops
and, shades of Vietnam, was reluctant to admit
            the insurgents had the support of much of the populace

There were many reports of ugly racism
                        against the Filipinos
& the US was stenched with violent racism inside itself.

Howard Zinn notes
            how every week 'tween '99 and '03 on the average,
            two blacks were lynched in the USA by
                        by evil-addled mobs—

And in the Philippines
there was plenty of chances for racists to spit and revile
                        as they shot and stabbed

Such things do not vanish
            but whisper from mind to mind
with the karma of the Philippines '99
            wending all the way to Vietnam '68

Gore, slaughter, subjugation, evil—
            not mentioned in most of the text books
                        then or now

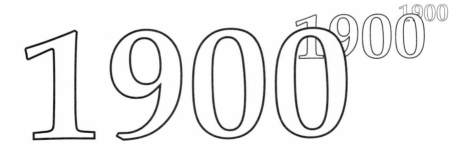

            America's seething century began
            with 75 million souls
                        and 6 million farms–

            Horses were still the main mode of travel
            and photos of '00 show broughams, carts and carriages,
            corn wagons, bundling parties

                    & the steamy nostrils of hippic sleighs
          till the Iron Heart began to pulse
                          with ground-drawn fuel

                    no websites
                    no cell phones
                    no nukes
                    no planes
                    no pavement
                    no radio
                    no tube
                    —sound like paradise? (It wasn't)

                    women could vote in only 4 states
                              & children worked long hours in mines

          You could get around the nation on trains
                              & there were steam engines on ships.
          Gas was the main energy
                    for appliances & street lights
                              till after '10.

     In February
          Andrew Carnegie
                    scribbled the amount he wanted
                              for his various steel companies
          at a dinner party

          (The history books aren't quite clear on the exact amount
          but it was something like $250 million)

          so that J. P. Morgan, in a matter of weeks
                    could set up the trust known as U.S. Steel

          enabling Carnegie in '01 to donate $5.2 million to found the
          NY Public Library.

     There may be a great library named after him also
     but Morgan was not much

          He dodged the
          draft
          in th' Civil War
                    giving $500 to a stand-in

then during the war
bought 5,000 defective rifles
                                        $3.50 each
then sold them to a general for
$22 per

They'd shoot off the thumbs of firing soldiers
                    —a fact not engraved on any of his monuments

March 2
    Kurt Weill was born

March 14
    Congress passed a Currency Act
                        —a gold standard for US currency
            that paper and other moolah
                            be redeemable in gold

On April 30 McKinley signed a bill organizing
    the Hawaiian Islands as a Territory of the US.

    Executive power was given to a governor
                    to be appointed by the President.

Over in France that year
            the work day for women and children
                                was limited to eleven hours

            in the inescapable pathway to 8

    & Arthur Evans discovered the Bronze Age marvels at Knossos
    leading to his four-volume work, *The Palace of Minos*

———————————————— **Casey** ————————————————

Casey Jones
was at the head of the Cannonball Express
at 3:52 the morning of 4-28
                    tracking through Mississippi

There was a stalled train
                    around a bend

What e. e. cummings later called the Worm Farm
                           was lifting its hatch

Casey got his fireman to jump
             and slowed enough to save his passengers

then himself was headoned
            and died a legend

•

The Beauty of Unions

Oh Unions!
Rise from the pain
Rise from the misery
Rise from the cruelty
        of angry owners

The International Ladies' Garment Workers Union was founded—
    to do something about
           women toiling 70 hours a week for 30¢ a day
    in airless sweatshops

Unions were determined to reach the masses.

That same year the American Federation of Labor
              was founded from 216 unions

Rise, O Unions, Rise

Eyeballing China

Countries with things to sell
kept eyeballing
      the 400,000,000 humans of China

(just as 99 years later they trembled
at the concept of selling
      1 billion refrigerators to China)

France, Germany, Japan, England,
          and the upstart USA

                                        thinking maybe they
                                              could cut it up
                    like shortcake at a church social.

The British and Americans
wanted something
              called the Open Door policy
                          in China

─────────────────── **The Boxer Rebellion** ───────────────

China had been ruled by the Empress Tzu Hsi
                          since 1861
She had a fierce dislike for
                    the nations of Europe.

There'd been a multi-century xenophobia already
                    and then, since late in the 1890s
                    a fear of Euro-shove
              when Russia, Germany & England
                          had taken land in China's north.

A secret society of young Chinese was formed
                                    called Yi He Tuan
              —translated as the Society of Harmonious Fists–
              AKA the Boxers

              dedicated to killing foreigners
                    and Christian converts

On June 21
              The Empress declared war
              on all the countries
                    hacking at her nation

And then on August 14
a force of troops from Japan, Russia, Germany, Britain, the US,
Austria-Hungary, & Italy
              sacked Beijing
                    and imposed what the textbooks call
                                    "harsh penalties"

          so that the drums began to thum thum thum

the fall of the mighty Ching dynasty
in power in China since the 1600s.

Manchuria was occupied by Russia
whose troops stayed behind as "railway guards"
(which helped lead in '04 to the Russo-Japanese War).

That same August
Nietzsche
passed from earth

In October Mark Twain returned from
several years in Europe

There were reporters at the docks
to scribe his remarks

He was upset with the war in the Philippines:
"I have seen that we do not intend to free,
but to subjugate,
the people of the Philippines.
We have gone there to conquer, not to redeem ...
And so I am an anti-imperialist.

I am opposed to having the eagle
put its talons on any other land."

Twain became a vp of th' Anti-Imperialist League of New York
& remained in the League for the rest of his life.

•

It was an election year
The "Hoosier poet" James Whitcomb Riley,
popular with the masses
wrote verse for
the presidential run of his good friend
Eugene Debs:

'An there's 'Gene Debs, a man 'at stands
An' jist holds up in his two hands
The kindest heart that ever beat
Betwixt here an' the jedgement seat.

The Republican VP had passed away
& when Teddy appeared at the convention wearing his wide-brimmed
Rough Rider hat

20k began to chant, "We want Roosevelt!"
throbbing in the nation's mind
for his fighting in Cuba

The Republicans ran on the prosperity ticket
"A Full Dinner Pail" was one of their mottoes

so that in November William McKinley picked up his second term
defeating William Jennings Bryan
who lost on a platform
condemning
Imperialism

7.2 million to 6.35 million
with the Socialist Debs getting 94,768
and John Woolley, the Prohibition candidate 209,166

November 30
46-year-old Oscar Wilde
passed away in Paris from encephalitis
from an ear infection

The yellowy sneer-press danced at his death
spitting at him for poverty
and hinting he'd killed himself.

December 28, Carrie Nation
smashed into a bar in Wichita,
chopped up furniture
and a oil painting by John Noble

Those were the months she toured Kansas bars
with her "Home Defenders Army"

In a lecture she said,
"You don't know how much joy you will have
until you begin to smash, smash, smash."

Carrie tore down

35

but others were more creative–
    Benjamin Holt of America invented the tractor!
        A hamburger came off the griddle in Connecticut

    the Kodak six-shot Brownie camera for $1
    plus the first textbook on limnology,
        (the biology and physical aspects/features of lakes)

    & rolled onto the linen of time:
    February 5, Adlai Stevenson   March 1, Basil Bunting
    October 3, Thomas Wolfe
    December 27, Marlene Dietrich

    Doubleday censored the sex & swearing
        out of Theodore Dreiser's first novel, *Sister Carrie*

    Chekhov finally finished his *Three Sisters* late in the year
    Joseph Conrad, *Lord Jim*
    & Frank Baum, *The Wonderful Wizard of Oz.*

        Seethe onward, o Century!

On 1-27
    the streets by the Grand Hotel in Milan
    were covered with straw
            so carriages might not disturb
                    the great composer

    on his thanatothalamium

    Giuseppe Verdi
            who passed that day

Five days before the great Verdi
Queen Victoria
            had gone to the soil.

            The stolid, ultraimperialist Victoria was gone
            & her rake-eyed
                        party boy son Ed VII
                                    began nine years
                                    of pre-war bassaridia, horse racing & fun.

It was the year the great water diversions
                                    in the West began–
On May 14
        The California Development Company
        finished a canal draining from th' Colorado River
                        running down 'tween California & Arizona
                                                            into Mexico

                to bring water into the Imperial Valley
                (then a desert)
                            suck suck slurp slurp cash cash.

Ragtime was hot that year but the
American Federation of Musicians
                    urged its members not play it.

The Socialist Party was formed in the US
            It seemed to millions that a formal
                        system of sharing could be built

September 2
                Vice President Roosevelt
                        came up with the Stick Motto
                            one of machismo's finest sentences:
                                "Speak softly and carry a big stick
                                            and you will go far"

        a very mnemonic apothegm from a West African tribe
                        though the people's memory stopped at "stick"

Then on the 6th
        a thin young man from Cleveland
                    named Leon Czolgosz

his hand wrapped up in bandages
to hide a gun

came up to William McKinley
at the Pan-American Exposition in Buffalo
and fired

Eight days later
the President died
singing, "Nearer My God to Thee"

Teddy was hunting in the Adirondacks
and rushed to Buffalo
to touch the Bible
at 42 the youngest to be sworn

The man from Cleveland was 24
and inked at once as an evil anarchist

"I killed the president," Leon Czolgosz said, "because he was the enemy
of the good people—the good working people."

(His father had belonged to the Polish branch
of the Socialist Labor Party)

It was learned that shortly before
he'd gone to Buffalo
he'd listened to a speech by Emma Goldman in Chicago
and, using a pseudonym,
had sought her out

The woman they called Red Emma
had to face the ghastliest sort of headline:

**ASSASSIN OF PRESIDENT MCKINLEY AN ANARCHIST.
CONFESSES HE WAS INCITED BY EMMA GOLDMAN.
WOMAN ANARCHIST WANTED**

Goldman was arrested in Chi
and grilled

Though most of the left condemned the killer
the publisher of *Mother Earth*

refused totally to separate herself from
               the young man so disturbed by the war
                             in the Philippines

      There was a big roundup of anarchists
      suspected of conspiracy

      and throughout the nation
      what the textbooks describe as an
                    "anti-immigrant hysteria"

Leon Czolgosz had purchased his Iver Johnson revolver
                    for $3.10 from the Sears catalogue

His final words before he was electrocuted
         on October 29, 1901,
               were to condemn the Philippines war,
                     plus three short sentences:
"I am an anarchist. I don't believe in marriage. I believe in free love."

October 16
Teddy Roosevelt invited the moderate black leader
         Booker T. Washington
principal of Tuskegee Inst.
             in Alabama

into the White House for advice on
         "African-American and Southern appointments,"
         which set off a vast klan-esque shudder of anger
                        in the cracker South.

Yet all in all a good year for genius:
         Thomas Hardy's *Poems of the Past and Present*
         Strindberg's *Dance of Death*
         the premiere of *Three Sisters*
                  at the Moscow Art Theater

then noon on the Cornish coast
         December 12th
         a guy tapped out three clicks
                on a transmitter

      which were heard 1,800 miles away
      in Newfoundland

by Guglielmo Marconi
through a speaker
he held to his ear

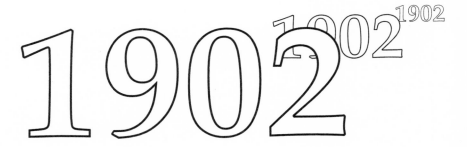

January 24
    Denmark agreed in principle to sell the Virgin Islands to the USA
        (The US wanted the islands
                    as part of a "walk softly/big stick"
                        guardway to the Panama Canal)

May 12–October 13
    United Mine Workers
    with 140k members
    went on strike in the coal fields of Pennsylvania

    unsafe conditions and low pay

    The Teddy Bear boy ended it in the fall
    by threatening to send soldiers to work the mines

    The owners o' th' mines
            agreed to the creation of a commission
                        to investigate the strikers' plight

    —the road to low pay is graveled with commissions.

May 20
    Cuba became an independent, yet compliant-
    to-American-business-interests nation
    (Don't forget that the US invaded or intervened in Cuba
                    in 1906, 1913, 1917, 1933, 1961)

It was the year
        Enrico Caruso
                laid down a few arias on newfangled gramophone disks
                (against his advisers' advice—so much for advisers)

                in a hotel room in Milan
                ten arias in two hours
                        with the accompanist sitting on a packing crate

                It was a big hit in London
                & ended the wax cylinder records of Thomas Edison

June 28
        The Isthmian Canal Act passed
                        allowing the financing o' th' Panama Canal

July 1,
        Congress passed the Philippine Gov't Act,
        declaring those islands an unorganized territory

September 28
        Émile & Alexandrine Zola arrived at their Paris apartment
        a bit damp and cold
                        so the coal fire in their bedroom was lit

        He was found the next day dead on the floor
        and she, being higher, on the bed, barely lived

        The right wing crowds that usually haunted him
                                with spits & derision
        stayed away from his funeral

        It's possible he was murdered
        since when they ran two tests on the stove & the room
        exactly as he had died
                        three guinea pigs survived
                                in cages on the floor
                                        where he had lain

1902
        the US government
        began a program o' irrigation
        modeled after the Mormons'

in Utah

A bureaucracy,
        the U.S. Bureau of Reclamation—
would build big tall dams
on the Colorado, Sacramento, Columbia, the Snake
& send aqueducts 100s of miles
            over desert & mntn
    to irrigate
            & provide power

It made
Arizona, Idaho, California
        rich

—————————————— **Muck** ——————————

Muckraking began in October!
with Lincoln Steffens' "Tweed Days in St. Louis"
                in *McClure's*

and then in November
    the first installment of Ida Tarbell's
            The History of the Standard Oil Company
                        also in *McClure's*

It was becoming clear
    that banks were more and more controlling things

& that business conglomerates
            were eating the economy.

        There was a big interest
                    for a few years
                        in articles
                            that laid bare the truth
                behind the harumphs

            though it allowed the smug & the liberal
            to blame the robber barons
                        rather than the system itself.

It was the same fall that Lev Davidovitz Bronstein
    escaped from Siberian exile to London

by doing the old leave-a-dummy-in-bed maneuver

He'd been in prison & in Siberia four years

He picked up a fake passport
            and called himself Trotsky
                        after the German for "defiance"

His nickname was "The Pen" in vanguard circles
                                    for his quick way with words.

When he showed up at Lenin's doorstep in London
he was welcomed by the future chairman's wife
                                    Nadezhda

who shouted, "The Pen has come!"

    It was also the year of the gas-powered lawnmower
    the first Rose Bowl game
    Lenin's *What Is To Be Done?*
                (Answer: *Dictatorship of the Proletariat*
                            though exactly what that preposition "of"
                            should mean
                                    never was really determined)

    Gustav Mahler's *Symphony #5*
                and Doyle's *Hound of the Baskervilles*

    plus uh-oh-time for human nature in
                        Joseph Conrad's *Heart of Darkness*

    William James *The Varieties of Religious Experience*
                (His philosophy was pragmatism—
                that in a complicated universe something is true if it is
                useful and consistent with "experience")

    It was the year Teddy Bears became popular after Roosevelt
                                    refused to shoot a baby bear

    Alfred Stieglitz curated "An Exhibition of American Photography
                arranged by the Photo-Secession"
                at the National Arts Club in New York City
                (Photo-Secession was meant to present photos
                as an art form

rather than mere point & click
at Aunt Mildred's wedding)

and the oldest known set of laws
The Code of Hammurabi was discovered at Susa in Iran

In January
a Colombian attaché in D.C.
inked a lease for perpetual use by the USA
of the ten-mile-wide canal zone

but afterward
Colombian gov't tarried too lengthily
in signing the formal agreement.

It should be recalled the canal
was at the time called the Colombian Canal

'03 was the year
the activist known as Mother Jones
organized a march of children
working at textile mills
revealing the evils of child labor

and the issue became an Issue.

Early in the year Jack London's *The Call of the Wild*
set in the Gold Rush of '97
brought him instant fame at 24
perfect for the first-fame
glorybuzz

when everybody is all smiles
                    to greet you at least once

The sort Chekhov got in '84
                    around the same age.

London was a socialist from his teens
& lectured across the country
                    on the evils of exploitative capitalism

Among his books:
People of the Abyss
    set in the English slums &
The Iron Heel
    an apocalyptic view of the rise of fascism.

He was too much a racist
    but identified with the
                    crushed outcasts of the system
& managed to mix his Marxism
            with a fascination for Social Darwinism.

His 15-hour writing periods
            rivaled George Sand's in length!

He helped get Sinclair's *The Jungle* published
        (after it was serialized in the socialist paper *Appeal to Reason*)

& his vehement, humorous description of a scab
            found its way into IWW songbooks

                              •

There was not much help from the US for a famine in
                                distant Russia

& when that Easter
there was a hideous pogrom
            (the Russian word for "devastation" or "massacre")
in Kishinev
        a town in Bessarabia in southeast Russia

the Russian Orthodox church
            did nothing to stop it

though they were begged.

49 were killed & 500 hurt
as the killers roamed
          the Jewish quarters
ripping up feather beds
                    looking for money
so that the streets
               flew thick with zigzagging pinions.

It's always a bit of a mystery
          why some evils trigger ink & uproar
                    & others nearly none
but news of the evil in Kishinev
          spread across Earth

—Pogroms occurred regularly from '03 to '06
and spurred emigration to the US and Palestine

May 2, Benjamin Spock was born
          who did more than any American
          to begin the multi-century path
               of cleansing the cruelty (passed on & passed on)
                    from the raising of children

———————————— **The LA Water Scheme** ————————————

The Owens Valley stretches many miles
     in a more or less southerly way
'tween the Sierra Nevada to the west and
          the Inyo Mountains and Death Valley to the east

Engineers from the U.S. Bureau of Reclamation
came to the Valley
          to help build an irrigation system—

The residents of the Owens Valley
who had grabbed the old irrigation system
                    the Paiutes had created

now looked to be
wealthy from

46

                a gov't assisted
                        irrigation system
                                w/ current technology

Meanwhile some rich & well-placed developers
                                (and developer-helpers) in LA
were eyeing the Owens Valley
                250 miles away
                as a source

They purchased water rights
                pretending they were developing a resort

    & began to sneak-seize the water
                in order to expand LA into the
                        San Fernando Valley
                                over land they were purchasing

        By the following year, 1904
        the LA water conspiracy
        began to succeed in turning th'
                        Owens reclamation project off.

        The newly formed LA City Water Company
        issued a report which said:
                "The time has come
                when we will have to
                supplement the supply
                        from some other source."

        The source was the Owens Valley
        where there was water enough
                in the Sierra snow-melt runoff
                        to feed a million showers
                                & lawnsprinklers in LA

    One water-suck, named Eaton,
    lied to landowners saying he represented
                        the Bureau of Reclamation

    You can read the fine book *Cadillac Desert*
                        by Marc Reisner

to gather the memory
                of the water-fibbers

(The developers
    and the water-grabbers
    have been skeletons for decades,
                        but here are some of them:
                Moses Sherman, trolley magnate
                Henry Huntington, another transportation greeder
                Edward Harriman, Union Pacific Railroad
                Harrison Gray Otis, of the *Los Angeles Times*
                Harry Chandler, *LA Times*

    & others in the power structure of Southern California
    from th' banks, railroads, newspapers, utilities, land developers)

They created an artificial water shortage
while the city bought up 40 miles of water rights

and on September 7, '05
        the bond to build the aquifer passed by a big margin in LA

——————————— **The Bolsheviks Are Formed** ———————————

From secret socialist groups
all over Russia
        delegates quietly came to Geneva in July
for the second congress of the
All-Russian Social Democratic Labor Party.
They kept apart from one another in public
and from the Russian émigré community
                        in Switzerland

The congress was soon adjourned to Brussels
but there were tsarist informers
and hostility from Brussels officialdom

        so the congress moved again,
                        with 57 delegates,
                                to London.

This was the congress that saw the famous split
'tween the Bolsheviks (Lenin's "majority")

and the Mensheviks

with Lenin winning out over L. Martov
                    by a slim margin
though on many issues
            Lenin's group was outvoted.

            The grim, stark
                    necessity of Revolution
            was brought
                    to the fork of Absolute Reality:

            Wage and hour reforms wd never be enough—
            the Answer was Rev.

    Ergo, the socialists would have to work
                        apart from the circuits of th'
                                    regular unions.

    The Party structure would be centralized
    with membership limited to those fully trained in Marxism

    & Mr. Lenin was given control of
                    the party paper *Iskra* (*The Spark*)

                        •

In October of '03
    President Teddy Roosevelt
    stealth-agitated with Panamanian nationalists
                to forge an uprising in th' isthmus

            It worked

    In November the nationalist army declared an independent Panama
    while US ships on November 2 stopped Colombian troops from
                        landing and quelling the Pan revs

    "I took Panama," Teddy later said.

October 22
    The Amalgamated Copper Co of Montana closed its doors
    with more than half the workers of Montana out of work,
            in "a bitter labor dispute"
                    to use the pain-masking parlance of historians

November 6
    US recognized th' independence of Panama
    and on the 18th
    US signed th' Hay-Bunau-Varilla Treaty,
        allowing US total control over the Canal Zone

        though it was later noted that
        no actual Panamanian signed the 1903 treaty

        The country's rep had been a Frenchman
                        close to those who had failed
                            in the previous attempt
                                by a French company to build the canal.

    Work to finish the 40 miles of locks began in 1904.

November 18
    Warships steamed to Nicaragua after 2 Americans, plus 100s
    of Nicaraguan revs, were killed by dictator Jose Santos Zelaya

December 1,
    The first western, *The Great Train Robbery*
                        was filling theaters

O. Henry's "The Gift of the Magi" was published
O. Henry had lived in NYC since let out of prison in Texas in '01
                penning his famous flow of American tales
                            w/ a Coleridgean indifference
                                    to the flow of cash

─────────────────── **Kitty Hawk** ───────────────────
December 17

    It was morning in the dunes of a lonely beach
                        near Kitty Hawk, N.C.
    when a couple of bicycle mechanics from Dayton, Ohio,
                Orville and Wilbur Wright, shook hands.

Cold wind-spurts blew
        Orville strapped himself face-down
        by wire, cloth and struts
                of a biplane called the *Flyer*
                        propelled by a tiny motor

but the first try flopped to the beach

Then, at noon, the fourth try—
        Wilbur got up to an altitude of 15 feet
& slipped o'er the strand for a 10th of a mile
                then thud-landed

a 59 second trip
        to make mere Icarus a myth

though at the time just 3 newspapers inked the act.

W.E.B. Du Bois *The Souls of Black Folk*
Helen Keller *The Story of My Life*
        The *Works of John Ruskin* in 39 volumes began to be published

        Erik Satie's *Trois Morceaux en Forme de Poire*
        A guy named Milton Hershey
                opened a chocolate factory & company town
                                in Pennsylvania
        a Dutch physiologist Willem Einthoven
                came up with the electrocardiogram
        William Harley
        and the three Davidson brothers:
                built the first Harley-Davidson motorbike

        Fly & Surge, O America

There was an hour long ovation
      at the Moscow Art Theater on 1-17
           for Chekhov's *Cherry Orchard*
              The very ill author
                    stood coughing by the footlights

              flowers by the hundreds & gluts of
              overly florid praise, he noted,
              as if he were already
                    doing the trillion-year saraband
                  on e. e. cummings' worm farm

February
    Japanese attacked Port Arthur, an area in southern Manchuria
                              controlled by the Russians
            Chekhov wrote a friend
            he was thinking
                of volunteering as a medical officer

February 29
Teddy selected a seven-human commission
            to oversee the building of the Panama Canal

April 22 (or 23) (others say May 4), 1904
    the French Panama Canal Co property
            (including the unfinished Panama Canal)
                was formally transferred to the United States

That same spring
Helen Keller graduated from Radcliffe College—
          Blind and deaf from scarlet fever in childhood
          nevertheless Keller learned, French, Latin, Greek, math, *et al.*
          & now, at the age of 24

she was a socialist
& bound for glory!!

Madama Butterfly opened at Milan's La Scala
The crowd hissed and booed
& the critics flowed hissy ink

Giacomo Puccini
pared away at the second act
(a bit too long at 80 minutes)
wove it again w/ post-hiss inspissated genius
& threw it back to the people in triumph

Never Give Up

July 2
Chekhov
died late at night
at Badenweiler in the Black Forest

His wife Olga Knipper was with him

In her diary she noted how
a black butterfly

came into the room
& beat against the lamp
as she stood
at 3 AM
by his cooling face

On July 25
25,000 textile workers went on strike in Fall River, Massachusetts
where children worked long hours for the low pay & exhaustion
of an evil system

This was the year a National Child Labor Committee was set up
to seethe for adequate child labor laws.

October 24
The first subway opened in New York City
& the first olive green subway cars
slid in a surprising silence

from the Brooklyn Bridge
     along a diagonal up through Manhattan
                   to Broadway and 145th St

Speaking of Broadway, it was the year of
Little Johnny Jones, by George M. Cohan
     —the first production commixing songs, dances and a story line—
     and some tunes that lasted:
          "Give My Regards to Broadway,"
              & "The Yankee Doodle Boy."

Max Weber published *The Protestant Ethic and the Spirit of
Capitalism*
     interweaving the development of highly structured greed
     with protestantism

while in the USA
there remained just six great "combinations" of railroads
consolidated from over 1,000

& each of the six
     was allied with either Rockefeller or Morgan.

Trustbusting
Ted Roosevelt
took on J. P. Morgan's Northern Securities railroad holding company,
     which the Supreme Court ordered broken up in 1904

to public praise
     and put TR in the books,
          flawed as he was,
               as a trustbuster

November 7
Ted Roosevelt won 32 states in the election
          against a conservative Democrat named
               Alton Parker.
Just before the vote,
     in a move he no doubt later regretted
          TR promised not to run again in 1908

The president helped fashion a fad for *jiu-jitsu*
and brought a Japanese instructor
          now & then to the White House

November 24
    the first gallery to exhibit photographs
                was opened by Alfred Stieglitz and Edward Steichen
                                        in NYC

New in '04:
    the tea bag
             (in small muslin pouches)
                    the Gillette safety razor
                           Thermos bottles

    & th' first speed limits in the States:
    10 in populated places   15 in villages   20 open roads

                    Cézanne began painting Mont Sainte-Victoire

Frank Lloyd Wright's Larkin Building in Buffalo
Mahler's 6th, *Kindertotenlieder*—the tragic symphony
Henry James' *The Golden Bowl*

Born in '04:
    March 1 Glenn Miller
    April 24 Willem de Kooning
    April 22 J. Robert Oppenheimer
    June 2 Johnny Weismuller
    July 12 Pablo Neruda   July 14 Isaac Singer
    October 2 Graham Greene   November 17 Isamu Noguchi

    while in St. Louis the exposition made famous the newfangled
                            hamburger and ice cream cone

                Swirl, O Century, swirl!

1905

On January 9 (the Old, Julian Calendar—13 days behind the Western,
Gregorian Calendar)
the hideous event ever known as Bloody Sunday
which was avidly studied by Revs of the time
in the sense of the world as tinder
awaiting the *iskra*, the spark
as a prolegomenon poof-up to socialism's triumph

300,000 workers under th' leadership of a priest named Georgy Gapon
marched on the Winter Palace
to deliver a petition to Tsar Nicholas II

The demands were those anyone could support:
an 8-hour workday, more money, the right to vote,
and a parliament.

Many were humble, carrying icons and pictures of the tsar
& singing Christian hymns

Bang bang replied the Tsar
& soldiers opened fire, with 100 protesters dead in the snow

Lenin and the revs used the ghastly shootings
to rally the workers

There were massive strikes in cities all over Russia
Peasants rioted and burned estates—
They called the burnings "illuminations"

Then radicals and socialists came to NY's Lower East Side
when the revolution faltered
looking for that strange American exceptionalist mix
of roses and gold.

February
 with the forests of the nation in danger of
 manic chop-down
 Congress and Roosevelt
 set up the United States Forest Service
 and a system of Forest Rangers
 one of the hamster man's lasting legacies

June, 1905
 Sailors on the battleship *Potemkin* arose in mutiny
 a story caught in '25 by the great Sergei Eisenstein

 They killed the captain
 and ran up the red flag of rev
 while nearby, the citizens of Odessa on the Black Sea
 at the mouth of the Dniester
 staged a general strike

———————————— **ARISE, O WOBBLIES!** ————————————

On July 7, 1905
 200+ socialists and trade union workers
 met in Chicago
 to overthrow capitalism

They called themselves the Industrial Workers of the World
&, for a reason lost in the chrono-mists
 came to be known as the Wobblies.

They organized unskilled, exploited nonwhites, immigrants
women, migrant workers
 those who were not allowed in the skilled-worker craft unions
 of the American Federation of Labor

Arise arise on the shores of America
Wobblies Wobblies

The Wobblies were known for
 the fierce tactics of direct action
 and for their wildly dynamic leaders.

They wanted OBU! One Big Union
to enable the workers

to own production & distribution

> thus
> Society
> would be
> TRANSFORMED

through on-the-job acts
which, in the elegant words of historian Joyce Kornbluh,
"would wage effective war on the great combinations of capital."

> The IWW had an impact
> > much greater than its numbers
> (just like the ruling class)

> Dues were kept extremely low
> > so as not to exclude
> so at its height had 100,000 dues-payers

> *Arise arise on the shores of America*
> *Wobblies Wobblies*

> The Preamble to the IWW Constitution
> became famous for
> > its clear, revolutionary prose:

"The working class and the employing class
have nothing in common.

There can be no peace so long as hunger and want
are found among millions of working people and the few,
who make up the employing class,
have all the good things of life.

Between these two classes a struggle must go on
until all the toilers come together
> on the political as well as on the industrial field,
and take and hold that which they produce by their labor,
through an economic organization
> of the working class
> without affiliations with any political party ..."

> The money-maddened brokers of power
> wanted to laugh at it

especially ignore it
but they couldn't

Arise arise on the shores of America
Wobblies Wobblies

From 1905 to say around 1920
they had their heyday run
They owned what Americans call "guts" —
They REALLY
did want a rev.

Much of it was done through education:
Billions of words! Galactic fire-squalls of ink!
& they attracted some of the best graphic artists & cartoonists

There were thousands of meetings in ethnic halls
National newspapers (printed in fifteen languages)
Union halls with well-stocked libraries
and a school in Minnesota
The Work Peoples College

There were summer camps for "junior Wobblies"
& the very very popular *Little Red Songbook*

Joe Hill was a famous IWW songwriter
Other Wobbly poets & tune-creators
were Richard Brazzier, Ralph Chaplin, Covington Hall,
Laura Payne Emerson, and T-Bone Slim.

IWW songs filled America's air
on picket lines, in hobo jungles, and from the dais
at thousands of meetings

& Chaplin's "Solidarity Forever"
had a destiny as America's premier labor tune

For a while
it looked as if the Wobblies
were rowing the Boat of Betterment

Seize Power & Sing
on the shores of America
O Wobblies!

•

September 5, 1905
    Roosevelt helped set up the deal
            for Japan and Russia to sign the Treaty of Portsmouth,
                ending the Russo-Japanese war
                        —and getting himself the Nobel Peace Prize

———————————————— **Out of the Brow** ————————————————

A young clerk in the Bern patent office
leaped from Athena's brow
        like the Zeus of numbers!

It was his "I Wanna Hold Your Hand" year

All in a year the young genius Albert Einstein
            published a group of epochal papers:

1. *Zur Elektrodynamik bewegter Körper*
   On the Electrodynamics of Moving Bodies

2. *Ist die Trägheit eines Körpers von seinem Energieinhalt abhängig?*
   Does the Inertia of a body Depend on its Energy Content?

    These two led to what became known as
                        The Special Theory of Relativity
            that the speed of light is constant
            and velocity has meaning only in the sense
                        that it's relative to the looker
            and his genius proof of the equivalence
                            of mass & energy
            speeding to the equation that everyone knows, $E = mc^2$

                    a subject much more vast
                    than *dichtung=condensare*
                            can trace in a few lines

3. *Eine neue Bestimmung der Moleküldimensionen*
   A New Determinaton of Molecular Dimensions
            submitted to the University of Zürich as his doctoral thesis

4. *Über die von der molekularkinetischen Theorie der Wärme geforderte*
   Bewegung von in ruhenden Flüssigkeiten suspendierten Teilchen

60

On the Motion of Small Particles Suspended in Liquids at Rest Required
by the Molecular-Kinetic Theory of Heat

which explained Brownian motion
(the zigzaggy erratic whirlagig of
                    microscopic particles
first noted in 1827
by the English botanist Robert Brown,
who saw microscopic particles suspended
                    in tiny pockets of fluid inside pollen grains!)

Einstein brought it a set of equations
which allowed
                    the size of molecules & atoms
                              to be determined

5. *Über einen die Erzeugung und Verwandlung des Lichtes betreffenden*
   heuristischen Gesichtspunkt
   On a Heuristic Point of View Concerning the Production and
                    Transformation of Light

which explained how light is emitted in
                    quanta, small bursts rather than continuous waves
& how light could be regarded both as a wave and a particle—
         —a unit of light as a particle will come to be called a photon.

Dance from the Brow, O Einstein!

And then at the
         Salon d'Automne in Paris
                    the group they called *Les Fauves*
                    wild beasts of the brush
                              (a term coined by Louis Vauxcelles)
                    starring Henri Matisse
                    Derain, Dufy, Vlaminck, and later the great
                                        Georges Braque

———————————— **Changes in Russia** ————————————

Meanwhile in Russia
by summer's end

after all the strikes and fervor
his magnificence the past-dwelling tsar Nicholas II
tried to create a Duma
                    —a democratic assembly—
with only recommendative powers
                    which didn't float well
                              in the riled-up political climate

By October 8
      with Japan having won th' war with the Russians
      & the tsar's ultra-right structure
                              weakened & stunned

      the Russian railway workers held a strike, which
      paralyzed the country—
            Again the demands had the merit of eternity:
            an eight-hour day
                    the institution of a state insurance system
                              freedom of press and assembly

      They also demanded the abolition of the death penalty,
      a national assembly,
                    & the right to demonstrate—

      Finally Nicholas II had to make concessions.

      On October 17, he agreed to call for a parliament
                    the Duma
                              granting them freedom of speech and assembly
                    real legislative power
                    and wider group of voters to elect Duma members

      This was the tsar's "October Manifesto"
                    & after centuries of stifling autocracy
                              wild celebrations ensued

                              •

Meanwhile in the USA
18 football players were killed that fall
Roosevelt threatened to ban it unless violence were curbed

New in '05:
      Sinn Féin formed
            —Gaelic for "ourselves alone"

Saltimbanques by Picasso
The Bathers, Cézanne
The Marlborough Family, John Singer Sargent

In Kansas City a developer named J. C. Nichols
                    began his Country Club District
an exclusive residential area
with Italian fountains and imported statuary
plus covenants restricting sales to blacks
                    The KC Plaza set off plazas in other cities.

                In Chicago the Rotary Club was begun by
                                Paul Percy Harris
                    biz types and professionals who met
                    in rotation in members' offices for fellowship
                            and to do good work in communities
            —all male till a Supreme Court spank spank in '87
                                made them accept women

Freud's *Three Essays on the Theory of Sexuality*
George Santayana *The Life of Reason*

Frank Lloyd Wright's Unity Temple in Oak Park, Illinois
        Oscar Wilde's posthumous *De Profundis*
            the Audubon Society was founded in the USA
                    first use of term "hormone" by E. Starling in England
                            & the first neon signs

1905 born:
    Mar 2   Marc Blitzstein
    April 24   Robert Penn Warren
    June 20   Lillian Hellman   June 21 Jean-Paul Sartre
    Sept 18 Greta Garbo
    Dec 9 Dag Hammarskjold   Dec 22 Kenneth Rexroth

THE '05-'06 | COKE LINE

1905
cocaine was still in Coca-Cola

1906
no cocaine in Coca-Cola

(caffeine takes its place
though non-"active" components of the coca leaf
remained in the Coke formula
with the accepted drug caffeine)

In Britain the Labour Party was formed.
Up to then the party of reform had been the Liberals
—really the Rich Liberals—
since only the wealthy could get on their ticket

The Labour Party
had one main goal: getting friends of labor elected
and soon the pluto-headed Liberals withered

Words Forcing Change

February

Upton Sinclair's *The Jungle* was published

(It had first been serialized in the *Appeal to Reason*

the nation's most successful
rural socialist weekly
published in Girard, Kansas
—in the southeast part of the state—
with a circulation
        in times of campaigns & crises
                        of up to 4 million)

Sinclair spent two months in 1903
in Chicago slaughterhouses as a laborer
        a ghastly experience

            of tubercular steer meat
                        sent forth as steak
            & hogs with cholera
                        stuffed into sausage

    filth everywhere
    & the odors of rotting meat
                        disguised with chemicals

    In *The Jungle*
    an immigrant from Lithuania
    Jurgis Rudkus
            is brought to grimness
            in the ghastly, unsanitary & evil
                        Chicago stockyards

            so that he turns to socialism
                        as a path from the evil

    five publishers turned it down
                        the next two years

    till finally, in early '06
                it was published

    (the publisher sent page proofs
                        to President Roosevelt
            & soon gov't sleuths
                confirmed what Sinclair had written

    so that th' Pure Food & Drug Act
    & The Meat Inspection Act

                    were passed just a few months
                              after the muckrake novel happ'd)

                    Sinclair was ambivalent
                    "I aimed at the public's heart
                    & by accident I hit it in the stomach"

On March 17
        Teddy Roosevelt used the
                    term *muckraker*
                    for investigators
                    describing
                              injustices in US

April 13
        Samuel Beckett
                    rolled out onto the linen

In April
        when Maxim Gorky came to the USA
        the Russian ambassador
                    tried to get the US to halt him
                              on the grounds he was an Anarchist
                    (There was a law at the time, believe it or not,
                              that prevented anarchists from coming
                                        to the land of gold)
        Gorky came with his interpreter & lover Maria Andreyevna

        There was much attention from the media
        & a banquet in his honor
                    attended by Mark Twain
        where Gorky announced that it was now
                    "time to abolish tsarism"

        The Russian ambassador
                    then told the press that the woman with Gorky
                    was not his wife

        and Gorky and Maria
                    were tossed on the nonce
                              from praise to vilification

        & even Twain refused to attend
                    a second banquet in Gorky's honor.

Gorky spent the summer in the Adirondacks
> where he worked on his novel *Mother*
>> and a play, *Enemies*

April 18
> the San Francisco earthquake
>> killed 450, wrecked 25,000 buildings
>> (some texts say 28k buildings destroyed)
>>> a city-sacking fire
>>>> & 225,000+ without homes

April 28 great math-man Kurt Gödel waxed wailing upon the linen of
> time

May 7
> Congress voted the Alaska Delegate Bill
>> Alaska could send a non-voting member to Congress

June 3
> the singer/dancer Josephine Baker
>> came to life

————————— **The Shooting of Stanford White** —————————

June 25
> The architect Stanford White
>> was killed by Harry Thaw during a supper performance
> on the roof of Madison Square Garden

An actor was singing "I Could Love a 1,000,000 Girls"
> but the melody froze on his lips
>> as Mr. Thaw, scion of a Pittsburg railroad fortune
> fired at his rival.

White, a very famous architect
> (Madison Square Garden was one of his works)
and the sadomasochistic Thaw, were examples of a demiworld
of wealthy men
> who are fatally attracted to teenage show girls.

Three years before, Evelyn Nesbit, then 16,
> a model & dryad of the stage

who starred in one of Charles Gibson's "Gibson Girls" paintings

had been drug-raped by White
and then she apparently had taunted Thaw
           with the tale of the naked Mr. White
                    at her side in crumpled sheets
& the ageless Iliadic themes
          of jealousy & death commenced.

There was a famous trial (Thaw walked free)
          which had its time of fame & sleaze
               that trembles ever more faintly
                    in the sloshings of futurity

June 29
    the Railroad Rate Act was brought to law
    giving the ICC authority to set rates for
               interstate shipments

and to intervene in the weird accounting practices of the railroads–
inspect books
        and to set up better accounting rules
            —one of the good laws of Teddy's reign

———————————— **Triumph, o Rand School** ————————
1906

The Rand School of Social Science was founded
                on East 19th with 90 students
        the first major workers' school

and it survived in a hostile nation
        for a number of decades

(By '17 it purchased a six-story building at 7 East 15th
near Union Square

The Rand School ran Camp Tamiment
    as a workers' summer school and camp
             in Bushkill, Pa.)

Thrive, Rand, Thrive

June 30
This was the day the Pure Food and Drug Act was passed
It required that contents be listed on the labels of food and drugs
one of the keystone laws of th'
Progressive Era to try to control
the depredations of capitalism
(and most of all to weaken any arrival of Socialism)

1906
"suffragette" coined for women campaigning to vote in England

July 12
Th' guilty verdict of September '99 against Alfred Dreyfus was
annulled
and Dreyfus was days later reinstated into the French army
and awarded the Legion of Honor

September 22
21 were murdered in Atlanta, in what they always
call in the chronos a "race riot"
but really just white mobs
raging four days in the places of blacks.

A few months later
Pitchfork Ben Tillman
right wing slime from South Carolina
spat praise for lynching
from the US Senate floor

September 29
US assumed military control of Cuba under the Platt Amendment
after election disputes caused a "revolt"

November 4
Charles Evans Hughes (R)
beat Not So Mellow Yellow William R. Hearst (D)
for Gov of NY
by 60,000 votes

November 9
Roosevelt traveled to Panama
the first President to visit foreign soil

Late in the year the U.S. Congress
moved against Roosevelt
                    on the conservation front

The '07 appropriations bill for the Dept of Agriculture
rescinded the Pres' right to set up forest preserves
                    in all the Western states (except California
                              where forest preserves were popular)

In February of the same year Teddy ordered
the Forest Service
            to work all night
                        for ten days

defining some 17,000,000 acres
                        of new federal forest
before his privilege to create
                    ran its term

Those who look at forests
                and see naught but 2x4s
                sneered at Roosevelt
                        for creating "Midnight Reserves"

        but it proved once again
        that temporary power & a ticking hour
                        can forge fresh good

December 24
      The first radio broadcast with sound,
      from the Massachusetts coast
                        some music, a poem, and talk

      made possible by the radio vacuum tube—
      the thermionic valve (or diode), and the triode,
                              which enabled amplification.

December 30
      Paul Cézanne
            then shrouded in silence
                        joined the universe at 67

●

Charismatic Bill Haywood of the
                    Industrial Workers of the World
and Western Federation of Miners pres Charles Moyer
were accused of bomb-killing the ex gov of Idaho Frank Steunenberg.
Defended by the great Clarence Darrow,
Haywood ran as a Socialist for governor of Colorado
                                        awaiting his trial in jail.

In 1907 he was acquitted
& Big Bill went back to ceaseless work
                    building the Wobblies, where
Strikes were the rehearsals
                    for the Big Strike.

Haywood's syndicalist faction
                            took sway in the group
        Tens of thousands came to his speeches

                            •

Novum in '06:
"allergy" was coined by Austrian pediatrician Dr. Clemens von
            Parquet
& Jack London's *The Iron Heel*
            which spoke of a friendly socialist system
                            of peace & prosperity
        & warned of the rise of fascism in America

    Charles Ives' *Central Park in the Dark*
        Maxim Gorky's play *Enemies*
            Mark Twain's *What Is Man?*
            bard Robert Duncan born January 6
                and don't forget the first Victrola
                        and Kellogg's Corn Flakes

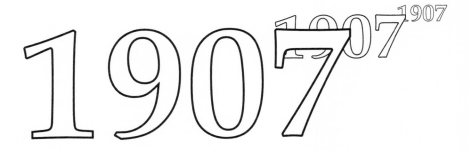

The bids for construction of th' Panama Canal
were opened in January

Roosevelt decided the government
could best do the project
which was placed under the Army Corps of Engineers
with Maj. G. W. Goethals in charge
till it was opened on 8-15-14

In early February
the famous "shifts" riot at the Abbey Theatre in Dublin
at the premiere o'
J. M. Synge's *Playboy of the Western World*
triggered by the line,
"If all the girls in Mayo were standing before me
in their shifts"

Reviewers called it decadent and obscene
How dare Synge's plays speak in working class vernacular
in tones derogatory to sacred Ireland
& the Irish Literary Renaissance?

Mr. Yeats confronted the shifts-shuddered rioters
outside the Abbey
and calmed them down
no doubt furthering his distaste
for Irish chauvinism & the masses/asses synapse.

It was part of a glorious line of first-night hissing
Aeschylus' *The Archers*
Carmen, La Traviata
Chekhov's *Seagull*
and soon Stravinsky's *Rite of Spring*

the Armory Show ...
                    The yes yesses
                    while the hiss hisses

———————————————— **Typhoid Mary** ————————————————

A NY City health official named Dr. George Soper
was investigating a case of typhoid fever
                    in a wealthy home
                                and cast his eye on a cook named Mary Mallon

Mary Mallon fled
                    & the newspapers picked it up

Soper sleuthed she'd caused the fever in a bunch of houses
                                            where Mallon cooked

She was captured in March of '07
                        and linked to 25 typhoid cases, with one death.

                    They forced her to live in a hospital off Manhattan
                    and she was freed in '10 after she promised to stay away
                                                        from food
                            but then she continued to spread it
                            till they locked her for life
                                    in the hospital

                            & thus another
                            American fantasy figment

                        Typhoid Mary

——————————— **The Second International, 1907** ———————————

There was a meeting of the Second International
                                    in Stuttgart

with the decision
                    for all Socialist parties
                    to support voting for women
                    but also to cease cooperation
                                with "bourgeois suffragists"
                                who were unconnected

with the rev

This caused strains in the American movement
major then, minor later
nonexistent now

──────────────── **Big Big Problem** ────────────────

"Don't try to make
people happy,"
Freud urged
a young socialist patient

"They don't want it."

1907
A group of hookers
in Barcelona
became a painting called *Les Demoiselles d'Avignon*

by Picasso
and Cubism 'gan

('08 Georges Braque had an exhibition that Matisse said resembled
"little cubes"

& at the 1911 Salon des Indépendents Guillaume Apollinaire
hailed the new style of Cubism)

April 21
A group of political clubs merged to become the Sinn Féin League

May 1
Many Labor Day demos in Europe
including a General Strike in Warsaw

The great Rachel Carson
was born in Springvale, Pa. on May 27

──────────────── **Heave $, Ho** ────────────────

There was a business panic that fall
beginning with a drop in copper prices

& a big run on the Knickerbocker Trust Co
October 22

NY financiers scarfed together enough cash
(plus the Federal gov't transferred money to NY banks)
so that depositors
stopped sucking out their $$$

J. P. Morgan "hated heights" as they say
& made big money from the stock crash.

———————————— **Panics** ————————————

Panics, of course, are the dry heaves
of the American Dream
(although, like visits to the dentist,
most tend to forget them at once)

Here's the flow of
business panics:
1837
1857
1873
1893
and now 1907

& in the boomlets 'tween heaves
Americans loved to sing a song called
"I Have Got It Made in the Shade"

November 16
Okhahoma became th' 46th State

December
In an act that did not reverberate through
the picket fences and church socials of America

Vlad Lenin, leader of the Bolsheviks
left Russia for the second time
to Finland

where he worked around the clock for rev
and night found him so anxious
he took huge walks
to tire himself to sleep

The newspapers called it the Great White Fleet
on December 16 when 16 American ships
sailed out of Virginia around the
world to flash US power
unto the Aeons

We're great
We're wonderful
We're tough
We're a power
Don't fuck with us
We're the States!

An American zoologist
first cultured tissues
His name was Ross Granville Harrison
Or was it C. Ross Harrison?
—textbooks are sometimes garishly various

Ivan Pavlov's *Conditioned Reflexes*
William James, *Pragmatism: A New Name for Old Ways of Thinking*

Tunes of 1907:
John Bratton's "The Teddy Bears' Picnic"
Jean Sibelius, *Symphony #3*
Gustav Mahler, *Symphony #8*

Linen-roll '07:
Feb. 21 W. H. Auden
May 12 Katherine Hepburn
May 26 John Wayne
July 7 Robert Heinlein

and the helicopter (by a Frenchman),
Armstrong linoleum,
canned tuna

Sing, my Nation, sing!

January 21
    Repression-heads on the New York City Council
    passed the so-called Sullivan Ordinance
                banning smoking (by women only)
                in public places

                gotta keep them in their libidinous places
                            (this joke of a law lasted just two days)

March 4
    Near Cleveland, in Collinwood,
                a school fire killed 180 kids
                            and 9 teachers

─────────────── **The Great Rent Strike** ───────────────

It was the year of the Great Rent Strike in New York City!
which spread from Manhattan to Brooklyn, Harlem
                            and Newark
coordinated by the Socialist Party—
sympathetic truckdrivers refused to evict—
        with the Socialist Party naturally much attacked in the press
                    for being against decency &
                            the freedom to rent-gouge.

Once again the Agitators lacked the $
        & the will
                to leave behind a Structure
                        to stand behind the Gains
and there's not much mention of
            the Great Strike 'o '08 in the histories

even though now we salute you
o Great Strike lost in the time-mist!!

•

The heavyweight Jack Johnson
   was married to a white woman
and wasn't hesitant
    to mention it loudly.

    Black dongs
    in white sarongs
      still brought lynchings
        in th' blighted South.

Crackers hated Johnson
    whose favorite authors were Victor Hugo
        & Shakespeare

One of his title defenses
  had to be held outside the US to

  get around the lynchers
  and state laws banning interracial sporting events

He beat up on white guy after white guy
till 1915
   when what they called a "white hope"
   finally defeated the 37-year-old champ
       in his fading physique

July 7
   The Muslim Turkish nation
      known as the Ottoman Empire
   governed Anatolia, SE Europe, North Africa,

                      and the Arab Middle East

from the 14th century
        —in the finality of the Byzantine Empire—
to the early 20th C.
It tended to be run by a vicious ruling class
                 headed by a Sultan

but a group called the Young Turks
                   grabbed control in 1908
& ran the Empire for a few years
secularizing the gov't
restoring a parliament
         & a constitution
& allowing the emancipation of women

(There were some grim aspects of the Young Turks
        as we shall see
            when we trace what they did to the Armenians)

The slang phrase "Young Turks" caught on in the West
            & is used to this day
                 in America

August 14
    There were "racial troubles" in Springfield, Illinois,
        & Governor Charles Deneen declared martial law

August 27
    Lyndon Baines Johnson was born in Stonewall, Texas

October 1
    The Model T Ford
        loved by the masses
           as the Flivver or the Tin Lizzie

durable, lightweight, flexible,
        & able to bump-skip on country roads

with its 20 hp 4-cylinder engine

$850
    affordable to the many
        & easy to fix

1908
Isadora Duncan
came to the States
         with her dance troupe

She based her revolution in Dance
on the natural grace of bodies moving in Beauty
It was ancient, she said, from the form-loving Greeks
& so when she showed a nipple or knee
                    she could claim those ancient roots
         She was an advocate of free love
         a political radical
                    & a stunning emblem to the women
                         who wanted to smoke, strut, paint,
                              write, dance, & fuck more freely.

It was the same year the
Boy Scouts were founded in England
by cavalry officer Robert Baden-Powell
'cause the Empire was mightily
         worried for the quality of fighting boys
                    in the recently ended Boer War
         where it had taken 450,000 Brits to stomp down 40k Dutch farmers

They wanted boys in better condition
                    more able to kill
                         more muscular at the offing trough

It was a brilliant move
to train young men for courage, self-reliance
respect for rank, comradeship
survival skills,
         & fun in the out-of-doors.
By 1910 there were 100k Scouts in Britain.

———————————————— **The Fall Campaign** ————————

Roosevelt
selected his
successor

his Secretary of War William Howard Taft
who had been

the civilian governor of the Philippines
                     & then his Secretary of War

& so on November 3
Taft pulled 7.68 million votes
              to William Jennings Bryan at 6.4

                 •

The Motion Picture Patent Company was formed that December
by Thomas Edison and others

Edison had built the first studio in 1893
       and had patented or acquired much of the early film technology

He sued his rivals
       and beat them down with huge legal fees

Then he formed the trust known as the Motion Picture Patent Co:
where inventors pooled their patents
             though most of it was owned by Edison
                      and his Biograph Co.

   Edison's company used
             vehement legal means
                 and even physical force
                     to wreak its will
   It helped drive
       the film world
             from the East to the West
'cause Hollywood was a long train away
             from Edison lawyers & goons

   (Finally in '15 the gov't snuffed the trust
             under the Sherman Anti-Trust Act)

Linen-roll '08:
    Simone de Beauvoir Jan 9
    Thurgood Marshall   July 2
    Olivier Messiaen Dec 10
    Elliott Carter   Dec 11
    plus Bette Davis, Joan Crawford, Milton Berle, Salvador Allende
    Joseph McCarthy, James Stewart
      Edward Teller, Theodore Roethke & Richard Wright

Novum sub sole '08:
    The first silencer on a pistol
            and Gideon Bibles in hotel nightstands

    plus, the first horror flick,
                Dr. Jekyll & Mr. Hyde.

    a German guy named Johannes Geiger
                (with Ernest Rutherford)
    invented the Geiger counter
    which measures the particles flying out
                    of radioactive substances

    Georges Braque's cubist landscapes at L'Estaque.
    Toscanini and Mahler debuted at the Metropolitan Opera
    Woodrow Wilson's *Constitutional Government in the United States*
                    and, oh yes, General Motors

————————————————— **The Ashcan School** —————————————————

On the U.S. art scene
    yahoo critics dubbed them the
    "The black revolutionary gang" when "The Eight"
                    showed at the Macbeth Gallery in NYC:

    Everett Shinn, John Sloan, George Luks, William Glackens,
    Robert Henri, Arthur Davies, Maurice Prendergast, Ernest Lawson

    They were later known as the Ashcan School
    and turned their canvas away
                    from the moneyed raiments
                            of middle class hacks

    It was the effort at realism, say, in the novels of Dreiser
    not afraid to depict the down-tone side of life,
    waterfront citizens, Broadway crowds, weirdness and pov

                    nor afraid to be radical, as when, say,
                    John Sloan joined the Socialist Party in 1908
                    & later worked for the great *The Masses.*

More novum:
    The paper cup and the electric iron

plus MSG as a taste enhancer in Japan
                                 & two more subways open in NYC

                    & the *Count of Monte Cristo*
                            was completed near LA
                     in the trend to get out of NYC to the West

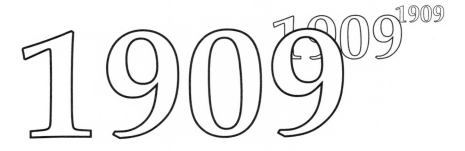

——————————————————— **The NAACP** ———————————————————

On the hundredth anniversary
                    of Abe Lincoln's birth (Feb. 12)

60 black and white intellectuals
met in NYC
& formed a committee that in the months ahead
                    became the National Association
                    for the Advancement of Colored People

    The previous year had seen
    the dreadful riots in Springfield

    & there comes a time in the time-track
    when you work for good, no matter the danger

    W. E. B. Du Bois, the author of *The Souls of Black Folk*
    was determined to contradict
                    people like Booker T. Washington
                    who wanted blacks to be content with jobs
                                        instead of social equality

There comes a time—

Jim Crow laws made everything poorly separate:
schools, housing, hotels, restrooms, theaters, cemeteries
—therefore the NAACP

There comes a time—
   You can look in photo archives
   at the shiny-eyed trash
         gathered about a lynching tree
            as if it were the homecoming parade
               —therefore the NAACP

There comes a time
   when minds set free set afire set bold set forth
            —therefore the NAACP

All Glory to the Dream

Hit-Filth

In a series of years ('09-'13)
      not noticed at all
               in the church socials of America
      or really anywhere at all
Hitler was filthing it up in Vienna
slurping anti-Semitism into his psyche
            and starving as a no-tal commercial artist

FUTURISM!

From Milan, Italy came an energy flow
         with ghastly but interesting prose

In a manifesto published that February
            in *Le Figaro* in Paris
         Filippo Tommaso Marinetti wrote:

   "We will glorify war—the only true hygiene of the world—
   militarism, patriotism ... the beautiful ideas which kill, and
   the scorn of women."

   It had a kind of élan
            and a clunky sense of design
                  this thing called Futurism

It celebrated speed & machines
　　　　anticipating the eager acceptance of the Grand Prix
　　　　　　　　　　　　　　& stock car races

　　　　and had a flair for the Manifesto
　　　　　　such as the one called
　　　　　　"The Pleasure of Being Booed"

　　　　but it also maybe helped lead to fascism
　　　　　　　　　　& the hemic spatters of the trench

March 4
　　William Howard Taft was sworn in as pres
　　　　　　　then Roosevelt went on a tour of the world.

　Not many months in office
　the muckrakers tore into Taft

　One Richard Ballinger became the Sec of the Interior.

　Ballinger greed-drooled to give
　　　　　some of the most valuable lands in Alaska
　　　　　to Guggenheim and Morgan monopolists

　Mr. Ballinger had dismissed a young investigator in the Interior Dept
　who had challenged the forkover to greed

　　　　There was a Congressional investigation
　　　　and Taft was shown to have backdated documents
　　　　　　　　　and his pres'cy was
　　　　　　　　　　　　muck-weakened

April 6
　Robert Peary the first known human to get to th' North Pole

April 10
　The fine iambo-anapestic chanter
　　　　　Algernon Charles Swinburne
　　　　　　　began tuning his lyre in the w.f.
　Ah, Swinburne! how wild wends to wan!
　so shocking you were in youth
　　　so staid in the
　　　　　post flip-out
　　　　　　pad of Watts Dunton

but we can still taste the
                kissing chaos
                        of your iambo-anapests!

                He weaves and is clothed with derision
                He sows and he shall not weep
                His life is a watch or a vision
                Between a sleep and a sleep!

May 17
    The Ballets Russes
            had its world premiere in Paris

    with Anna Pavlova, Vaslav Nijinsky (on leave from th' Imperial Ballet),
    Michel Fokine and founder Sergei Diaghilev

    a synthesis of painting, music, drama
                            with ballet
    (Pablo Picasso, Igor Stravinsky, Jean Cocteau
            just three of the names that threaded the weave)

─────────────── **So Much for Freedom of Speech** ───────────────
                        May 23

        New York City police broke up an
        Emma Goldman lecture
        because it "wandered away" from its
                            advertised topic
    "Modern Drama, the Strongest Disseminator of Radical Thought"
        when she spoke of Joan of Arc & martyrs.

        The audience was angry with the police
                        & several were arrested

─────────────── **A Mortarboard for Freud** ───────────────
    Sigmund Freud came to the USA
    to Clark College in Worcester
                for lectures and an honorary doctorate
    Freud's lectures titillated the media
                        and psychoanalysis became a fad
                                then a fact

86

July 12
    Congress passed a resolution for the 16th Amendment,
           the imposition of income taxes
                which went to the States to be ratified

——— The Great Wobbly Free Speech Struggles ———

From their founding in '05 to WW1
    the Wobblies were
        a ceaseless vector
           against the capitalist class

The right wing arrayed itself against them:
police, company mobs, the army, courts, establishment newspapers.

When towns, counties and cities passed laws preventing their free
    speech
        the Wobblies defied the laws

For instance, in Spokane '09
a law banned street meetings

& an IWW organizer was arrested—
A Wob-flood
    marched to Spokane's main drag
        and began to speak
           one by one

till 600 Wobblies were arrested
The jails were horrible, and two Wobblies died there
but finally
    the IWW won
        & could speak in downtown Spokane.

In Fresno in '11

another protest for the right of free speech
again the jails were packed

and Wobblies were singing and giving speeches
    to supporters and the curious
        gathered outside the jail

Fire trucks were brought
and hosed the prisoners
                    with icy water
                              to stop their singing

The Wobblies propped up mattresses to ward off the water
and kept on singing
          till the water was knee high in their
                                        entrapments.

When it was obvious that
more and more Wobblies were coming to Fresno
                    to commit civil disobedience

the power structure relented
                    and rescinded the ban on speaking in the streets

There were other Free Speech struggles
                              in many other cities.

          How many of our cherished freedoms
          to march & speak in the streets
          are owed to th' Wobbly men and women
                              of 1909?

July 27
     Orville Wright set a flight duration record of 1 hr 1 min 40 sec

September 27
     Pres Taft set aside 3 million acres of oil-rich land for conservation
                    including something called Teapot Dome in Wyoming

November 18
     Warships were sent to Nicaragua after 2 Americans, plus 100s
               of Nicaraguan revs were killed by dictator Jose Santos Zelaya

——————— **The Shirtwaist Makers Strike of '09-'10** ———————

Let us sing the Shirtwaist Makers Strike
                    known as the "Uprising of 20,000"
from the genius of teenage immigrant women

November 22, there was at big rally at Cooper Union
                                    8th St. & 3rd Avenue
Clara Lemlich, one of the *farbrente maydelekh*
                                    the burning young women
                                                arose to speak in Yiddish:

           "I have listened to all the speakers,
           and I have no further patience for talk.
           I am one who feels and suffers from the things pictured.
           I move we go on strike."

15,000 walked out the next morn, growing to 20

                    The NY Women's Trade Union League
                                    surged to glory
                    & the male-dominated ILGWU
                                    was thrown off guard

     There was a forgivable optimism
     among Women radicals
                    who came forward to
                    teach the strikers the facts of socialism
                    no doubt envisioning
                              an American proletariat
                                        to force a new economy.

There were 20 halls where the strikers were headquartered
The WTUL coordinated the
              picket lines, raising money, bailing out strikers,
              setting up parades, getting articles in sympathetic papers,
              paying out benefits
                              & signing up women for the union.

Cap-slime hates this sort of thing
but knows, if anything, how to coöpt

The Socialist women who came aboard
& the Women's Trade Union League both
              pledged support for the central issue:
              recognition of the union
                              and the closed union shop.

           This cross-class strike
                    was pocked with tergiversation

and what we shall call here
soc-baiting

(the baiting of Socialists)

This came about when the Women's Trade Union League
picked up the support of a few
wealthy fellow travelers
notably Alva Belmont, suffragist and rich,
and Anne Morgan, daughter of financier J. P. Morgan

Anne M wanted to ban Socialists in public meetings
to keep them from teaching "their fanatical doctrines."

WTUL refused to defend the Socialists in its midst
so that some resigned and criticized the WTUL

An activist named
Theresa Malkiel was the chief target of Anne Morgan's sneers

Malkiel wrote a fictionalized autobiography
Diary of a Shirtwaist Striker
& had pointed at "mainstream activists"
including suffragists
as Class Enemies

The Strike ended in Feb. 1910 without a closed shop agreement
Socialist women blamed their former allies the WTUL

The shirtmakers' strike
showed in vividity
the problems of cross-class efforts
to make a change in money.

Novum '09:
the invention of plastic
the first Lincoln head pennies

In France the bacteriologist Charles-Jules-Henri Nicolle
found the spreader of typhus:
the body louse!

Plus that year a cure for syph!
but too late for Baudelaire, Rimbaud, Nietzsche
and countless millions of
th' belesioned

(a German bacteriologist Paul Ehrlich
 injected sick rabbits
            with an arsenic-based chemical compound
which, after adjusting,
                        began to heal the rabbits.
Demand for the sex drug was overwhelming

It was the main cure till
            the penicillin of the 1940s)

Also Novum:
   The first Kibbutz in Palestine
               and the electric toaster in the USA

   Mahler's Symphony #9, *Das Lied von der Erde*
   Gertrude Stein's *Three Lives*

   & D. W. Griffith pulled off an Ovidian metamorphosis
               on child actress Gladys Smith—
                           voilà Mary Pickford!

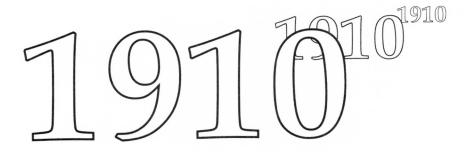

   A big strike in Chicago
               'gainst Hart, Schaffner and Marx

   The anger of workers
                  growing and
   there comes a time when you strike
                     against the mean, petty tyrannies
                                 of boring bosses
   the filthy air, low pay
               and the prospect of an early death
                              in the whispering dirt

The Wobblies were very active in the strike
plus Leftists of a number of shadings
        all of it leading to the formation of the
                        Amalgamated Clothing Workers of America

Rise, o Unions Rise!

Song to Being Indefatigable

This is a song to Florence Kelly
who was active in the settlement house movement
                in the era '10 through '20

ceaseless ceaseless O Florence Kelly

She never gave up, & was key to the passing of
                minimum-wage laws for women.

For several decades she lived at Lillian Wald's
                Henry Street Settlement

She was an important part of the creation of the
                US Children's Bureau in '12

ceaseless ceaseless O Florence Kelly

& the law known as the
        Sheppard-Towner Maternity and Infancy Protection Act o' '21

ceaseless ceaseless O unsung agent of the Rose

    phantom of a sacred struggle
            & a member of the Socialist Party
            Florence Kelly

Halley's Comet

That spring and summer
Halley's Comet was streaking the heavens

with sky-scads of 'noia
        kicked up by the tabloids
over the chance of poisonous comet-gas
        skulling the skies
and the ancient fear of Armageddon
        armed the addled

American genius Mark Twain was fading
        in Redding, Connecticut

"I came in with it, & I'll go out with it"
        he said
and with the comet just coming into view
        he passed on April 21

It wasn't all 'Geddon that year as
        the Boy Scouts of America
        were founded

and June 19
        in Spokane, the first Father's Day

and how about June 25
        when the Mann Act passed,
        prohibiting interstate transport of women
        for "immoral purposes."

June 25
        Congress set up the Postal Savings System
        responding to citizens' distrust of savings banks

In late August
        Teddy Roosevelt gave his speech on "The New Nationalism"
        & the Square Deal Policy: a graduated income tax,
        a bigger federal role in working conditions,
        a strong army and navy, plus tariff revision

        kill 'em abroad, chill 'em at home

1910 in Mexico

There was an uprising against dictator Porfirio Díaz
led by Francisco Madero

with the help of Indian rev Emiliano Zapata
and bandit-rebel Pancho Villa

American cap-slime
had sponsored Mr. Diaz' dictatorship
since 1876

He was their personal dictator
kept the native population in poverty
while foreign capital (Mostly American)
ooze-flooded into Mexico

so that by 1900
it owned most of the mines, oilfields, sugar and
coffee plantations and cattle ranches

while th' French owned much of the textile industry

Meanwhile on October 1
two evil explosions at the downtown LA printing plant
of the *Los Angeles Times*

which set tanks of ink afire
& killed 21 men

Who did it?
There was a big investigation by private eye William J. Burns.

That fall Woodrow Wilson, 53,
in his first race
won the New Jersey governorship

As president of Princeton
he helped it grow

& tried, without success, to abolish the snobbish
Princeton social clubs

& replace them with a system somewhat modeled on
Oxford/Cambridge college with a resident faculty.

Wilson picked up much ink for his struggle

He was from a family of Presbyterian ministers
& began a kind of reformist tenure as gov of NJ:
biz regulation
   & concern for workers in unsafe conditions
in the sentiment of the era
    for mild reform

November 8
 Victor Berger the first socialist elected to Congress
          from Milwaukee

 During his five terms
 he pushed for public jobs
    old age pensions shorter work days
    held hearings on the McNamara–*LA Times* bombing case,
    and later the Lawrence 1912 strike

 & was one of the first to bring a class perspective to debates in
  Congress

November 10
 Leo Tolstoy
    joined Anna Karenina
      at the age of 82

Women after 1910
  more women worked
  more became clerks in stores
  more became high school teachers
  more into civil service

 There was much i-yi-yi-ing that emancipated woman
    wouldn't go to church
      refuse to marry
        would spread birth control

 Dress lengths went up to midcalf by '15
     & short, bobbed hair became popular

  After '10 the social stigma against makeup
     ebbed
  & smoking for women,
  ai-yi-yi'd in the past as
      "the gesture of the brothel"
         became big biz

Novum Sub Sole '10:
   Principia Mathematica
            first volume, of a 3-vol work

by Bertrand Russell and Alfred North Whitehead

a great effort to
commingle math and logic
            then lincoln logging it into a systematic structure

which inspired Ludwig Wittgenstein
            who went to study under Russell in Cambridge
            and gave the world-mind his
                  Tractatus Logico-Philosophicus

Stravinsky's ballet, *The Firebird*

John Philip Sousa and band began a world tour

E. M. Forster, *Howards End*
Edward Arlington Robinson's "Miniver Cheevy" in
      The Town Down the River

There was a tango craze also
the Manhattan Bridge opened in NYC
roller skating came to public perception
                        as fun
the bard Charles Olson was born on December 27
and the Tom Mix flick, *The Ranch Life in the Great Southwest*

The Masses

January

One of the century's finer magazines began
The Masses it was called
        & it strutted in the time-track
                till the cap-slimes
                      & war-heads
                 crushed it in '17.
    Max Eastman was editor
    Eugene O'Neill wrote theater criticism
    There were brilliant cartoons by Art Young
              and artwork by Sloan, Becker, Minor et al
                     —art that stays alert even now—
  & John Reed on the IWW & th' Mexican rev

The Masses masthead:

"This Magazine is Owned and Published Co-operatively by Its
Editors. It has no Dividends to Pay, and nobody is trying to make
Money out of it. A Revolutionary and not a Reform Magazine; a
Magazine with a sense of Humor and no Respect for the
Respectable; Frank; Arrogant; Impertinent; searching for the True
Causes; a Magazine directed against Rigidity and Dogma
wherever it is found; Printing what is too Naked or True for a
Money-making press; a Magazine whose final Policy is to do as it
Pleases and Conciliate Nobody, not even its Readers—There is a
Field for this Publication in America. Help us to find it."

January 7
    the NY state supervisor of banks closed the sinking Carnegie Trust Co

January 21
    Robert La Folette founded th' National Progressive Republican
        League

January 25
    The US cavalry was sent to the Rio Grande to preserve its "neutrality"
    during the Mexican civil war, and to protect US territory from
        "insurgents"

──────────────── **The Triangle Shirtwaist Fire** ────────────────

The top three floors of 25 Washington Place
                                at Greene Street
just off Washington Square
were rented by the Triangle Shirtwaist Company

where on a Saturday morn, it was March 25
500 workers, mostly young women
were turning out shirtwaists—
the sheer, clingy blouse
            that was all the rage
                    from the Gibson Girl drawings
                            of Charles Dana Gibson

It was a ghastly place to work.
At the end of a shift
they made the women walk out
            single file
            past a watchman
                    to have their pocketbooks searched

Just at quitting time that Saturday
a fire began on the 8th floor
                    in a pile of sheer sheer cutaways
                            under a table
& floofed at once to hell height

500 tried to flee.
The cap-slime who owned the factory
kept the doors to the stairwells locked!

Some escaped by the elevators
but many crowded out upon a fire escape
which collapsed!
                and flung them downward
                            like rice off a spoon

            Many others leaped to their deaths
            from flaming windows

Some of the bodies were burning as they fell
The fire department's life nets didn't work
                as the women hit the pavement
                thock   thock   thock
                startling the nearby horses
                            who trembled in their harnesses

                146 lay crushed
                No greater symbol of evil
                against workers
                            had there ever been

——————————— **The McNamara Brothers** ———————————

That April two brothers, John & James McNamara
active in the International Association of Bridge and
                            Structural Iron Workers
were indicted for the *LA Times*
                bombs that had killed 21

All over the nation
                unionists
                depicted the McN's as victims of
                            frame-ups
After all,
Harrison Gray Otis, head of the *Times,* hated unions
                    & vom-railed ceaselessly against them
(& there'd been a big-scale effort to organize the *Times*)

Labor Day 1911 was renamed McNamara Day

April 11
        The great socialist leader Jean Jaurès

proposed his plan
for a socialist France
which proved the value of
political blueprints
when, over the decades,
a good portion of his plan
was brought to life!

(The founder of the the newspaper *L'Humanité*
Juarès wrote his doctoral thesis in Latin on
The Origins of German Socialism
in the Works of
Luther, Kant, Fichte & Hegel)

May 4
Chancellor Lloyd George in England introduced a
National Health Insurance bill!

May 15 in the U.S. the
Supreme Court dissolved Standard Oil of NJ
for antitrust violations

The dour, always-praying J. D. Rockefeller's empire
was broken into 34 separate companies

———————————————— **Mexico in '11** ————————————————

Throughout '11, there were glorious uprisings all over Mexico

Pancho Villa, for instance, in Chihuahua
Emiliano Zapata in Morelos

and then, May 25, dictator Porfirio Diaz resigned
after which there was,
in textbookspeak,
"ten years of turmoil"
but the need for a system change, at last, had been fingered

1911
The radical lesbian physician Marie Equi
known for her work with working-class women & kids
helped found the Eight-Hour Day League
in Oregon

Mahler

The Austrian perfectionist Gustav Mahler passed May 18 at 50
His attentiveness to perfect sound
     sometimes made his orchestras angry

He was in demand as a conductor
& the director of Vienna Opera for ten years
    though vampired by the anti-Semitic press

till finally in '07
   he came to the U.S. to work at
      the Metropolitan Opera & the N.Y. Philharmonic

A genius composer of 7 song cycles, 9 symphonies and on his tenth
       when seized by the Scythe Man

"My time will come" he said

He combined snatches of pop tunes, mil marches, birdcalls,
       in his work

   walked with his own flashlight—
    & told Trouble to "go bake a bagel."

May 23
  The opening of the New York Public Library

May 29
  The American Tobacco Company was ordered dissolved
  by the Supreme Court
  because of antitrust violations

    and the first Indianapolis 500 was
      won on May 30 by Ray Harroun in a Marmon Wasp

August 23
  Someone stole the Mona Lisa
     from the Louvre
    & left her frame
    at the feet of the *Wingéd Victory at Samothrace.*
  The great bard Guillaume Apollinaire
  was arrested by mistake
    in a complicated tale
      for being vaguely connected

101

THE POETRY LIBRARY

with what the fuzz were convinced was an international
                                    band of museum thieves
but which really didn't exist
            —you can read all about it in Francis Steegmuller's
            fine tome, *Apollinaire, Poet Among the Painters.*

Marc Chagall began his *Hommage* to Apollinaire
(the thief turned out to be an Italian named Peruggia
                        who wanted to return it to Florence)

Speaking of Italy
            that country's thirst was utterly slakeless
                        that year
                        to seize Libya from Turkish control
                              in the brakeless fade of the Ottoman Empire

After all, did not France control Morocco?
and had not Rome grabbed Tunisia from the Ottomans in 1881?

Italy attacked
with the first use of aerial bombardment
                              —grenades from planes

Right wing militarism
                  went up to the berserker level
to split the Socialists
                  with Benito Mussolini coming to power
                        and toppling the Liberal government

July 1
Surl' scene among Euro-imperialists:
when the German gunboat *Panther* arrived in Agadir, Morocco,
allegedly to guard German "interests" which seemed threatened
                        by the French "involvement" in Morocco

& then on November 4
the Agadir "Crisis" ended

when Germany let France have its will in Morocco
while France gave Germany territory in the Congo

                        Africa
                        sliced
                        oozing

November 5
    Italy took Tripoli and Cyrenaica
                then carved up a total win on November 26

Meanwhile on November 21
    what the textbooks say
                were "Suffragette riots in Whitehall, London."

and in early December
    in Los Angeles
            it looked as if Socialist Party leader Job Harriman
                    was going to be the next mayor.

He'd won a plurality in the November primary
and was favored to win the runoff election on December 5

All the Labor and Socialist movement
        had backed the McNamaras
                as being framed for the
                        murderous fire bombs

until, December 1st, in an uh-oh! heard across the land
the McN's pleaded guilty

It turned out that top officials of the International Association
                  of Bridge and Structural Iron Workers
had done about 87 bombings
to force the National Erectors Association to recognize the
union

James McN had put dynamite outside the printing plant
just to damage the building
        but drums of ink poofed to hate-flames.

        The effect was instant
        Job Harriman's fortunes fell fatally
            in the election for mayor
                (see Louis Adamic's fine book *Dynamite*
                    for the tragic minutiae)

Novum Sub Sole '11:
    C. F. Kettering developed the automobile starter motor
    Albert Einstein in Germany
        figured out how much light was deflected

when it passed through the gravitational field of the sun

the word schizophrenia first coined, in Switzerland

Ernest Rutherford
    proposed that the atom has a central nucleus
                    orbited by electrons—

and in Britain the ghastly law known as the Official Secrets Act
It was now a criminal offense for government officials
                to disclose certain categories of information

so that, to this day, the
                government can do anything it wants
                        & prosecute those who reveal it

    The next year something called the "D Notice" committee
    was set up to "guide" the
                    press on national security issues

In painting
Kandinsky, Matisse, Picasso, Chagall, Braque, Gris
                boating in the time-track with
                        brush stroke oars!

"Alexander's Ragtime Band," Irving Berlin
Petrushka, by Igor Stravinsky
Der Rosenkavalier Richard Strauss

& Anna Comstock's great great
                    Handbook of Nature Study

It was the year that
    Hollywood happened
    with David Horsley's first studio
    and 15 other companies also that year

the first Keystone Max Sennett comedy
plus *Anna Karenina*
            and Sara Bernhardt's *La Dame aux Camélias*

        Rilke began the *Duino Elegies* (till 1922)
        Ezra Pound's *Canzoni*
        D. H. Lawrence *The White Peacock*

Joseph Conrad *Under Western Skies*
Theodore Dreiser *Jennie Gerhardt*

Worms and linen:
Carrie Nation began smashing paintings in Hades, June 9 at 64
Hubert Humphrey linen, May 27
Ronald Reagan linen Feb 6   & Elizabeth Bishop on Feb 8
Marshall McLuhan linen, July 21
E. F. Schumacher linen, Aug 16

Dance in the Time-Track, O Nation!

Early in the year
    Ted Roosevelt decided to run for th' Repub nom
                "My hat is in the ring," he said

    He was, he said, worried about social upheaval
                —the Socialists, the Wobblies
                        the entire proposal for Enforced Sharing—

    but was he really?
        Com-fear is always a face-brace for the moaning bemoneyed.

    Senator Bob La Follette of Wisconsin
                    was running as a Progressive Republican
    & there'd be bad blood in the time-flood w/ Roose'
                        whom he was not to support in the fall

Also early in the year the
    Social Democrats won in Germany
                —antiwar, urging solidarity among workers,
                    but facing a vehement German military
                            still shoving toward war

On January 6
New Mexico became the 47th state

─────────────── **The Bread & Roses Strike** ───────────

And then,
in the middle of the month
one of the greatest strikes began
in Lawrence, Massachusetts.

where the American Woolen Company ran four mills
The workers, mostly women, were
English, Irish, Russian, Italian, Syrian, Lithuanian, German, Turkish,
Polish, Belgian, Portuguese, French-Canadian
and at least 12 other nationalities

with an average wage a little under $9 a week.

There was even less money one cold day
in the envelopes passed out to Polish women weavers
so they halted the looms and left the factory.

The next day another 5,000 at another mill
marched to a third mill
& shut off the looms

Soon there were 25,000 strikers.

IWW organizers rushed to Lawrence
and helped hold the strike together

There was a Committee of 56
according to Bill Haywood
"representing 27 different languages"

The workers demanded a 15 percent wage increase,
plus a 54-hour work week
with double pay after 54
and no punishment for those who had struck.

Women befriended each other across ethnic lines
sang songs all the time
held numerous parades

In one some women carried a famous banner
                              "We want bread and roses too"

The strikers had to feed and give winter fuel to 50,000
so soup kitchens were set up
                              & donations came in from all over the nation

The mayor of Lawrence sicced in the local militia
                              who clubbed & beat the women & children
and the governor sent forth the state police

Local church leaders sneered at the strikers
The AF of L was against the strike.
One AFL leader said, "This is a revolution, not a strike."

Late in January
        a parade of strikers was attacked, a riot ensued,
                              & striker Anna LoPizzo was shot to death

A witness said the police fired the shot
but an IWW organizer Joseph Ettor & poet Arturo Giovanitti
                                                        were arrested

Also at January's close
        Syrian striker John Ramy was bayonetted to death

At the height of Bread & Roses
        there were up to 10,000 pickets
                        walking in an endless pain-chain
                                                past the mills

—————————————— **Children** ——————————————

The NY Call, a socialist paper,
                proposed to place strikers' children with sympathetic
                families in other cities

                100 children of strikers on Feb 10
                were met at Grand Central Station
                by 5000 Italian Socialists singing the "Internationale"
                                                and the "Marseillaise"

        Allons, enfants de la patrie

Le jour de gloire est arrivé!

More and more children
                    were being sent to safety
till the authorities banned children from leaving Lawrence
and soldiers beat women and children in a military truck
                    after they were grabbed at the train station
                                                February 24

                    What a disgrace.

At too long last the
        American Woolen Company
                offered pay increases, time-and-a-quarter for overtime,
                            and no reprisals 'gainst strikers

        March 14 on the Lawrence Common
                10,000 workers agreed to end the walk-out
        (& Ettor and Giovanitti months later were found not guilty)

By springtime of '12
                275,000 New England textile workers
                            had gotten pay increases.
and Massachusetts soon passed the first minimum wage law.

        Joe Hill wrote his famous song, "Rebel Girl"
                inspired by strike leader,
                                        Elizabeth Gurley Flynn

            Arise, O Genius of Unions!

1912
    The first U.S. Montessori school opened in Tarrytown
    based on *The Montessori Method*
            by Italian psychiatrist Maria Montessori
                emphasizing self-education & individual initiative

February 12
    The Manchu dynasty was out in China
            and a provisional republic was created

February 14
    Arizona became the 48th state

108

March 1
   the first parachute jump in the USA by Albert Berry

March 19
   In US the Excise Bill became law
            taxing the net income of businesses

————————————— **The Titanic** —————————————

The huge *Titanic* on its maiden voyage
         hit an iceberg off the coast of Newfoundland on 4-15
                                                and slowly sank

2,224 were aboard, & 1,513 died
            because the owners did not provide enough rafts

               Isidor & Ida Straus
               owners of Macy's
                        & A. & S. Straus
                           department stores

            were on the ice-slashed ship

            Come on! Come on!
            they shouted at Ms. Straus
                     Get in the boats!

            but she called for them to go
                     and stood arm in arm with her husband
                     as the last boat left
                     to sink in the final cling

April 22
   Lenin was in Austria
            & wanted an inexpensive way to reach his people
                                    formed *Pravda* (Truth)

1912
   The violence crowd
   sent marines to Honduras, Nicaragua, Cuba and Honduras

   ⟶ In Honduras in Feb to protect banana companies

⟶ To Cuba in May after Afro-Cubans rose up against racial
discrimination

⟶ To Nicaragua in August to stomp down the revolt against
US-installed pres Adolfo Diaz
(The US remained in Nic till '33)

1912

was the year of *Sons and Lovers*
D. H. Lawrence eloped with Frieda von Richthofen
They lived in Europe, Ceylon, Australia, Tahiti, Mexico
and then New Mexico
to cure his tb

Revised edition of the 1899
Theory of the Leisure Class
by Thorstein Veblen

One might peruse Chapter XI
"The Belief in Luck"
wherein the author placed his fingers
on one of the support struts
of American "exceptionalism"

Plus, the key phrase, "conspicuous consumption"
clicked to life
to limn some parts of the new America

The pamphlet, *What is Anarcho-Syndicalism?*
by William Foster and Earl Ford,
published by the Syndicalist League of North America,
in Chicago,
in September.

The anarcho-syndicalist view
was of a nation based on natural production units
to be created by "boring from within" mainstream unions
eschewing electoral politics
& modeled on the French, Italian and Spanish
syndicalist experiments.

Late May in Paris
Vaslav Nijinsky
premiered his art-shaking dance
to the *Prelude à l'Après-midi d'un Faune* of Debussy
(itself based on Stephane Mallarmé's poem of '76)

with Vaslav engaging in probably the
    first onstage mimic beat-off
        since the ancient Boeotian goat dance
(except in ancient Boeotia they probably actually did it)

Nijinsky choreographed it himself
resplendent in golden sandals
as an eros-addled faun
    in the midst of seven cute nymphs
        one of whom was bathing

A kind of flirtation was danced
    then all of the damsels departed
leaving a scarf
which Nijinsky sniffs
    in a famous move

He spreads it out
    then lies upon it
sliding his hand
    down near his Clinton

    and spurt-writhes

There was considerable booing in the audience
and, while some papers praised the ballet
the reviewer in *Le Figaro* the next day complained of
"a lecherous faun, whose movements are filthy & bestial
    in their eroticism

    and whose gestures
        are as crude as they are indecent."

June 22
    at the Republican convention in Chicago
The Teddy man pitched a new "Progressive Republican Party."
but when Taft won the vote

Teddy's supporters walked out
to meet in a nearby auditorium

& founded the Progressive "Bull Moose" Party

July 2
At the Democratic convention in Baltimore
Woodrow Wilson triumphed on the 46th ballot
(He needed ⅔ of the votes to win
by virtue of the Democratic rules of the time)

August 5
The founding convention
of the Progressive Republican Party
nominated the hamster man

Not long thereafter
a reporter asked him how do you feel about running
& Roosevelt replied, "I feel as fit as a bull moose!"

Some Progressives did not trust Teddy's real intentions
There were too many tycoons
in the Roosevelt apparatus for instance
so that some felt he was
not strong enough on the trust issue

All three were fans of big biz

Wilson sought to distinguish 'tween a trust
"an arrangement to get rid of competition"
and bigness, i.e., a biz that "has survived competition by
conquering
in the field of intelligence and economy"

The Progressives supported suffrage
while wince-minded Wilson
would not come out for it!
feeling it was an issue for the states!

—Racism and women's rights
not visited at all by
the whitebread campaign o' '12

112

September 27
    W. C. Handy's "Memphis Blues"
                —first Blues to be published in the USA

October 14
    Teddy Roosevelt bullmoosing in Milwaukee
                                was shot but not killed

November 3
    Kansas, Arizona and Wisconsin
                        voted women's suffrage

November, Woodrow Wilson was elected
                    because of the Taft-Teddy Republican split

                Wilson 6.29m
                Roose 4.2m
                    Taft 3.48m

                Debs doubled his showing, to 900,000
                6% of the voting
                the best Sharing vote before or since

December 2
    Supreme Court dissolved the Union Pacific merger with Southern
        Pacific

Novum in '12:
    Speaking of "What is it?"
    Austro-American physicist Victor Franz Hess
                            discovered cosmic rays

    & the Consumer Price Index began
                as a guide to set cost of living adjustments
                                    for U.S. wages

    Jung's *The Psychology of the Unconscious*

    and a German named Max von Laue showed that
                            crystals
                                scatter x-rays

    One Casimir Funck
            coined th' word "vitamin"

Marcel Duchamp's *Nude Descending a Staircase, II*

plus Robert Delaunay, Giorgio de Chirico,
           Pablo, Gris, Kandinsky
           and Georges Braque, first "papiers collées"
               in the zone of rowing sea-boxes of genius

Henry Cowell's *Tides of Manaunaun*
and Schoenberg's *Pierrot Lunaire*

and the tune, "It's a Long Way to Tipperary"

Edna St. Vincent Millay's *Renascence and Other Poems*
         and the great Constantin Brancusi's *Mlle Pogany*

Jung's *Psychology of the Unconscious*

Also in '12 Alfred Wegener's
      theory of Continental Drift
         to the sneers of colleagues

Poetry: A Magazine of Verse
         founded in Chicago by Harriet Monroe

Worms and Squirms:
Tennessee Williams on March 27   Woody Guthrie July 14
August Strindberg pitchforking in the w.f. May 14
John Cage, linen, September 5
grim-destiny'd Milton Friedman, linen, July 31

and in Milan Benito Mussolini began to edit the socialist paper
    Avanti

January 9
    Richard Nixon was born in Yorba Linda, California

January 11
    the last horse-drawn bus in Paris

February
    The famous Armory Show at th'
    New York City 69th Regiment Armory
    organized by Arthur Davies of the Assoc of American Painters and
            Sculptors
    gave the nation its first view of the avant garde of Europe
    Picasso, for instance, & Matisse, Braque, Brancusi
                                    et al.—
                                    1,300 works

    including the Ashcan artists and artists associated with
                        Alfred Stieglitz's "291" gallery

    Some people howl-mewled in agony

            Duchamp's "Nude Descending a Staircase"
            was called "an explosion in a shingle factory"

    yet 300,000 paid to see the future

February 2
    Grand Central Terminal opened

———————————— **The Great Paterson Strike** ————————

        We hold that it's sacred
                    to read about strikes

such as the one that began on February 25
in Paterson, N.J. with 300 factories
  where silk was woven and dyed
     & 25,000 humans were employed

It was a great strike
begun in the spiritual energy
   of the Bread & Roses triumph in Massachusetts

The broad-silk weavers began it
to block an increase in loom assignments from 2 to 4
     (looms they each had to tend)

There's no limit to the exhaustion
     factory owners seek

Then ribbon-weavers and dyers' helpers joined
    and the strike became the largest in Paterson's
    history

The IWW rushed again to help
   & radicals from Greenwich Village
      & people from the Socialist Party

Women played leadership roles
     in the strike that closed the mills
       for five months
Finally it came down to money
There was not enough to feed their families
    and so it faltered

though frightened owners held off increasing
     the loom assignments to four
       for about ten years.

Too often the workers lose
     in Blake's Satanic mills
& there was too much blame-dabbing
   by upset leftists
    over why the great strike failed

Was it the Socialists' fault? Was it the Wobblies?
Was it them dang Greenwich Village hay-heads?

     Bill Haywood was tossed from the Socialist Party
     executive committee

116

& Helen Keller
wrote in the NY *Call*

how she regretted "the ignoble strife between two factions
[the SP and the Wobs] ... at a most critical period
in the struggle of the proletariat."

February 25
the 16th Amendment, authorizing levying of taxes, was ratified.

February
a right wing general named Victoriano Huerta
grabbed power in Mexico

and had the elected president Francisco Madero
            murdered

            dissolved congress
            and spread right wing nuttery.

Just as United Fruit strangled control o'er Guatemala
        Rockefeller interests liked the conservative Huerta
                for the promise of a Mexican strangle

        though Wilson, after he was sworn in March 4,
                                would want him gone.

——————————— **The Inauguration** ———————————

        Like an up-tight professor
        who doesn't want to show too much Bacchus
        in front of his students

        Wilson refused
                to dance with his wife
        at his Inaugural Ball

March 31 J. P. Morgan passed down, at 75,
                        for pitchfork duty on the w.f.

    Dante himself
        may have handed J. P.
                a finger-melting ouchy pouch
                    in the bolge where white-hot money
                                harms hands

April 1
   Ford installed its first moving assembly line in Detroit

April 8
   There had been no State of the Union speeches to Congress
   for 112 years
         Woodrow Wilson rebegan them

———————————————— **The *Alcools* Decision** ————————————————

         Not long before the great tome
                  Alcools, Poèmes 1898-1913 was published
         on April the 20th
         Apollinaire went to the printers
         and asked them to take out all the commas, quote-marks,
         periods & punctuation

———————————————— **Hissing in Paree** ————————————————

   At the premiere of Stravinsky's *Le Sacre du Printemps*
   at the Théâtre des Champs-Elysées
                  in Paris

   with Vaslav Nijinsky's choreography

   the audience perhaps expected more of a
                  moon-june-spoon-croon sweetness

   & not a startling polyrhythmic April is the Cruelest Month
                                    tone knife.

   It was a remarkable evening of hisses and whistles
   though Nijinsky's dancers were so well rehearsed
                  they were able to perform to the plan
                  even though the music could not be heard.
   Stravinsky, seated in front
                  fled to th' backstage

      Carl Van Vechten recalled
            how someone behind him used the top of his head
            as a drum

118

with his fists

In '14 *The Rite* again was performed
and Stravinsky was carried in triumph
                              on the shoulders of fans

            One moment's shriek
            is another moment's tweak

May 29
    One further step away
                from landed royalty in the US
                the 17th amendment to the Constitution
                was ratified
    transferring election of US Senators from State Legislatures
    to popular vote

June 4
    British suffragette Emily Wilding Davison
    tumbled herself 'neath the King's horse Anmer
        during the Epsom Derby
                    and died

June 7
    the "Pageant of the Paterson Strike"
                            at Madison Square Garden
            organized by John Reed and writers for *The Masses*
            for the striking silkworkers

        It was a "big success"
            but failed to raise money
                or stir the actual masses
                    showing how
                    art, social action, money, power & victory

            do not always hold hands

                            •

        This was the year a group called the Women's Political Union
        led by Harriet Stanton Blatch
        began to canvas in New York State
                        for a referendum on women's right to vote
                            and in '15 the referendum lost!

(but passed later on in '17)

Each Spring
　　　　the parades in NYC for women's suffrage

grew bigger and bigger

Washington Square to 57th Street

　　　　bigger and bigger

　　　　　　till there were 500,000 in 1913.

　　　　This was the year
　　　　th' Antisaloon League
　　　　set off a
　　　　drive to ban
　　　　liquor through
　　　　a Constitutional Amendment

　　　　The WCTU
　　　　joined them.

　　　　Get ready for moonshine

September 13
　　　The Underwood-Simmons Tariff
　　　　　　　lowered tariff rates
　　　with an accompanying income tax
　　　　　of 1% for $20,000 up to 6% for 50,000 and above

──────── **The Great Colorado Fuel & Coal Strike** ────────

　　　　The dour, mean-souled Mr. Rockefeller,
　　　　grabby, vicious, prone to prayer,
　　　　owned the Colorado Fuel & Iron Corporation
　　　　　　　　　　　(with his family)

　　　　11,000 miners worked in the dirty danger
　　　　Italian, Greek, Serb, and eastern Euro immigrants
　　　　　　　　　　　for the most part

120

feudally quartered in company-owned towns
for low pay
& domination by bosses

There's something about mines
(from ancient Egypt on)
that brings out the urge to encroach.

The Strike began in September
after Rockevom henchmen killed
a union organizer

The great United Mine Workers organizer, Mother Jones
helped the strikers

but she was arrested
held in a "dungeonlike cell"
then banned from Colorado

We'll pick up this tale of
Rockeslaughter
when we get to 1914

October 17
The Serbs invaded Albania

October 28
European countries– Britain, France, and Germany—
would not recognize the right wing Huerta gov't in Mexico
till the U.S.A. showed its hand

Then on November 3
Wilson demanded that General Huerta leave

———————————— Water to LA ————————
November 5

Six years it took to build the LA Aqueduct
through many tunnels & 223 miles

till the first water came down the sluiceway
into the San Fernando Valley

                    the aqua vita of the bulldozer

O'er th' years
LA sucked
            more and more water
from the Owens Valley
so that even normal
                    desert plants
                            could not survive

with lungkilling clouds of alkaline dust
                        that floof from the sucked-down floor
                                            to this day

but, as Marc Reisner has noted
            "In the West ...
            water flows uphill toward money."

November 17
    the first ship through the Panama Canal

———————————————— **The Federal Reserve** ————————————————
                    December 13

            Congress passed the Owen-Glass Act
            creating the Federal Reserve System

            & a Federal Reserve Board to set monetary policy
                        plus 12 district Federal Reserve banks

and seven days later
            the first crossword puzzle
                    in the *New York World*

'13 Novum:
    Proust's *Du Côté de chez Swann*
            Vol 1 of *À la Recherche du Temps Perdu*
            written in the corklined writing room of his Paris pad
            on the way to seven volumes
                        he was 41

    Camel cigarettes were lesion-launched
                        with a huge ad campaign
                    peppermint Life Savers

122

                    the Duesenberg
                              Quaker Puffed Wheat
              Actors Equity

The American Cancer Society
       Th' B'nai B'rith formed the Anti-Defamation League in NYC
            a British scientist, Frederick Soddy coined "isotope"
                    E. McCollum in the US iso'd Vitamin A

Sigmund F: *Totem and Taboo*
Guillaume Apollinaire's *The Cubist Painters*
                  and the first readymade, Duchamp's *Bicycle Wheel*

Rachmaninov's *The Bells* Debussy's ballet *Jeux*
          Anton Webern's *Six Bagatelles*
                  Shaw's *Pygmalion*

The first feature film, a western,
          The Squaw Man
          shot in Los Angeles

       was a big hit

with a producer, Sam Goldwyn, formerly a glove merchant
and a so-so playwright named Cecil B. DeMille

                              •

A young socialist genius
       named Chaplin made 35 movies for Mack Sennett
       and Sennett hired Fatty Arbuckle as a Keystone Kop

The foxtrot became popular
                  in the dance world

Rolled upon the linen in '13:
              Danny Kaye Jan 18
              Woody Herman May 16
              Gerald Ford July 14
              Jesse Owens Sept 12   Norman O. Brown Sept 25
              Albert Camus Nov 7
              Benjamin Britten Nov 22
              Delmore Schwartz Dec 8   Muriel Rukeyser Dec 15
              Willy Brandt Dec 18

              Roil, O Century, Roil!

In January
    The IWW singer Joe Hill was arrested near Salt Lake City
    for the murder of a Salt Lake City shopkeeper
                          which had occurred a couple days earlier
    It was likely a frame-up
          for his IWW work
              (Hill was convicted in June
                    & sentenced to die)

January 27
    Pres Oreste of Haiti abdicated during a revolt
    The US marines came ashore to "preserve order"
              (One General Zamon was elected pres a few days later)

February 13
    American Society of Composers, Authors and Publishers
                                (ASCAP) in NYC

———————————— **Margaret Sanger** ————————————

had been a housewife with kids in Westchester,
but had insisted on moving to Manhattan in '10

She worked as a nurse on the Lower East Side
Joined the IWW
    & became a militant

She learned from Emma Goldman
               the politics of women's bodies
& began to write and speak on issues such as venereal disease
             In '12 she began a series o' articles on sexual
             matters for the *NY Call*

with a big response from working class women.

Then, from March to October of '14
Margaret Sanger published *American Rebel*
                              a feminist newspaper
Its motto was *No Gods, No Masters*
& it sang in the time-track of anticlericism, free love,
                              & working class women.

Editorials promoted birth control and the ultraleft,
sparking out at "bourgeois feminists"

In th' July issue she published an essay, "In Defense of
          Assassination"
for which the Post Office stomped out her mailing privileges

In August Sanger was indicted for violating the
                    Comstock Postal Act of 1873
                    and she fled to Europe and
                         American Rebel never returned to life

          The police can usually kill a publication
          through indictments

———————— **The Colorado Coal Strike Continues** ————————

The Rockefellers tossed the miners
                    from their company-owned shacks
                                        after the strike began
They set up tents in nearby hills
                         and kept the picket lines going

Rockie hired a detective agency
          which raided the tent towns with Gatling guns and rifles
& Governor Ammons
          sent the National Guard
                    to shake the strikers
The Guard, whose wages were paid by the Rock's,
brought scabs to the mines
          & strikers were arrested by the hundreds

but, even in the cold cold weather of the winter o' '13-'14
                              the strike struck onward!

President Wilson meanwhile
        was paying attention to Mexico
                during those months

He wanted Huerta out
        and cut off military aid
though old man Rockefeller and other conservatives
                liked him

The US Atlantic fleet had gone out on winter maneuvers
        and came to various ports on the Mexican coast
Some sailors went ashore in Vera Cruz to get some gas
        They were arrested & brought through the streets
After their release Pres Huerta refused the US request
        for a 21-gun Mexican salute of the US flag
                as an atonement for the arrests

Four days later there was fighting
        19 Americans perished
           and 126 Mexicans

──────────── **The Ludlow Massacre of April 20** ────────────

Only by keeping the images alive
        in text & song
           does a massacre teach tomorrow
as Euripides keeps alive the women of Troy

The tent town lay quiet
        in the smoky dawn
           near Trinidad

Soldiers and Rockegoons encircled the strikers

The National Guard was positioned in the hills
        overjutting the biggest striker tent town

The guard began to fire machine guns at the tents
where a thousand men and women and children
           were residing

The miners fired back
& women and children dug pits under the tents
                                                to escape the bullets

At darkfall the forces of Rockefeller
                            came eviling with torches down the hillside

to arson the tents
                    with miners and families
                                    fleeing up nearby steepnesses

Goony war whoops gooned the smoke
13 were shot dead

Then, as rosy-arsoned dawn arose,
a telephone man
                    lifted an iron bed above a pit

        and found
        twelve children and two women
                            twisted and charred in desperate thanatos

                    This was the Ludlow Massacre
                    from the mind of Rockevom

─────────────── **The Shelling of Veracruz** ───────────────

Around the time the lineman found the bed-pitted bodies
Mexico severed diplomatic relations with the US
& American warships were firing shells at Veracruz
& then the US seized the port
to prevent German munitions coming ashore for
                                        Huerta's troops.

─────────────── **Ludlow Shaking the Nation** ───────────────

Word of the Ludlow Massacre shook the nation
the 21 dead, including 11 children
                    seemed a much greater tragedy
                            that the shelled victims at Veracruz

        Rallies all over the nation

Upton Sinclair was arrested
in a silent picket at the Rockefeller offices
at 26 Broadway
Other pickets at Standard Oil offices in San Francisco
Max Eastman, editor of *The Masses*
took the train to Colo to write the strike.

In Tarrytown Wobblies picketed the Rockefeller estate,
& four Wobblies died when a bomb went off in a Lexington Ave
tenement—the speculation was that
it was being made for Rockefeller's townhouse.

Barrels of neg-ink
forced the Rockefellers
to do a big public image campaign
and to institute a company union in Colorado coal mines.

Weak efforts, but they semaphored
a slight liberal shift
among important capitalists.

The miners began an armed rebellion
but Pres Wilson sent the U.S. Army into so-Col April 28

after which the strike waned
but left a line of remorse
all the way from Ludlow '14
to Attica '71

•

This was the urn-of-prophecy year that
Mohandas Gandhi departed South Africa
after 20 years there
to India

He had developed his *satyagraha*
"firmness in truth"
his program of passive resistance

against the ghastly apartheid in S.A.
and now brought satyagraha to India
to peel it free from
the grabbers of England.

128

May 7
     Mother's Day, the 2nd Sunday in May,
                    established by resolution in Congress
     after a six-year campaign by one Anna May Jarvis
     a suffrage struggler
               who felt she had neglected her mom

1914
     W. C. Handy's "St. Louis Blues"
               and Edgar Rice Burroughs' *Tarzan of the Apes*

     It was the year of recession
     much unemployment
                    losses of jobs

                    Don't worry
                    guys
                    war's a-comin'

June 11
     In Niagara Falls—brokered by Argentina, Brazil and Chile—
     delegates approved a new Mexican gov't
     and a peace agreement was soon signed 'tween the US and Mexico

June 13
     Greece stomped Turkey out of Chios and Mytilene
                    in the continuing dissolution of the
                                        Ottoman Empire

———————————— **Killings in Sarajevo** ————————————
                    June 28

          Archduke Francis Ferdinand of Austria
          heir to the ozymandian throne
          and his wife
               the Duchess of Hohenburg,

     were assassinated in an open car in Sarajevo
                         the main town in Bosnia
     by an 18-year-old student named Gavrilo Princip
                    who wanted to bye bye the Hapsburg rule
     & win freedom for Serbia.

A month later Austria-Hungary declared war on Serbia
an act that triggered
creepy links
that led to WWI and millions of skulls
on Europa's fields

July 16
Pres Huerta fled into exile, replaced by the *pro tem* Carbajal,
till August when Carbajal also was put to flight

July 29
Russia mobilized over a million troops.

July 30
The great socialist Jean Jaurès
author of the 8-volume
Histoire Socialiste de la Révolution Française
was murdered in Paris at 55
by an ultranationalist bonk-bonk

after Jaurès had repeatedly called for the unity of Euro-Soc's 'gainst war

------------------------ **Mobilization Mania** ------------------------

Testosterone levels were high
'mong the military of mighty
Europe
after A-H declared war on Serbia

All of Europe's nations seemed to strut around
like roosters
Bombledoodledoo!
Bombledoodledoo!

On July 30,
the Germans said to the Russians,
Well, if you, Russia, don't demobilize within 24 hours,
we gonna mobilize too
& on August 1 Germany declared war on Russia,
while France prepared its bayonets
& on the 3rd Germany declared war on France

Choo choo choodledoodledoo!

                    the troop trains
                    were on their way
                        choo choo

        Railroads
        were as unstoppable
                as the triremes to Mitylene
                        once were for Athens

        so that the war became certain
        because the
                troop trains
                    choo choo
                could not be called back
                        choo choo choo

August 4
        US declared neutrality in the
                tale of slaughter
                        to be known as WW I

        In fact, the war in Europe did not impinge at all
                        on the first traffic lights, in Cleveland,
                                        on August 5

─────────────────── **Crazed with War** ───────────────

August 6
        Austria-Hungary warred on Russia
        and Serbia and Montenegro warred on Germany

August 10
        France made war on Austria

August 12
        Britain declared war on Austria-Hungary

On August 15
        the Panama Canal opened.
                The USA had agreed to turn it over to Panama in '99

August 20
        Germany occupied Brussels

August 23
  Japan warred on Russia

September 26
  the Federal Trade Commission was set up by Congress

September 27
  Russians crossed th' Carpathians to invade Hungary

October 12
  to November 11 the first battle of Ypres in Belgium
  —the Germans struggling to snap the Allied line

October 15
  Congress passed the Clayton Anti-Trust Act, giving labor unions
  bargaining power in negotiations with management

  This somewhat strengthened the Sherman Antitrust Act,
                                        around since 1890.
  It exempted unions from the anti-trust law

  Big biz had spurted in size for 20 years
  with power blocks forming
                  and all types of industry
                  railroads, farm equip, public utilities,
                                        tobacco, oil
          controlled by single corporations

          For instance, the baleful
          monopolist, J. D. Rockefeller
                  hirer of goon-squads
          had once owned
          85 percent of domestic oil, and 90 of exports

October-November
  The Germans came to
  the little Belgian town
                  known as Ypres

  for th' first battle of WWI (there were three such battles at Ypres)

By early November
  Russia, France, Britain

132

bared their guns on Turkey
                    and the weak Ottoman empire
          (which was supporting Germany).

Meanwhile on election night
     in New York's Lower East Side
                    it was party time!
They danced through the cobbled streets till dawn
when Meyer London
          whose father had worked in an
                              anarchist print shop
was elected a socialist to the
                    U.S Congress!

London said,
          "As a Socialist
          instead of denying the existence
                    of the class struggle
          I seek to minimize its bitterness"

(London was trapped inside
                    one of those ghastly sociologic sandwiches
          he wasn't left enough for the left
          nor right enough for the pro-war right

and the Zionists disliked him because
          he refused to endorse a home for Jews in Palestine.

Dems and Reps united behind a single "patriotic" candidate
                              and axed London in 1918

though in '20 he rewon his seat
but then odious gerrymandering
                    so much a tool of the Republicrats
                              axed him again in 1922)

                    Meanwhile, nothing can prevent
                         the fine knowledge
                              of the night-long party
                                   in the Lower East Side
               when the socialist Meyer London
                              knew glory.

November 23
    US troops were withdrawn from Mexico
                after another buzz of control

    Wilson allowed racist sleaze in his cabinet
    to set up separate
            dining and restrooms for black and white workers
            & to work in separate rooms

    The thought of being supervised by a black
    was almost as horrifying a thought
                to a Wilsonian racist
    as a black dong
        in a white sarong

        Senator La Follette spoke up for black gov't workers
        but Wilson wince-whined onward
                  and did nothing

December 2
    the Austrians took Belgrade
        (which was reoccupied by the Serbs on the 14th)

December 14
    John Muir died
        the "Yosemite Prophet"

    who led the successful campaign to protect Yosemite Valley
    from mining & logging
            till it was declared a national park

    1892 he helped cofound the Sierra Club
                     its first president

        He sang the wilderness
        spoke up for outcast animals
            such as the wolf & the grizzly

December 21
    the first German air raid on England
            south coast towns bombed

Linen 1914:
    William S. Burroughs Feb 5   Tennessee Williams Mar 26
    Joe Louis May 13
    John Berryman October 25

Dylan Thomas on October 27
Jonas Salk on October 28

Novum in '14:
 Ernest Rutherford
 gave the name proton
 to the charged nucleus of hydrogen
 which was then seen to be the fundamental atom
                                    (little did they know!)

         and all of reality seemed
         made of protons & electrons
         (till the discovery in '32 of the neutron,
                     and then, later, many more particles)

Mussolini founded *Il Popolo d'Italia*
Ted Roosevelt's *History as Literature*

and in England
         the Vorticists appeared!
         with Wyndham Lewis' *Blast: Review of the Great English Vortex*

Henry Bacon's Lincoln Memorial in DC
Marcel Duchamp's *Bottle Back*
Henri Gaudier-Brzeska's *Hieratic Head of Ezra Pound*

Charles Ives' *Three Places in New England*

 Robert Frost's *North of Boston*
 The Single Hound, posthumous poems of Emily D
 James Joyce, *Dubliners*
             after nine years struggling with publishers
         and the elastic brassiere was invented by Mary Phelps Jacob
             in NYC.

There were
79 lynchings in the US

     Thanks, hicks

& it was the baleful year
         the French used poison gas
                 from rifle grenades

             Drift Perilous, O Century!

1915

January 3
  Th' Germans on th' western front first used gas-filled shells
                                                 Thanks, Germans.

January 12
  The House of Representatives
                     stomped down a proposal for women's suffrage

On January 17
  Ralph Chaplin
              poet & IWW organizer
                        wrote "Solidarity Forever"
                   to the tune of "John Brown's Body"

January 19
  the first German Zeppelin raid
                        on the eastern ports of Britain

January 28
  The nihil-nope of nativism
                        still mean-spirited the Senate
  which passed a bill to limit immigration
                    including a literacy test
                        which, to his credit, Wilson vetoed
                              & the House failed to override

January 31
  Germans used poison gas for the first time in the East
                              attacking the Russians

  (Th' French used gas in '14
                  rifle grenades

  but the Germans were the first to use it a lot

in Ypres in '15
chlorine, tear, mustard, phosgene)

February
Germans in Zeppelins began bombing Britain
Then, in March, English airplanes started
bombing German troop trains

The Germans announced
sub warfare
to break the Allied naval blockade
of Central Powers

On February 10
Wilson warned Germany the
US would hold it accountable for
deaths and/or property loss in sub attacks

March 3
D. W. Griffith's right-wing Klanophilic film
The Birth of a Nation
ope'd in NY

a 3-hour flick
with a sympathetic rendering of the forming of the Klan
(Griffith was the son of a Confederate Colonel)

March 21
Germ Zep's raided Paris

——————— **IWW Agricultural Workers Organization** ———————
April

The IWW Agricultural Workers Organization
in Kansas City, Missouri

was a big success

with 18,000 sign-ups by the end of '16

Some believe that the success of th' IWW ag org
was a big, unspoken reason
for the U.S. gov't's ceaseless
          persecution of the IWW
                    during and after the First World War.

April 22
    at Langemark near Ypres, Belgium
                    in the second battle of W1 there

    the Germans used poison gas in cylinders the first time
    wearing helmets with gas masks
    & grrr-storming the French and Canadian troops
    along a four-mile-long cloud of green-yellow chlorine

    Losses were heavy
                    Thanks, o war-slime!

Both sides began using gas
After masks were in use, gases were invented
                    to penetrate the skin

———————————————— **All Quiet** ————————

    The gas trapped soldiers in trenches
                    in slow pain wrenches
    They rarely tell the truth about war
    Homer, Herodotus, Tacitus,
              & Kipling too

· Erich Maria Remarque
          later noted
                    how thousands of Germans might die on a day
                    but the news dispatches would say

          All Quiet on the Western Front

    The British public in '15 was not told of the slaughter

          All Quiet on the Western Front

    Nor were the revellers

at the strawberry festival
            at the First Christian Church

All Quiet on the Western Front

•

It was the year of the Klan Revival
        by the Georgia sleazopath, William J. Simmons

      The Klan dry-heaved in the American time-track
        from '22 till 1939

           (& then another heave in the '60s)

   hating Negroes, Catholics, Jews, Internationalism,
Darwinism, the fossil record,
               &, tremble O Universe, jazz too!

--------------- **Cyclical Mass Violence** ---------------

The century began to have
        cyclical slaughter
as, beginning in April and throughout W1
the Turks slaughtered Armenians
      —somewhere 'tween 600k and 1.2m
          out of a population of 2.5m

Shame in the Time-Track, O Turks!

May 7
   The Cunard Line's *Lusitania* was sent to the bottom
     by German torpedoes
off Ireland

  1,195 (or 1,198) drowned
       (128 Americans among them)

The Germans justified it on grounds that
                    the ship was carrying munitions

While Teddy Roosevelt gave out a huge skree for war
Wilson negotiated with Germans
who said they'd pay reparations, and no more attacks

                    —& war was averted for now

May 24
    Thomas Edison presented the "telescribe"
                    a device for recording telephone talk.

May 27
    was the date Turkish murd-heads
            began to deport Turkey's 1.8m Armenians
                            to Syria and Mesopotamia
        —⅓ deported   ⅓ killed   ⅓ evaded

July 2
    The US Senate reception room was destroyed by bomb put there
                            by a German professor

July 27
    Direct wireless service commenced 'tween the US and Japan

    the same day
    a rev in Haiti
    w/ president Vilbrun Sam killed by a mob
            & naturally the US Marines
                had to land
                    "to restore order"

The end of July was the moment
            the Germans first used flame-throwers
                        on the trench-gored Western Front

———————————————— **Leo Frank** ————————————————

        In June the governor of Alabama
        had commuted the death sentence
        of Leo Frank
                an Atlanta, Georgia factory owner

                    & a Jew
        convicted of raping & murdering a 14-year-old white girl
                                    who worked at his factory
        (& very likely innocent)

        Demagogues demagogued dipshittedly
        & in August
        a group of thugs
        seized him from prison
                        & hanged him

        The rope & his clothing
                        were sought-after trophies
        & someone counted 15,000 crackers
                                cracker-flowing past his body

August 30
        US protested to Germany
                        which ordered its subs and ships
        to warn enemy passenger vessels before sinking

September
        Margaret Sanger returned after year of exile
        to face trial for sending smut through the mail
                        in *Women Rebel*
                        The d.a. then dropped her case

September 8
        the illustrious totalitarian tsar Nicholas II
        took personal control of Russian forces

September 10
        Tanks were first used by the British
                        designed to crush barbed wire
                        cross trenches
                                be impervious to machine guns
        with soldiers swooping in behind them

Duchamp Debarks
September 15

Marcel Duchamp
        arrived from Europe
                in a blaze of fame

Reporters met him at the NY docks
                as if he were Mark Twain

The great artist carried peculiar gifts for the nation
the seeds of Dada
the frozen glyphs of the new Muse Retentia
the kiss of frozen dust
& the multi-planed visions
                of Braque & Picasso

September 16
    Haiti became a US protectorate

October 9
    Austria-Hungary captured Belgrade once again, in Serbia

October 15
    American bankers, led by J. P. Morgan's bank loaned $500m
                        to England and France.

A Big American Relief Effort

Before America's entrance in the war
there was a big US effort
        by a group called the
Committee for Relief of Belgium

5,000,000 people were helped

A mining magnate & engineer named Herbert Hoover
headed the effort
        & became famous for the goodness of it

The Death of Joe Hill

None of the witnesses to the murder
i.d.'d Joe Hill as the

killer who fled the scene
His impending execution on November 19
became an international cause—
The Swedish gov't, even President Woodrow Wilson
intervened on his behalf.

Shortly before the raising of the rifles
in Utah
he wired IWW sec-treas Bill Haywood,
"Don't waste any time in mourning—organize."

You will eat (you will eat), bye and bye (bye and bye)
Blam!
In that glorious land in the sky (way up high)
Blam!
Work and pray (work and pray), live on hay (live on hay)
Blam!
You'll get pie in the sky when you die (that's a lie)

Thousands attended his funeral service in Chicago
lining the streets and singing his songs

A year of genius:
Alban Berg's *Three Pieces for Orchestra*
& "Pack Up Your Troubles in Your Old Kit Bag"

Duchamp's *In Advance of the Broken Arm*
& he began *The Large Glass* or
The Bride Stripped Bare by Her Bachelors, Even

the dysentery bacillus was iso'd
E. C. Kendall isolated thyroxine from the thyroid gland
& Einstein's general theory of relativity

Cathay Ezra Pound
Virginia Woolf *The Voyage Out*
D. H. Lawrence *The Rainbow*
Maugham's *Of Human Bondage*

'15 flicks: *Les Vampires Carmen*
Fatty and Mabel's Simple Life (with Fatty Arbuckle)

Linen and scythes:
Orson Welles May 6
Saul Bellow June 10
Ingrid Bergman August 29

Arthur Miller Oct 17
Booker T. Washington reaping the perma-wheat Nov 14
Frank Sinatra linen on December 12

Shine, O Nation

February 21–Dec 18
    On the Western Front
        Germans attempted to capture th' French city of Verdun
        —The Germans & French each had 400,000 deaths
        in the famous First Battle of Verdun
        & both countries
            shielded the numbers from their people

    & innocent horses too
    by the tens of thousands
        lay shelled to death in scenes
        not even Stendahl could have caught

March 9
    The Mexican guerrilla leader Pancho Villa led
    a predawn attack on
        the U.S. garrison town of Columbus, N.M.

    The history texts vary—either 16 or 19 Americans were killed
            & over 100 Villistas
    Why an invasion?
    perhaps to draw the US into the Mexican civil war
        (Villa was warring 'gainst Venustiano Carranza)
    or to get even with an arms dealer in Columbus who'd burned him

    or perhaps he actually thought he could
        begin a campaign
            to set up a warhold

144

in N.M.

One week later
   General John J. Pershing
   with 12,000 troops
   pursued Villa
       ever deeper into Mexico

   Villagers helped him escape
      —& Wilson withdrew the troops after a year

―――――――――― **Dada Comes to Zürich** ――――――――――

    They came to the wealthy, liberal city of Zürich
                from the slaughterous zones of trench
      like boats on a scroll

     in the year of Dada

   Lenin lived at #12 Spiegelgasse
     a little street in the red light district
       & just down the hill at #1 was a nightclub
   that changed its name
       to the Cabaret Voltaire

   The soul-boats had come ashore
        from the violence of Europe
   There was a German actor/playwright named
   Hugo Ball and his girlfriend, the singer Emmy Hennings.
   From Bucharest in Rumania came
   the poet Tristan Tzara
      & maskmaker/artist Marcel Janco

   There were the Alsatian artist Hans Arp
   a chanter named Richard Huelsenbeck from Berlin
          & others

   It was Hugo Ball that, moving fast,
      founded the Cabaret Voltaire
        in February

Emmy Hennings sang songs,
                    with Ball on piano
& there were pictures by Hans Arp on the walls.

She had the kind of shraily voice
                    that either drove you insane
                              or thrill-chilled your ears

        "The Cabaret Voltaire, "
                    wrote Hugo Ball at the time
        ... has as its sole purpose to draw attention,
        across the barriers of war and nationalism,
        to the few independent spirits
                    who live for other ideals."

They had a Russian evening
and then a French evening
in which the concept of "simultaneity"
                    1st written by Apollinaire
came to Zürich
          the same weeks as Verdun's slaughter

Hans Arp:
"Revolted by the butchery of the 1914 world war
          we in Zürich devoted ourselves to the arts.
We were seeking an art ... to cure the madness of the age
          & a new order to restore the balance
                    'tween heaven & hell"

Someone thought of the name *Dada*
          two syllables with enough
                    force to move around the world
                              in a matter of months
(They argued the rest of their lives over
          who thought it up, and exactly when)

────────────── **The Birth of Perf-Po** ──────────────

There were Dada evenings at the Cabaret Voltaire
where poets chanted poems
          & put on "ballet-theater" performances

Marcel Janco made masks

146

which seemed to give
the performers the power of
The Other

They donned then danced
with strange Otherly arm and body wails
tuned to the ghastly lyre of war

"Nightmare" was a name of one of the ballet-simultaneities
&
"Despair of Celebration."

One night at the C. Voltaire
was devoted to Hugo Ball's phonetic poems, *Lautgedichte,*
the placed was utterly packed
and Janco and Ball had
outfitted themselves
with shiny blue cardboard cylinders
on the legs
& big gold cardboard collars
hanging down like wings
to be flapped by raising & lowering the arms

Then the performers began to sing-shout
—a holy, mind-freeing rinse of nonsense
to laugh away
the stench of the trench

a Rinse heard as far away as
San Francisco

On another night
Tristan Tzara, Richard Huelsenbeck, & Marcel Janco
put on the world's first *poème simultané*
singing and shouting their lines together
just down the hill from V. I. Lenin.

There were art exhibits of works by
de Chirico, Max Ernst, Kandinsky, Klee, Picasso

& a magazine called *DADA*
inspired by the great hieroglyphic collages of Max Ernst

Though the Cabaret Voltaire

barely made it into 1917
it offered proof of some sort of Jungian Dada Mind
as the D word spread
almost instantly
to the US, Germany, France, & Italy

―――――――――――――――――― **Verdun** ――――――――

The spring that Dada
emerged in dancing blue cylinders
the war's 3rd year of floundering blood-hell
battered all Bibles

as in February in northeast France—more ghastly evil of slaughter
in Verdun
and along the Somme River in France, more ghastly slaughter & evil

and Russia, ghastly losses in the Carpathian Mountains
so that, by year's end,
while their armies were crouched down
in trenches of slime

leaders in war rooms or castles
drew circles of schemes
for the edge of
a nonexistent victory

―――――――――――――――― **The Easter Uprising** ――――――――
April 24–29

there was the uprising in Dublin by Irish Republicans
for full independence
led by Patrick Pearse and James Connolly

They captured the General Post Office in Dublin and declared the
Republic of Ireland

There were only 1,000 of 'em
and a huge force of Brits landed to stomp it down

—w/ bombardment for four days, till finally the Irish surrendered

148

Pearse, Connolly and 13 more were executed "summarily"

> but it was the uprising
> to turn fate
> > toward the long-luckless Irish

> as Yeats noted in his great poem
> "Easter 1916"
> how
> "a terrible beauty is born"

──────────── **Wobblies Again Defend Freedom** ────────────

> Everett, Washington on the Puget Sound
> with its 35,000 residents
> was a place to ship out timber

> In May 1,400 shingle cutters went on strike
> & Sheriff McRae made some arrests

> The IWW in Seattle sent one James Rowan
> > to organize in Everett

> When Rowan arrived, he stood to speak and was arrested

> The Industrial Workers of the World
> > once again arose to defend
> > > the Constitution's freedoms

> 41 Wobblies arrived by ferry on Oct 30

> Right at the dock a sheriff's posse surrounded them
> and they were thugged and beaten badly

> On Sunday, November 6, another 250 Wobblies
> > > arrived by ferry
> > to challenge the sheriff's repression
> > > at a public meeting

> The Sheriff was drunk, and his deputies began to shoot
> > at the Wobblies while they were still in the boat

> Some Wobblies shot back

and why not?

Ai, before the ferry could depart
5 were dead, 6 missing, & 27 passengers were wounded

On the gunfiring shore
lay one dead deputy, one dead lumber official
                                             & 24 wounded

There was a big national stir
They called it the Everett Massacre

24 IWW-ers were put to trial
but they defended themselves with vehemence,
                              so that charges were dismissed.

Because of the One Big Union victory
the timber workers
                 gathered the courage at last
                 to get better working conditions & wages

As the Wobblies termed it
         "the timberbeast became a lumberworker"

That spring
    Monet began his waterlilies series
                              in Giverny

& in May
    US Marines were sent to the Dominican Republic
                 and then, in July, the Marines swooped into Haiti

June 1
    Wilson's pal, the Boston attorney Louis Brandeis,
                 was finally okayed by the Senate for the Supreme Court

         Rightwingers & anti-Semites
                      had struggled mightily
                           to stab him out of there

              in that he was too liberal, plus
              was there anything more terrifying
                              to ordnungoids

than a Liberal Jew with Power?

as when, slowly, too slowly
Brandeis was able
to pull the court away
from overt right-wing ugliness

June 10
Charles E. Hughes was nom'd for pres at th' Republican convention

June 15
Wilson nominated again for pres by the Democrats in St Louis

1916
Provincetown Playhouse in Mass
produced Eugene O'Neill's first play

July 1–November 19
Battle of the Somme
offensive by French and English which in six months gained 5 miles

Brit/French deaths were 620k, Germans 450k

July 17
Wilson signed the Federal Farm Loan Act,
a banking system for loans to farmers

July 22
There was a Preparedness Day parade in SF
—one of those rev-up events
urging the nation to war.

A bomb blew &
9 were killed
The authorities
framed railroad union activist Tom Mooney
& a man named Warren Billings

Mooney they sent to die, and Billings got life
It was one of those cases
where, even after the frame-up was totally shown,
cap-slime kept the innocent in jail

Even President Wilson urged mercy, so that Mooney's death
            sentence

                                                            was null'd.

For twenty years they rotted
                    in cages
    till at last in 1939
            they were freed

        (& so few recall the injustice
                        at century's end.)

August 25
    Congress created the National Park Service

August 31
    a New labor law
    giving the 8-hour day to interstate railroad workers!
    a goal of labor unions since the 1880s

    —before now they had to work ten hours before overtime pay began

September 1
            By the Keating-Owen Act the interstate transport of
                    child-labor goods
            was made illegal, plus mine work by children
            and nighttime work for those under 16 banned
            plus daytime work had to be 8 hours or less

September 7
    the Workmen's Compensation Act passed

                            •

The radical physician Marie Equi
reworked Margaret Sanger's birth control pamphlet
improving its medical accuracy
                and then right-wing repressionists
                arrested them both in Portland
        at a birth control demonstration
                            the summer o' '16

This year and the next
    Emma Goldman (of IWW) and Margaret Sanger (of SP)
    visited clinics in Holland
          where women were fitted with diaphragms
    & they saw how
    European unions and socialist parties were promoting
        contraceptives.

    The Sanger/Goldman synapse
    came up with a plan for civil disobedience
    in the US,
          handing out banned leaflets about contraception
    while opening banned birth control clinics

        The guys at the top of leftist groups
                yawned
                but women union members
                        were eager for it

        It wasn't many years after
                the risks that Goldman & Sanger took
        there were birth control leagues
                across the nation

October 16
    Margaret Sanger opened the first birth control clinic, in Brooklyn

    It was the year the
    socialist feminist birth-control advocate Rose Stokes
    was arrested distributing birth control info at a rally at Carnegie Hall.
    She also wrote a play about the sexual double standard,
                    The Woman Who Wouldn't.

                  •

    Einstein's General Theory of Relativity
    on which he'd labored 11 years
          was smuggled out of wartime Germany
              where he was antiwar

    In the general theory of relativity
    he told the world that
          mass generates a gravitational field that curves space!

while in the States,
        Woodrow Wilson
                hungry for a big place in history

shoving shoving shoving
to build a much bigger army & navy

& Teddy R, growling
                for mid-life glory
kept shouting
        from the sidelines, "Kill the bastards!"

as if some bullets, vile battle
                & bayonets dried brown with brains
                        would grant him eternity

1916–1917
    even though the conservative President Venustiano Carranza
    was against it—There was a Mexican constitution passed
    which has been described as
    "the most far-reaching attempt the world had seen to establish
                            a welfare state."

- all land was declared the property of the state
- it guaranteed an 8-hour working day
- and profit-sharing
- a minimum wage
- compensation for industrial injuries
- the right to organize unions
- & right to strike
- and church was banned from owning property

──────────────── **The No War Man** ────────────────

On November 7
Woodrow Wilson

was reelected on his summer o' '16 slogan
"He kept us out of war"

9.1m votes for the dour professor
8.5m votes for Charles E. Hughes

Some "German moderates"
warned Wilson that fall
that Germany might well resume
U-boat warfare unless
he could mediate a peace

so after the election
the President tried to broker a settlement

In England, John Maynard Keynes warned his nation
was running out of credit with America

The 18th of December Wilson sent forth a "peace note"
asking the warriors to list their goals in the gore

noting that "the objects which the statesmen of the belligerents
on both sides have in mind
are virtually the same"

In this note he called for a new League of Nations
"to insure peace & justice throughout the world."

Early in '17 the English replied quietly & politely
while the Germans were dismissive

1916:
Jeanette Rankin, a pacifist Republican from Montana
became the first woman in the House of Representatives
hooray!

Then, on December 13/14
the legendary snuff-out of Grigory Rasputin
whose randy behavior
& hypnotic hold over Tsarina Alexandra
made some tremble with hatred
especially when the autocratic tsar was gone
so often running the army

Court insiders came to believe
                that Russia would revert almost at once
                                to a constitutional monarchy
                                        with the Rasp' man gone

so they invited the Rasp' to Prince Yusupov's pad
Here, try some of our poisoned almond & chocolate pastries

                Rasp' kept breathing

The good Prince then shot Grigory

                Rasp' kept breathing

Finally someone else shot him

                Rasp' barely breathing

then they carried him out to a hole in a frozen canal
                                & offered him to the water

Novum '16:
        Ferdinand de Saussure
        published his lecture notes
                A Course in General Linguistics

how language sounds are arbitrary signs
that define one another through their relations
                more than through their meanings.

                a line of thought
                that would lead
                        heh heh

                60 years later
                        to Language Poetry

Lenin's *Imperialism: the Highest Stage of Capitalism*

                With soldiers flipping out in the
                        slimy horror of the War 1 trenches
                a guy named F. W. Mott expounded the theory of shell-shock

                & the techniques of plastic surgery
                        leaped forward in the warpy gore

Charles Ives' *Symphony #4*
James Joyce *Portrait of the Artist as a Young Man*
Franz Kafka *Metamorphosis*
Bound East by Eugene O'Neill
            Sandburg's *Chicago Poems*

    & let us not forget
    windshield wipers, Lucky Strikes & Lincoln Logs

'16 linen & permasleep:
        Henry James on February 28 at 72
        Jack London November 22, at 40
        Milton Babbitt May 10
        Walter Cronkite
        François Mitterand Oct. 26
        Eddie Arcaro February 19

    Flicks: *Intolerance* directed by D. W. Griffith
            Love and Journalism by Mauritz Stiller

On January 9
    the Germans elected to restart submarine warfare February 1st

    Apparently the reasoning was this:
    it'll take US a long time to mobilize,
    and by then,
            with their increased subs
                    the Germans will have interdicted supplies
                                    to England and Allies

        and therefore before America
                        arrives out of breath
        the Kaiser

will have already won!

Then came

The Zimmerman Telegram

On January 19
a coded message was sent from

German Foreign Secretary Arthur Zimmermann
                              to the German Minister in Mexico.

It urged a German-Mexican alliance so that
if the US declared a war against Germany
        when the Germans rebegan their unrestricted submarine
        warfare on February 1
        the Mexicans would invade the American Southwest

        & then, when peace came
        Mexico would be awarded the territory "lost" in
                              New Mexico, Texas & Arizona
                              back in 1848

The telegram was intercepted and de-coded by British naval
        intelligence
and sent to Washington,
                where it was released to the press on March 1.

There was a big big outcry in America
& a factor that led to war on April 6

January 22
    Wilson went before Congress
        with a plan for a "world league of peace"

        Meanwhile they called it the "turnip winter" in central Europe
        where stomachs rumbled like distant shells

On February 1
    Germany declared unrestricted sub warfare
                    in a baleful arrogance spasm
                            that would lead to Hitler & Total Evil
Two days later

158

the US liner *Housatonic* was destroyed by a German sub off Sicily
& U.S. sliced relations

March 2
    The Jones Act or the
    Organic Act for Puerto Rico
            in which it became a US territory,
                        its residents having the rights of US citizens

March 8
    US troops landed in Santiago, Cuba
                    putatively at th' request of the gov't there

On February 23 Old Calendar/March 8 Western
                a big strike of 80,000 workers
                            in Petrograd
                                    over shortages of bread
The next day, Feb 23/March 9
                    it spread to the city's centrum

then Feb 23/March 10
    the Petrograd strike reached 200k strong

    and then there was a mutiny of Russian troops
            after millions 'pon millions
                    had died in the war

Leon Trotsky was in NY when the rev began
                and headed toward Russia, arriving in May

On March 1 (or March 14) the Duma established a provisional gov't
                            headed by Prince G. E. Lvov.

March 2/March 15
    Tsar Nicholas II abdicated
                his throne.
                        Bye.
And on the 22nd
    the US recognized a Russian gov't headed by Aleksandr Kerensky

March 31
    the US at last acquired the Virgin Islands,
            to keep them from German hands, and to guard the
                    Panama Canal.

When the revolution surged to Russia
America surged almost instantly to war

There are three Reasons the texts give for America's
declaration of war:
- Zimmermann telegram
- overthrow of Tsar
- sinking of five US merchant vessels by German U-boats

another reason: behind the scenes shoving
by those who like war
by munitions makers
by money-loaners to Europe
& some, not all, in the military

WWI was very very good for American biz

England bought billions
& the usury of American banks
made Dante weep

April 1917
Germans said its sea wolves would sink ships bringing supplies
to their enemies
and they had sunk some merchant vessels

The *Lusitania,* sea-bottomed early in '15
bore falsified cargo manifests

—it was carrying tons of bullets and weapons

―――――――――――――――――― **War** ―――――――――――

In his speech asking Congress for war
on April 2
Wilson promised
that regular Americans
would not have to make
financial sacrifices

Two days later

The US Senate voted war on Germany
& then April 6
            Congress voted for war

(There was a struggle over raising the scratch
                        to join the slaughter.
Senator La Follette & his allies fought hard
for steeply graduated income taxes
                        & inheritance taxes
though wincy Wilson quailed at having the war-caste
                                    actually paying for wars

Much of the financing came from Liberty Bonds
            exempt from federal taxes

Bankers bought a lot
The Fed Reserve decreed that Liberty Bonds
            could be counted as assets
                        against which to issue notes)

———————————— **The Question of Involvement** ————————————

Did the USA have to do it?
I'd say Debs was right
& the editors of *The Masses*

It *was* the schemes of munitions men
The moil of the profit-batty
The surge of the serially aggressive
The worship of war
                as a cleansing Christian thing
                            by the German Kaiser
& those puffed up with power like Wilson
            who pitched
                    white hot horseshoes
                            into the Abyss.

The Socialists were right after all
when they met in St. Louis that April
to issue
        what was known as
                the St. Louis Resolution:

"We call upon the
                workers of all countries
to refuse support
                to their governments
                                in their wars."

But a few hundred thousand leftists
                & a few million leaflets
were nothing against
                the crackdown to come

―――――――――――――― **The Great Sealed Train** ――――――――

Lenin left Zürich on April 9
He'd hoped to get back through England
                                then by sea to Murmansk in the north
but the British said no

so he took a German offer
                to hasten home in a sealed train
                                from Zürich through Germany
                                Sweden and Finland
They hoped he would moil the minds of Russian troops

Lenin schemed in Petrograd
                from April 16 till July
when a Bolshevik *coup d'état* fell apart
and he fled to Finland

Lenin returned in October
and from quarters in the Smolny Institute
led the struggle
                that grabbed the gov't on November 6

―――――――――――――――― **Pitching the War** ――――――――――――

In the US
there was a big public relations effort
                                to pitch the war

There were pro-war rallies & meetings,
        plus mass intimidation of the left

The war was hawked to the people
                    like Fuller brushes
& left bitter brush swabs
                    in many peoples' memories

though the majority, for certain,
                    began singing the "Battle Hymn of the Republic"
                                        & "America the Beautiful"
                                                        in their hearts

April 14
        preparing to crush dissent
                    Wilson ordered creation of a
                                Committee on Public Information
                                        to control and censor the news

On April 16
        Food strikes in Berlin

& April 17
        on the Western front, a mutiny among French troops
        & another mutiny April 29
                        & more through the summer

─────────────── **The R. Mutt Readymade** ───────────────

In the war-swirl of April
Marcel Duchamp
entered his piece called *Fountain*
in the Society for Independent Artists
                            exhibit in NYC
—a urinal signed "R. Mutt"

Stieglitz took a famous photo of it
                    but it was banned from the show

May 16

Congress passed the Sedition Act
   with serious penalties for those who hindered the war

The S. Act listed more deeds to be punished
     which before had been considered only unpatriotic

It was aimed at th' IWW
   which up to then
   had taken care
     to place its opposition to capitalism
       rather than, in particular, to the war

Western biz-oids and conservatives were hot
     to stomp down the Wobblies

In Washington and Montana Federal troops
raided Wobbly headquarters, broke up meetings
     & patrolled freight cars for migrant activists

May 18
  Congress then passed what was called the "Selective Service Act"
    because so few had surged forward
       to take up rifles

Parade

Four brilliant artists
Pablo Picasso, Erik Satie, Jean Cocteau & Léonide Massine
premiered the ballet called *Parade* in May

Picasso designed the sets & costumes
& Satie worked a year on the score
   with choreography by Massine
    —more evidence of what Guillaume Apollinaire
      called "simultaneity"

Though critics snicker-inked *Parade*
    it triumphed in the time-track

(In the program notes, Apollinaire
                first-flamed the word "surrealism")

May 29
    John Fitzgerald Kennedy was
                        born in Brookline, Mass

June 10
    Sinn Féin riots in Dublin

June 14
    Wilson sent a delegation under Elihu Root to Petrograd
                to urge Kerensky, then minister of war, to continue it.

———————————— **The Espionage Act of June 15** ————————————

An Espionage Act was passed
making it illegal to engage in
                        "disloyal acts" against the US

It defined treason or disloyalty
                as any attempt to create distrust in the military

    The government
            wadded up the Constitution
    & continued its war against the Wobblies
    raided IWW headquarters in Chicago
                        and wherever Wobblies were

    stole office equipment, records, buttons, leaflets—
                to chip the Wobblies' name from time
                                    like Akhenaton's

———————————— **Post Office Kills *The Masses*** ————————————

        The Espionage Act of June 1917
        allowed the Post Office to
        refuse to mail what it felt was promoting
        "treason, insurrection or forcible resistance
        to any law of the United States."

    The P.O. refused to mail the August issue of *The Masses*

It looked askance at the antiwar cartoons,
a drawing that laughed at greedy armsmakers,
& a poem by Josephine Bell admiring Emma Goldman
and Alexander Berkman's draft resistance

Gov't pressure caused *The Masses*
           (with a distribution of around 25,000)
                to lose their distributor

The Masses sued in Federal court, and won, thanks to
      a brave & liberal ruling by Judge Learned Hand
          but then the Post Office appealed
                  and won

Meanwhile when *The Masses* brought the September issue to be
   mailed out
right wing sleaze at the P.O.
        canceled its second-class mailing privileges
        because it had missed the August issue
            (because of the P.O. censorship!)

This drove it out of business
        in December of 1917.
Editor Max Eastman had raised $2000 to send John Reed to Russia
        to report on the revolution
        & Reed's first reports,
        the core of his great book
            Ten Days That Shook the World
        were just arriving in December
        when cap-gunge killed *The Masses*

Then the gov't indicted artist Art Young, editor/writers Max Eastman,
John Reed, and several others, including the poet Josephine Bell
              for conspiring to obstruct the draft.

T. Roosevelt

For his part, the hamster man wanted martial law
        & military censorship
           of publications

He also wanted to lead a division to France
but Wilson turned him down
        and Roosevelt attacked him

166

sans cease

all the way to his death bed

in 1919

June 16

The first All Russian Congress of Soviets was convened in Petrograd
(Soviet is the Russian word for "council")

June 19

King George V announced that the British royal family
were renouncing their German names and titles.
No longer would they use the German name Wettin—
from Prince Albert of Saxe-Coburg-Gotha,
Queen Victoria's husband—
but would take up a new name borrowed from Windsor Castle

June 24

the Russian Black Sea fleet mutinied at Sebastopol.

June 26

th' first US troops arrived in Europe, to St.-Nazaire, France
but saw little action

July 16

In Petrograd, demonstrations 'gainst the provisional gov't
as the Bolsheviks attempted an insurrection
but crowds were sparse
& Vladimir Lenin fled to Finland

July 21

Alexandr Kerensky replaced Lvov as prime minister.
In a big historical blunder
Kerensky tried to continue the war the people hated
sawed by left   sawed by right
& governed till October

July 31–Nov 10

the third battle of Ypres, Belgium
The British, at enormous death count, pushed forward 8 miles

———————— **Crushing the Wobblies** ————————

48 Wobbly halls were raided
by the Justice Department

167

                                                          on September 5
           5 tons of written material were seized
           then sifted
                        & a Grand Jury indicted 161 IWW leaders
           "for conspiracy to hinder the draft, encourage desertion,
           and intimidate others in connection with labor disputes."

September 9
     Great unrest at a British training camp in NE France
                        All was no longer quiet on the Western Front

October 6 (old Calendar/October 19 Western)
     The Petrograd Soviet elected Trotsky chair
     & Leon set up a committee to plan the Great Insurrection

October 7
     Lenin secretly arrived in Petrograd from Finland

October 15
     Mata Hari was executed in St.-Lazare, France
                              as a German spy

October 22
     the Congress of Soviets
     passed a resolution to
                    seek an armistice

October 27
     At dawn in western France the first shots fired by the USA
     the shell of the first artillery round was sent to President Wilson

————— **The Balfour Declaration of November 2** —————

British Foreign Secretary Arthur J. Balfour
           sent a letter to Lord Rothschild
                        head of the British Jewish Federation
     giving British support for a Jewish national home in Palestine

Mr. Balfour was hopeful that the declaration would
urge the millions of Jews in Russia
           to work for a victory
                        over the Central Powers

168

The next day three leading Zionists in London
were sent to Petrograd
             to rally Russian Jews to support the war

(It was one of those instances
where the results were vastly more important
                            than the reasons
as the Balfour Declaration later led to the League of Nations
mandate for Palestine in 1920)

November 3
       the Germans attacked the Americans,
                in the USA's first battle of WWI,
                            near the Rhine-Marne Canal in France

———————— **Ten Days That Shook the World** ————————

When Lenin returned in October
he led the campaign from quarters in the Smolny Institute
             that grabbed the gov't on November 6
when Lenin became the head of the
                Council of Peoples' Commissars

& nationalized all banks and property
             Saw to a major distribution of land.

As leader of the Petrograd Soviet Trotsky
when the civil war soon commenced
became Commissar for War
             and fashioned the Red Army

On October 26 of the Old Calendar
November 8 of the New

the Bolsheviks grabbed the winter palace
             to overthrow the provisional gov't

At the All Russian Congress of Sov's in Petrograd
the Mensheviks and others walked out
with the Bolsheviks left in control
Lenin formed a Soviet of People's Commissars
                            as new gov't

Lenin addressed the Petrograd Soviet at 3 pm
He told them the workers' and peasants' revolution
                                    had begun
& called for the abolition of private ownership of land
workers control of production
            an immediate peace with the Germans
                        and World Wide Rev

November 8 of the New
    Trotsky announced Russia would consider any peace terms.
    This was apparently a plan to force a general peace conference.
    It failed.

The Bolsheviks
            began at once to abolish the large landed estates
                                    (without compensation)
            took over the Romanov's holdings,
            & those of the church & monasteries!

Lenin: chief of commissars, Trotsky: prime minister

    Roll, o cap-eyes, roll:

Three Tough Commies
Stalin   Lenin   Trotsky

November 20
    Western Front
        Battle of Cambrai
                first major battle using tanks

November 26
    The Soviet gov't offered peace to Germany & Austria

December 5
    the Russians and Germans signed the armistice
                at Brest-Litovsk in modern Belarus.

December 7
the US declared war on Austria-Hungary

───────────────── **Beware of Offending Bacchus** ─────────────────

Anyone reading Euripides *Bacchae*
will sense the fee to be paid
　　　　　for disrespecting
　　　　　the human urge to party

Euripides was not a factor
on December 18
when th' Eighteenth Amendment
　　　　　　　　　was passed by Congress,
barring sale or distribution of alcoholic bev's—

It had its reasons:
The draining of paychecks by drunks
Fathers drinking up the dole
The violence caused by Bacchus
Husbands beating and breaking
Puritans not wanting people
　　　　　to "hang out" in bars
w/ fucking, orgies & loose living deemed Bacchus-abetted

—even a poet like Vachel Lindsay chanted for Prohibition
　though he did not hesitate to use the meters of the Bacchus
　　　　　　　　　he denied

& Bacchus was
　　　　　already dancing all moony
　　　　　　　in bootleg bathtubs

•

December 27
　The Bolshevik gov't allowed workers' committees to supervise
　　　　businesses
and it nationalized banks
　　　　　while cap-eyes all o'er the world
　　　　　　　　　waxed moony goony wide
New that Year:
　T. S. Eliot's *Love Song of J. Alfred Prufrock*
　　Sinclair's *King Coal*

171

Chaplin's *The Immigrant*
Modigliani's *Portrait of a Girl*

Edna St. Vincent Millay moved to G. Village
the year o' her first book, *Renascence and Other Poems*

New York the first eastern state to allow women to vote

There were race riots in East St. Louis, 39 blacks were killed, 9 whites

In Russia the revs
nationalized all art collections

Births and whacks of the scythe-man:
Buffalo Bill at 70 on January 10
August Rodin dies Nov 17 at 77
Edgar Degas on Sept 26 at 83
Scott Joplin on April 1 at 48
Robert Lowell born Mar 1
Lena Horne June 30
Robert Mitchum August 6
Dizzy Gillespie born Oct 21
Carson McCullers February 19
Indira Gandhi Nov 19
Kirk Douglas Dec 9

The Storyville district was closed in New Orleans
by the U.S. Navy
a place where prostitution was licensed
and jazz flourished
Some jazz players moved on to Chicago
and other places

What a year!

January 1,
    Wilson imposed a gov't takeover of the trains
    when they were slow & inexact
            in moving munitions & troops.

There was a Price-Fixing Committee
            headed by economist Robert Brookings

———————————————— **The 14 Points** ————————

Wilson outlined his famous 14 points on January 8
                            in a speech to Congress:
            which looked to a just & lasting peace
                    when the war to kill war had warred:

1. renunciation of all secret diplomacy
2. freedom of the seas
3. removal of economic barriers
4. reduction of armaments
5. an "impartial adjustment of colonial claims"
            (good luck on that, Mr. Wilson)
6. evacuation of Russian territory
7. restoration of Belgium
8. liberation of France and return of Alsace-Lorraine
9. readjustment of Italian frontiers "along clearly recognizable
            lines of nationality"
10. autonomous development for the people of Austria-Hungary
11. evacuation of Rumania, Serbia and Montenegro
            with Serbia getting access to the sea
12. self-development for non-Turkish peoples of the Ottoman
            Empire and free passage in the Dardanelles

13. creation of an independent Poland with free and secure access
     to the sea
14. formation of a general association of nations to guarantee the
     political independence of all states

January 26
leftists in the Social Democratic Party in Finland
grabbed power to declare the Finnish Workers' Socialist Republic

Bolsheviks occupied Helsinki on January 28, but the
FWSR was stomped down in March by Germans and Finns

January 28
By decree the Red Army was founded

January 31
The Bolsheviks
     adopted the Western Calendar—
               (making the writing of this book
                         80 years later
                                   a bit easier)

February 8
The Bolsheviks captured Kiev in the Ukraine
and Ukrainian leaders fled to the Germans for help

February
Sidney Webb and Arthur Henderson drafted
the Labour Party constitution
which was adopted with its famous "Clause IV"
     calling for "Common Ownership of the Means of Production."

———————————— **Waiting for Com-Rev** ————————————

          Since early December the peace conference
          'tween Bolsheviks & Germans
                    had stalled

          because Trotsky expected
                    the com-rev might come
                              to Austria & Germany

          Meanwhile the Germans

resumed their attack on Russia
                    so that at the end of February
                              Lenin ordered a deal

& March the 3rd
the famous treaty of Brest-Litovsk
                    was inked

which forked over Poland, Lithuania & some of
Belorussia to Germany

& which allowed independence to
the Baltic states and the Ukraine
& gave the Caucasus to Turkey

Russia thereby lost ¼ of its land in Europe
⅖ of its population
& ¾ of its iron and coal.

It was then that Western nations
intervened to try to snuff the Bolshies

(the Treaty later was nullified by the defeat of th' Central Powers)

──────────────── **Bye Bye Bolsheviks** ────────────────

On 3-6
The Bolshevik Party
changed itself to the
                    Russian Communist Party

──────────────── **The Huge German Offensive** ────────────────
March 21

The German spring offensive moved close to Paris
A huge gun
        made by Krupp
              hit the great city from 75 miles away

The Germans fired off 2 million poison gas shells!
and surged to break the arcing north-south line

of the Western Front
& scatter to the Atlantic Coast
no doubt hungering
to hun the shores of England
come fall

March 31
Pres Wilson signed a bill setting up Daylight Savings Time

──────────────── **Ghastly Flu Epidemic** ────────────────

Beginning that spring
a massive thock! thock! thock!
of the Scythe Man
as the ghastly Spanish influenza
swirled the globe in three ghastly waves
then vanished

It offed over 21 million
the great Apollinaire on November 9
as well as one of my uncles in Mountain Grove

& then, into the summer:
the Scythe Man still thocking
with his henchman Hunger:
National Food Kitchens in England in March
Food rationing in July there

June 17 food riots in Vienna

──────────── **Possibly Faulty Wobbly Court Strategy** ────────────
April

John Reed covered the five-month trial of
101 Wobblies for *The Masses*

The IWW used court-time explaining their dreams and concepts
and their rationale
for not supporting the war
while working for rev
The jury found all guilty

176

Haywood and 14 others got 20 years, and the rest ten years or less
The aggregate fines were $2,500,000   a huge sum in '18 currency

Big Bill jumped bail to Russia, where he passed ten years later

──────────────── **First *Masses* Trial** ────────────────

Also in April,
        the first trial of the fine American artist Art Young,
        plus the editors of *The Masses*
                ended in a hung jury

                but Wilson's repressionist network was not to give up
                & a retrial was scheduled in the fall.

──────────────── **Dollar-A-Year Men** ────────────────

        They had these things called Dollar-A-Year Men
        Big time capitalists
                        coddled into gov't
                                for a dollar per

        as when that March
        the one named Bernard Baruch
        took over
                the War Industries Board
        to oversee production & distribution
                                for the violence in Europe

        and, of course, these big time capitalists
        soon learned
                that being close to a wartime gov't
                        could have fine advantages
                                    for their purses

──────────────── **Americans Begin to Fight** ────────────────
                April

        90,000 Americans joined the battle
                    on the Western Front

       & the French-English trenchmen
               took heart

          at the fresh energy
             of young Americans

April 21
   air ace Manfred von Richthofen
         was shot down

June
   "Share or die!" the Bolsheviks shouted
   as they ordered the nationalization of industry
      and shudders zoomed through the board rooms of Wall Street

     Tremble, o Greed heads, tremble
         & Roll, o Cap-eyes, Roll!

June saw also the
   British and French troops hit shore in Murmansk
            on the northern coast of Russia
      to go against the Bolsheviks

Oddly enough, the Germans too sent
          2,000 troops to stomp down the Bolsheviks
         landing at Poti on the Black Sea
              and surging to the capital of
              the newly independent Georgia
          to defend it 'gainst the Russians
while in the north the British & French
           (plus soon over 5,000 Americans)
     took Archangel the next month, establishing a puppet gov't,
     fighting the Bolsheviks till October
               o' '19

The great Eugene Debs
    came to a jail in Canton, Ohio
                on June 16
    to visit three socialists who opposed the draft

    then across the street he spoke
                two hours to supporters

    Among his many sentences:
    "... That is war in a nutshell.
    The master class has always declared the wars,
    the subject class has always fought the battles."

    "The sun of capitalism is setting," said Debs
    and the sun of Socialism is rising....
        In due time
        there will come the hour to
        proclaim the emancipation
            of the working class
            and the brotherhood
            of all mankind."

               Go, Debs, Go!

    He was arrested within days
    for violating the Espionage Act
    in that there were draft-age kids in the audience
            & his language tended to
                "obstruct the recruiting or enlistment service."

    Wilson kept him in jail
            the rest of his term

·

There were new Postal Regs in '18
    the gov't could prevent mail delivery to dangerous individuals

    Postmaster Albert Burleson confiscated selected issues of various
    Socialist pubs, then suspended their 2nd class mailing permits
                                     because they missed issues.

    Rural socialist papers, dependent on mails, were stomped.

    Only about 10 percent of the formerly thriving rural socialist papers
    survived by '20

July 15
    Allies checked the German advance toward Paris
    and then till the big victory Nov 10
            the Allies forged a counteroffensive against the Germans
                                       on the Western Front

——————————— **Romanov Dynasty Ended** ———————————

The Whites were about to overrun Ekaterinsburg
where the Tsar, the Tsaritsa, 4 daughters & their son
                              were held in arrest

The local head of the Red Army
decided to kill the Tsar
        and end the rule of the Romanovs
                (in power since 1613)
He telegramed Lenin
& said if he didn't want him to do it
        he should reply but
        Lenin was silent

and so in the mid summer twilight of 7-16
the family
        plus their cook, doctor & staff man
were brought
           to the courtyard
               and down into a basement room

The daughters came clutching their pillows

& chairs were brought.

    Eleven men entered on a sudden
    took quick aim
        and the family & staff were shot

    They carried them up the steps
        laid them in a pit
            doused them with face-eating acid
            then dirt and lime and boards

        the facts of which stayed silent
            for 70 years

    Trotsky had wanted them to go on trial
    with himself as prosecutor

August 7
    Kaiser Wilhelm
        to Ludendorff:
            "This war must be ended,"

    but he wanted it ended
        at a point of advantage
            (which was not to come)

August 15
    US and Russia severed relations
    & by early September over 5,000 American troops
        had arrived in Archangel
            north of Moscow

    joining the British & French
        against the Bolsheviks

The US sent troops to Vladivostok also
    ostensibly to "protect" the Trans-Siberian Railway.

September 14
    Eugene Debs was sentenced to 10 years

        "Your honor," he told the judge
        "years ago I recognized my kinship
        with all living beings

and I made up my mind that I was not one bit better
than the meanest on earth. I said then, and I say now,
that while there is a lower class, I am in it;
while there is a criminal element, I am of it;
while there is a soul in prison,
                              I am not free."

(10 March 1919 the US Supreme Court upheld the sentence
                      in their early-Century right-wing drift)

————————————— **Roosevelt/Mercer** —————————————
                        September

Assistant Secretary of the Navy
Franklin Roosevelt returned from Europe
                              on Navy business
with double pneumonia

Eleanor was tending to his mail
              & found a packet of love letters from
                      her social secretary Lucy Mercer

They talked about divorce
                      but it didn't come about
He promised to give her up
though they saw one another secretly
                      for 27 years
                      till his Warm Springs stroke

October 1
    British and Arab forces took Damascus.
                    in the further grinding down of the
                                          Ottoman

October 3
    A German-Austrian letter was sent to th' USA via Switzerland
                    wanting an armistice based on Wilson's 14 pts.

On the 12th the Germans and Austrians agreed to retreat to
their own territory
              and on the 20th Germany gave up submarine warfare

On Oct 14 the Turks sent a message to Wilson
                      also wanting an armistice

October saw the 2nd trial of editors/poet/artist
associated with the great
                              leftist radical art mag *The Masses*

John Reed was one of the defendants
and traced with eloquent horror
                    the gore & gas & grime of trapping trenches
They asked him also 'bout class warfare
"Well, to tell you the truth,"
                              John Reed replied,
                    "it's the only war that interests me."

The jury hung 8-4 for acquittal

November 1
    British and French took over Constantinople

November 4
    The Allied conference at Versailles agreed on peace terms for
            Germany

―――――――――――――― **The Kaiser Abdicates** ――――――――
November 9

Kaiser Wilhelm II fled to the Netherlands
and the Social Democrat Philipp Scheidemann proclaimed a republic

Three days later the
Germans inked an armistice
            in a railroad car in a forest in Compiègne, France,

    ending World War 1

―――――――――――――― **Anschluss-Mania** ――――――――

November 12
    Austria claimed union with Germany.
            The term,
            which shuddered the world

was called "Anschluss"
though it was later forbidden by the Paris Peace Conference
and several connected treaties

It Was Over

The fighting had ended
50,585 Americans had died in battle
& another 62,000
                    from the ghastly Spanish influenza

A famous "bitterness and disillusionment"
                    began to spread through the nation

It influenced the Nation's great literature:
    Hemingway's *A Farewell to Arms*
        Dalton Trumbo, *Johnny Got His Gun*
                    Dos Passos, *1919*

and, post war, the Establishment still feared socialism
& responded with its usual twins: reform and repression.

                    •

A man named Adolf Hitler
had been blinded *pro tem* by a British poison gas shell
            on the Belgian front October 12

He was very very upset
                lying in his hospital bed north of Berlin
that the Germans had surrendered
& began his evil concoctions of
                        Blame

The Great Victory of
The Non-Partisan League of North Dakota

After being around for about three years
the Non-Partisan League of North Dakota
swept into office
        with a leftist platform
                in the November elections

184

It was wonderful

The State Legislature
        in '19 created the Bank of North Dakota
        the only state bank in the States
        (which exists to this day!)

    The law required all state and local gov't funds
    to be deposited in the State Bank

    & it was to supply low cost credit
    & serve as a clearing house
            & "rediscount" source for
                    all the state's banks.

    Unfortunately, the Dem's and Rep's banded together
    at the next election
            to snuff out the League

    but its bank remains
    Yes!

                    •

November too saw the Socialist Victor Berger
            re-elected to Congress
                    in Milwaukee on a strong peace plank

    The gov't had gone after the 2nd class mailing privileges
    of Berger's newspapers
    as it had *The Masses*

    & Berger, along with other Socialist Party officials,
    was convicted under the espionage act
    (a verdict later tossed out by the Supreme Court)

    Because of his conviction, the US House of Rep
                    twice tossed him out of his seat

    (though in the '20s he was able to
                    serve three more times in Congress)

The Spartacists

That fall in Germany
the group known as the Spartacists
under Karl Liebknecht and Rosa Luxemburg
                    sought to set up a leftist government
                                        modeled on the Soviets

November 28,
    Insurance companies nationalized in Russia
                    —roll yet again o cap-eyes:

Wilson Goes to Europe

Like a rock star
                Woodrow Wilson strutted off to Europe December 4
                to head the U.S. delegation
                                    at the Paris Peace Conference
                                                    arriving on the 14th

determined to save the world by his single voice
"Hubris loves to give birth to hubris"
            the great bard Aeschylus sang
                            in *Agamemnon*

Wilson's carriage passed beneath the Arc de Triomphe
                    in wild tossings of flowers
                                    & roars of approval
                                        as the hero of heroes.

This was the month that
        Western forces under French command
                    invaded Russia at Odessa and other Ukraine ports
                                    to put down the Bolsheviks

On December 20 in Berlin
        a conference of workers' and soldiers' delegates
                    demanded nationalization of German industries

Novum in '18
        Erik Satie's *Socrate*
                    —a treatment of Plato's dialogues
        Booth Tarkington's *The Magnificent Ambersons*

186

plus Kotex, Daylight Savings Time, the popup toaster (by Am-inv
Charles Strite),
the Raggedy Ann doll,
red/yellow/green stoplights in NYC
78 rpm is set for record players

& volleyball arrived in Europe from America
thanks to American soldiers

'18 linen, scythes:

Nov 7 Billy Graham
Mar 23 Claude Debussy at 55
Ella Fitzgerald April 25
Leonard Bernstein Aug 25
Richard Feynman May 11

O America

The weave of '19 had bitter threads!
It was a year of great unrest
with 3,000 strikes
& young minds weeping from war
on the way to the *Génération Perdue.*

For the first six months of the year
Wilson stayed almost continuously in Paris
working on the peace

January 3
Herbert Hoover was chosen as director-general of th'
Commission for Relief and Reconstruction of Europe

on his way up
on his way up

January 4
   Riga in Latvia was taken by the Bolsheviks

January 6
   Even on his death bed
   Theodore Roosevelt
                  lay scheming against Wilson
                              till he passed away, age 60

   The same day in Berlin
   a vast crowd demanding rev

January 10
   In Bremen, Germany
               the Soviet Republic of Bremen
                              was hoisted up as a concept

January 11
   & paramilitary right wing killers
                  hunted down and shot many revs
                              in Berlin

———————————————— **Rosa Luxemburg** ————————————————

Rosa Luxemburg
            was arrested at night
                  on January 15
& brought to the military command post
                  of the right-wing-nut Frei Corps
                              at the Hotel Eden
   She'd not expected death
   brought a suitcase
            and Goethe's *Faust* to read

   Her Spartacist co-leader Karl Liebknecht
                              was also shot
   & Rosa tossed in the
            Landwehr Canal
            by the zoo

near where now you can
       find a memorial plaque
              in her honor

January 18
    The Peace Conference began in Paris under
         French Prime Minister Georges Clemenceau

    the same month that Congress
    ratified the 18th Amendment
    which stamped out the
    "manufacture, sale, or transportation of intoxicating liquors."
              to go into effect January, 1920

January
    Sinn Féin set up its own national assembly, the Dáil Eireann,
    and decreed the independent "Free State" of Ireland.

    (Then, in 1920
    the British parliament
    passed an act to give home rule
         to a parliament in Dublin
    but six Protestant counties in north were not to take part.

    Sinn Féin, with its military wing headed by Eamon de Valera
    as president,
    and its civil wing by Arthur Griffith as v.p.,
    rejected the split

    That is, in the north a self-controlling province came to existence
        and Ireland was split in two.

        with two grim years of war 'tween the
        southern Republicans
          & and the British black & tans)

February 3–9
    White Russian Army under Anton Denikin routed
         the Bolsheviks in the Caucasus.

February 14
    Wilson brought the draft of the League of Nations Covenant to the
        Peace Conference in Paris

Wilson had promised
        a new time of abundance for labor unions
as a reward for their sacrifices during the war
        (which included forced purchase of war bonds).

After the war, there was hideous inflation
        & the workers were no longer counted
        'mong Wilson's obsessions.
There were copious strike funds
        built up during W1 full employment

Around 20% of US workers took part in the
        strike wave that year
3,000 strikes in the US
        for shorter hours, safer work & greater pay.

Among some workers there was a hope for an American revolution
        modeled on the Russian
Needless to say, the angry American power structure
        was having none of it
        & and began the Big Red Scare of 1919.

The Wave began in January with the New York City
        tugboat workers
which the gov't shortened by threatening to send in the US Navy

──────────── **The Great Seattle Insurrection** ────────

And then, in Seattle
        there was a general strike by 100,000 workers
        in February
        that thrilled revolutionaries
        around the world.
It began when 35,000 shipyard workers
        hit the bricks for a higher wage
The Seattle Central Labor Council recommended a citywide strike
They decided to shut down the city
        with different unions to take over necessary chores
        such as feeding the populace and preventing crime

On February 6 in the morning
        the gen strike struck

It kept to its plan for health & safety
      as firemen stayed on duty
            and the laundry workers
                    cleaned only hospital goods

Neighborhood milk dispensing posts were set up
and kitchens which cooked 35,000 meals a day
                 to be carried to union halls

The strikers established their own nonviolent police force
                and crime went down during the strike

From Feb 6 to 11 the unions ran the city

More respectable unions, such as the AFL,
          were aghast at such a "Bolshevik" action
      just when the AFL was
             picking up "respectability"
                 in capitalist realms

There were militant events
such as when longshoremen refused to load
weapons headed for troops fighting against
                 the Russian Rev.

By the week's close
1,000 soldiers and sailors came to town
              and crushed the strike

The Rose spread wide its petals for a while
as workers cooperatives were opened, and the new Farmer-Labor
    Party,
pro tempore, replaced the Dems as the second largest party
                 in the Puget Sound area

And then in the middle of the year
the shipyards closed, with wartime ship-need ended.

                •

February 28
    In a historically stupid move
    Senator H. C. Lodge began his party-serving bluster against
                the US entering the League of Nations

Lodge & Wilson were what they call
                    "bitter political enemies"

                        •

Another famous strike of early 1919
        at the textile plants in Lawrence, Massachusetts
                for 16 weeks
                        led by the great Christian pacifist A. J. Muste
                                fervent for the Social Gospel

        which won a 44-hour week for Lawrence workers
        and saw the founding of the Amalgamated Textile Workers of
                America

——————————— **1919–1933 Weimar Republic** ———————————

        The German Federal Republic was called that
        because in February 1919 the National Constituent Assembly
                        met in Weimar, a town on the Elbe
                                known for its liberalism.

        On July 31 a constitution was adopted, with a
        a seven year presidential office, and proportional representation
        in a federal system

        The Weimar Assembly accepted the Treaty of Versailles
                                (to the agony of the right)
        The National Assembly moved from Weimar to Berlin
                                in the spring of 1920

                        the Weimar Republic
                        surged in the time-track
                        It was known for its arts
                                & personal freedom
                while right-wing hate
                & Communist fate
                        clashed in the streets

March 15
        the American Legion was formed by vets of World War I

The Fascist Party

Mussolini was wounded in WWI
came back to Milan, edited *Il Popolo d'Italia*
organized fasci (groups) of working men
    to seethe for "revolutionary" changes
then in March the fasci merged
      into the Fascist Party

The Comintern

The Third International
    i.e., the Comintern
was convened in Moscow that March,
      to promote communist revolutions

It was an attempt by the Bolsheviks
    to take control of International Communism
with an org to replace the Second International of 1889–1914.

A big effort in the early history of the Comintern
was to unify American Communists,
    against their tendency to splinter and feud

The Comintern wanted to centralize Am-Coms by
    curtailing the autonomy of the many American leftist groups
      formed along ethnic lines & foreign language

The Bolshevization effort drove many ethnic activists away
      decades before the word "control-freak"
        was coined

Civil War in Russia

The White Army came across the Ural Mntns
    aided by Western capitalist roll-eyes

The Whites laid siege to polis 'pon polis

while Leon Trotsky minister of war
    waited for the snows to melt

In April as the Whites oozed upon the Volga River cities
of Samara and Kazan
        Trotsky attacked
            then retreated

(By November o' '19 the northern front was over
as the western nations [France, England, the USA] withdrew their
    support

but there was a Southern front
        so that the Whites came north to within 250 miles of Moscow

There were huge devastations
             & finally by April of '20 it was over

but millions were to die of starvation
        as the Bolsheviks finally controlled it all)

────────────────── **Bauhaus** ──────────────────

The architect Walter Gropius organized the Bauhaus
            in Weimar

Paul Klee taught stained glass
Kandinsky wall painting
Marcel Breuer interiors
    & Josef Albers was a student

The idea was to make things, even the quotidian,
more beautiful & pleasing
—that eye-thrilling design should
        be part of every day life for everybody

    Always under attack from right wing sleaze
    it moved in '25 to Dessau, then to Berlin
    till Naz-vom closed it in '33
        & some of its spirit
           moved to the States.

        •

    It was also the year of Herman Hesse's *Demian*
    His antiwar essays had angered many

His father had died
His wife had gone insane commixed
with the ai-yi-yi of W1
leading to the concept of the alienated hero
        trying to figure out what the hell is going on
       'tween flesh, spirit, soul, lust, reason,
               and happiness

in the oi   joy teeter-totter
              /\

Algonquin Group

Very witty writers & theater types
Robert Benchley, Alex Woollcott, Dorothy Parker, Franklin Adams,
Robert Sherwood, George S. Kaufman
       famous for causticity of turnéd phrase
           some of them leftists
(The playwright & short-story writer Dorothy Parker, for instance
covered the upcoming Spanish Civil War for the *New Masses)*
met for lunch every day
at the Algonquin Hotel on E. 43rd

The Round Table kept up its metabolism till '43
             in the boat named *Font* on the inky sea

Race Riots in April

Riots began in 25 cities in April
           and 38 died—
In Chicago whites stoned black kids swimming on the wrong side of
a segregated beach, and one was drowned

Soon white drool-heads were assaulting blacks around the city

In July, a white woman was raped in D.C. and police said they'd
             search every black man out at night

White soldiers invaded houses warrantlessly
           but blacks fought and shot back

Many black soldiers had fought the gas-hurling Kaiser
             with the finest valor

but as in Cuba and the Philippines
                    in '98 and '99
the military still treated blacks like dirt

    The NAACP complained there were no black officers
    so that by the end of the war there were 1,200 black officers
    out of 367, 000 blacks in the military
                        during the war

    yet in France they tasted a place
                        with no automatic racism

    and, in that tasting,
                        there was no turning back

There was an upswing of lynchings in crackerland in '19
        ten of them were black soldiers
                    some of whom were hung in their uniforms

                        •

April 4 a Soviet Republic was flagpoled in Bavaria
            lasting till May Day
            when Bavarian troops recaptured Munich from
                            th' Commies
April 7
    The Western forces evacuated Odessa
                    in the Southern Ukraine
    & the next day the Red Army entered the Crimea

April 10
    Emiliano Zapata
            friend of the small farmer
                    was shot in ambush by Venustiano Carranza's men

        —he'd taken large tracts of land from cap-slime
                        & given them to the landless
        & set up a system for rural agricultural credits

                    Zapata!

April 17

        Charlie Chaplin, Mary Pickford, Douglas Fairbanks
        and D. W. Griffith formed United Artists

owned by the creators!

&, in Russia,
          the film biz was nationalized

May 1 the snows were finally melted
          & the Red Army began its
                    counterattack
                         on the Whites

──────────── **Holy Toledo!** ────────────

In May, a strike by electrical workers in Toledo
Capitalists were rolling their eyes

                    in googoohood
               o'er an imminent Bolshevik takeover

     so Federal troops were sent there
               to halt what the *New York Times* saw as
               imminent grab of Toledo, shudder shudder,
                              by the Unions!

──────────── **Bombings in April** ────────────

          Forces unknown to this day
          mailed bombs
          One went off, aimed at an anti-immigration
                              politician in Georgia
                    and mailed from "Gimbels"
                         but blew his maid's hands off
          Others were found in the New York Post Office
          addressed to J. P. Morgan, J. D. Rockefeller,
                    & members of Wilson's cabinet

──────────── **The Palmer Bombing** ────────────
                    June 2

A bomb went off outside the home of US Attorney General
                    A. Mitchell Palmer in D.C.

A human was shredded at the site and suspected
of being a former editor of the anarcho-rev *Cronace Sovversiva*

This led Congress to vote money for a leftist stompdown
and dawned the career of J. Edgar Hoover as director of the
Justice Dep't General Intelligence Division

June 4
the US Congress passed the proposal for the 19th Amendment
American women at last allowed to vote

──────────────── **The Treaty of Versailles** ────────────────
June 28

The Treaty of Versailles was signed in France
with 440 clauses
formally ending the war

Germany had been excluded from the negotiations
but was summoned to Paris
& given the terms

Among the important ones:
- surrender of all German colonies for distribution under a system of
  mandates
- return of Alsace-Lorraine to France
- ceding Eupen-Malmedy to Belgium
- plebiscites to be held in Northern Schleswig
- the adjustment of Polish borders, with parts of East Prussia and
  Upper Silesia going to Poland
- ceding Danzig to be administered by the League of Nations
  (thus giving Poland a corridor to the Baltic)
- ceding a small area around Hultschin to Czechoslovakia
- ceding Memel (eventually seized by Lithuania)
- occupation of the Saar by the French for fifteen years, pending a
  plebiscite
- demilitarization of the Rhineland, with Allied occupation for fifteen
  years
- payment of a heavy sum of Reparations
- limitation of the German army to 100,000 men with no General Staff,
  no conscription, no tanks, no heavy artillery, no poison-gas
  supplies, and no aircraft or zeppelins
- limitation of the German fleet to vessels under 10,000 tons, with no
  submarines and no air arm

The Treaty
        said no no no
        to the Anschluss

and fingered Germany
as the sole cause of the Great War—

        the Treaty's language forced Germany to agree that
        "Germany accepts ... the responsibility
        of Germany and her allies for causing all the loss and damage
        to which the Allied and Associated Governments and their nationals
        have been subjected as a consequence of the war imposed upon them
        by the aggression of Germany and her allies."

        Germans hated the "war-guilt clause"
                        and Hitler later used it as a drum of evil

The Covenant of the League of Nations was in the treaty,
                & it excluded both Germany & the Bolsheviks.

Apparently there was significant outcry in England and France
that the Versailles Treaty wasn't harsh enough on the Germans.

        John Maynard Keynes
        (pronounced Kaynes)
        was a member of the literary set they called the Bloomsbury group.

        He had been the chief financial rep for England
                                at the Paris Peace Conference

        & resigned to protest the
        reparations forced on Germany

        In 1919 Keynes
        published *The Economic Consequences of the Peace*
        in which
                like a princess warning of clanking weapons
                                in a wooden horse
        he predicted that Europe would be wrecked economically
        from the fierce economic terms imposed
                                on Germany.

                        •

Woodrow Wilson successfully suggested that a Reparations Commission
be set up independently to set the amount Germany would have to pay.

──────────────── **The Great War Death List** ────────────────

Allies

United States - 50,585   France - 1,357,800
British Empire - 908,371   Russia - 1,700,000
Italy - 462,391   Belgium - 13,715
Serbia - 45,000   Montenegro - 3,000
Rumania - 335,706   Greece - 5,000
Portugal - 100,000   Japan - 300

Central Powers

Germany - 1,808,546   Austria-Hungary - 922,500
Turkey (Ottoman Empire) - 325,000   Bulgaria - 75,844

plus God knows how many
              million disemboweled neighings
                        of shrapneled & bulleted horses

                    on the mad-man fronts

                              •

        Things were still a bit
            like a kaleidoscope but
            Gone was the Hapsburg rule
            Gone was the Austro-Hungarian empire
                    & the trillion-laced lines from the
                                gold-topped castles of Vienna
            Gone was the Ottoman

        & by treaties to come
        Syria & Lebanon
                    went to the French
                        as "Mandates"
        Iraq, Transjordan & Palestine
                        to the British

Hungary lost more than ½ of its land
Austria ¾ of its, &
Poland was put back together
Yugoslavia was created of
                    Bosnia-Hercegovina, Dalmatia
                              & a new, bigger Serbia.

───────────── **The Little Blue Books Begin** ─────────────

The far-famed Little Blue Books
            began life
                    not long after Emanuel Haldeman-Julius
                        bought the Girard, Kansas
                                    Appeal to Reason

A teacher named Marian Wharton
at the Socialist People's College in nearby Ft. Scott
                                    asked for inexpensive texts

& Haldeman-Julius published 50 small paperbound booklets
        3½ x 5 inches in size

a group of socialist tracts
            and literary classics
                    which were advertised in the *Appeal to Reason*
                        for $5 the set

They were mass produced &
the public response was vast

More and more were published
Greek plays, how-to books, joke books, socialism, Russell, Sinclair,
                                    Darrow, James Farrell

To stay in print each book had an annual sales quota of 10,000
though Shakespeare & Ingersoll
                were among those allowed to stay in print
                            without the 10k figures

In '23 the project became the Little Blue Books
All in all, Haldeman-Julius put out some 2,203 books
such as Margaret Sanger's controversial 1919 book on birth control
till he went to the big subsurface printing plant
                                    in 1951.

Hail to the Little Blue Books &
Emanuel Haldeman-Julius!

—————————————— **Wilson Returns** ——————————————

In early July the President
came back from Paris
to New York City
with the Treaty of Versailles
as an American hero.
There was a standing ovation for him at Carnegie Hall
and when his train hero'd into Union Station in D.C.
10,000 were there to hail his greatness.

There was one big problem
for this modern day Achilles
He needed the Senate to ratify the Treaty
by ⅔ vote

and Wilson's political enemies
a main one Henry Cabot Lodge of Massachusetts
and also a senator named William Borah

combined in a drive against the League of Nations.

One factor was political
the Republicans wanted to shake up the Democratic structure
in power since 1912

but much of the blame was Wilson's
who behaved a bit like a pouting movie star
& refused to offer the good old American
"milk of kindness"
to his political foes

Much of the furor arose from Article X of the League of Nations
Covenant
which would have forced each nation
to come to the aid of every nation
that was attacked.

Would the Covenant, for instance impede America's sacred right
to invade Mexico
any time it wanted?

It's said that just a bit of compromise
                    would have brought the great United States
                                        to the League of Nations.

That summer Wilson said "Never!"
                    to accepting the Treaty
                              with the so-called "Lodge reservations"

                    Meanwhile right-wing nuts
                    added the League of Nations to its
                    enemy list—joining Jews, pacifists,
                    Catholics & immigrants

          plus, on a more refined level
          there was a fear of Europe
                              'mong Americans
          —Edith Wharton's characters
                    wincing with fascinated deprecation
          at the Old Nations—

          Meanwhile the president kept bringing Senators to his office
                              to give them lectures as to why
                              they should vote for the Treaty

June–July
     US, Canadian & French troops
                    withdrew from Northern Russia

          but US troops remained in Siberia
                              till early in 1920

July 27–31
     More race riots in Chi
                    then race riots and lynchings throughout
                                        the nation

———————————————— **Cracks in the Left** ————————————————

On September 1
     at the US Socialist party convention in Chicago
                         huge cracks yawned in the American left
          as factions factioning fractiously formed
          the American Communist Party and the Communist Labor Party

and left the Socialists to deny their own depletion.

There was a millenarian mind-flow
                          'mong American communists
who knew that Lenin & Trotsky
                          believed their manifestoes
& so were waiting for
          the Big Revolution
                    to circle the world

    & expected it any day to come to the USA.

Many leftists, however,
opposed the anti-electoral, underground and
dual-unionist
              directions of the
              Am-Coms

Hideous Inflation

Meanwhile there was hideous inflation
                          everywhere in America
& little was done to protect the buying power of workers.
By fall there were 4,000,000 workers on strike

The nation's first police strike in September in Boston
          Calvin Coolidge, then Gov of Massachusetts,
                    called in the National Guard to stomp it down

          Conservatives liked it
          liked it a lot
          This guy Coolidge
                    maybe he'll be president some day

September 22, a huge steel strike began
                          which lasted till January 20
In October, 60k metalworkers in SF Bay walked out
US coal miners struck in November
                    and the government sent in soldiers
          in December
                    to work the mines

In August a strike by railroad shopmen in Chicago

& a strike by subway workers of NYC—
                    The railway unions
                              badly wanted Congress
                                        to nationalize the railroads.

The Pennsylvania State Police, known as the "Cossacks"
              were used brutally to hurt strikers on picket lines

There was plenty of vigilante action by business groups & th'
              Ku Klux Klan
The courts winked and nodded,
                    and most of the gains the union workers
                    had gotten during the War
                                        were blistered away

————————— On the Road to Promote the Treaty —————————

Meanwhile Wilson
              realized that the Republican Senate
                              would not ratify the Treaty of Versailles

His lectures at Princeton were always packed
& he had a faith-healer's belief in his voice
so Wilson began a 10,000 mile trip across America
                              to talk to the populace

with his wife, a staff, and secret service guys
                              in a seven-car train.
He shouted ten speeches a day
              like the Trojan Stentor
                    to gather support for the Treaty
                    & the League of Nations

There was a "spotty" reception
                              as they say in show business
though on September 25
the reception in Pueblo, Colorado was enormous—
a 10-minute ovation
              & Wilson weeping at the lectern
                              in verbal vastness.
That night he was taken ill, with blinding headaches
& the Treaty Train rushed back to Washington
where in early October

he suffered a stroke
from which he never fully recovered.

That same month in Munich
Hitler joined a small nationalist group
called the National Socialist German Worker's Party

He was a good orator in open-air raves against Jews and
the Treaty of Versailles

September 27,
British troops moved out of Archangel, Russia.

October 27
From his sickbed
Wilson vetoed the Volstead Prohibition Act
which set the rules enforcing the 18th Amendment
but the House and Senate overrode it

————————————— **The First Palmer Raids** —————————————
November 7

The first Palmer Raids
in 18 cities around the nation
were deliberately conducted
on the anniversary of the Russian Rev

Agents of Attorney General A. Mitchell Palmer
dubbed by the tabs as the "fighting Quaker"
& oh so hungry to be president

raided radical offices
and seized literally tons of literature

The *New York Tribune* ran an 8-column headline:
150 ARRESTED HERE AS U.S. STARTS ROUNDUP OF "REDS"

"Fighting Quaker" Palmer
had come to office in the spring o' 1919

&, like Joe McCarthy 31 years later
was foamily fearful of Commies.

24-year-old J.Edgar Hoover
   became assistant to Palmer
      to slurp together info
         on revs and radicals

Hoover, who had once worked in the stacks
            at the Library of Congress
now took his skills
      into file card mania:
500,000 names were indexed
        plus biographical notes on 60,000 people—
the beginning of Hoovie boy's smear system.

     After these first Palmer sweeps
     249 aliens of Russian birth,
      including Emma Goldman and Alexander Berkman
         were put by the Feds on a ship to Russia.

Hoov' especially hated Emma Goldman
—a free love-ist, a radical and a woman

    Four days before Christmas
    Hoov' and Bureau Chief William Flynn
    went at 2 am to Ellis Island
      to gawk-snicker at Emma & Berkman
      & th' 247 others on the troopship *Buford* taking them
      to Russia

    Hoovie told reporters the next day,
      that "other Soviet Arks will sail for Europe,
      just as soon as it is necessary, to rid the country
      of dangerous radicals."

November 19
 Senate voted against ratifying the Treaty of Versailles,
 & therefore the USA could not join the League of Nations.

December
 On the 5th the Serbo-Croat-Slovene Kingdom (aka Yugoslavia)
      agreed to peace treaties with Austria and Bulgaria

 and on the 20th the House of Reps
      made a move to curtain immigration

John Reed's *Ten Days That Shook the World*
       flamed into print.
Returning from Europe
     he was tossed out of the Socialist Party
& became head of U.S. Communist Labor Party

Reed worked fiercely for Bill Haywood's
       "Industrial Unionism"
was indicted for sedition
     & late this year fled to Russia

Novum '19:
 the first helicopter flight

 H. L. Mencken's *The American Language.*
 A. N. Whitehead, *Enquiry Concerning the Principles of Natural*
  Knowledge.

 Marcel Duchamp *L H O O Q*
    the mustache that glyphed the century!

Modigliani, Kurt Schwitters, Picasso
     geniusing on the void trumpet

and bronze casts were made of the Degas dancers and horses—
      done in wax and plaster '90–'12

Thomas Hardy, *Collected Poems*
The *NY Daily News*
    joined the saffron blab-tabs

The great song of linen & oi:
Pete Seeger! Margot Fonteyn! Merce! J. D. Salinger!
    Nat King Cole!
Oct 22 Doris Lessing born
Dec 3 Pierre-August Renoir passed at 78
Primo Levi born July 31 Lawrence Ferlinghetti on Mar 24
Liberace born May 16

Flicks: *The Cabinet of Dr. Caligari*
      directed by Robert Weine
         & Abel Gance's *J'Accuse*

January 2
   the 2nd Palmer Raids
   in 70+ cities

   up to 4,000 detained, some say 10k, and finally 1k deported

   J. Edgar Hoover led these raids also
            the victims were handcuffed in pairs, then chained together:
                 secret hearings, then they were deported.

January 16
   The US Senate voted again against joining the League of Nations

   &
   Prohibition began 'neath the 18th Amendment.
   Temperance groups had struggled for it for 80 years
   & an Anti-Saloon league had started in 1895
   which grew during War 1 when drinking was deemed unpatriotic
          because of so many German-born Americans in the alcohol biz—
             This disregard for the stern message of Euripides' *Bacchae*
                                      was to last till December of '33

February 8
   the Bolsheviks took Odessa in the southern Ukraine

February 28
   Congress approved the Esch-Cummins Transportation Act,
   returning railroads to private ownership

                    (Wilson had seized them
                              for being uncooperative
                              & poorly run
                                        during the War)

March 13
    Right-wing grime in Germany
    supported by troops that had fought in the Baltic
                    grabbed Berlin & announced hegemony
    a scheme which failed
                    but soldiers in the uprising
                    painted a newfangled sign on their helmets
                              they'd brought from the Baltic:
                                                  the swastika

March 19
    After a big public campaign
                    by supporters of the League of Nations
                    for yet another vote in Washington
    the Senate this day
                    again rejected the Treaty of Versailles
    Not too bright of you, o Senate

March 28
    Bolsheviks caused the final collapse of
    Anton Denikin's White Russian Army.
    Bye, WRA

April 1
    Five members of the NY State Legislature
                    were expelled because they were Socialists

Two weeks later,
        at 3 pm
        two men were bearing a payroll of $15,776
        on the main street
                    of South Braintree, Mass

        when two guys standing next to a fence pulled pistols
        and shot the money-holders to death

        scrambled into a waiting auto
                              and drove thence

Bill Tilden

Six foot tall and full of charisma
Bill Tilden won the Wimbledon
        and the middle & leisure classes
                loved him with conspicuous consumption glee

till it was discovered he was gay
        and the same gentle classes
                ostracized him, and he died impoverished in '53

Sacco & Vanzetti

That spring
    an Anarchist typesetter named Andrea Salsedo
        was arrested by the FBI in NY
& held incommunicado eight weeks on the 14th floor of FBI building
Then his body was found on the pavement
           The FBI said he had committed suicide

Two anarchist friends of Salsedo
had started carrying guns
        and were arrested May 5
              on a streetcar in Brockton, Mass.
         & charged with killing the guards
         & stealing the $16,000 shoe factory's payroll
        two weeks before
             in South Braintree.

Their names were Nicola Sacco and Bartolemeo Vanzetti
They were carrying guns
They lied about their radical connections
In Sacco's pocket they found a draft of a handbill for an
anarchist meeting to feature Vanzetti as main speaker

They both had a long history of labor strikes
antiwar agitation, and a political stance
        that accepted revolutionary violence

They were supporters of Luigi Galleani's Italian-language anarchist
journal, *Cronaca Sovversiva,*
        viewed as the most influential in the USA in this field.

They were eventually charged with the murders
in the middle of the ghastly Red Scare o' '19–'20
        where just the concept of the "foreign born radical"
                        caused hemorrhaging cap-eyes

1920
    Babe Ruth signed a $125,000 contract
                    with the NY Yankees

June 10
    The Water Powers Act created the Federal Power Commission
                        to regulate power plants.

─────────────────────────── **First Dada Fair** ───────────────────────────

The *Erste Internationale Dada Messe*
        was held that June in Berlin

You entered the exhibit through a public toilet
        to face a young woman
                in a communion dress
                        reading sex verse

A model of a pig in German military uniform
hung from the ceiling

and there was a big banner
DADA FIGHTS ON THE SIDE OF THE REVOLUTIONARY PROLETARIAT

                sure it does

June 12
    the Republicans nominated
                lawyer & newspaper owner Warren G. Harding
                plus Calvin Coolidge for vp
                        in Chicago

                Coolidge was known mainly as the guy
                who had crushed the Boston police strike

The great Boeotian bard Hesiod
sang of the first three things created:
first Chaos, then Earth, then Eros.
All three were in evidence in the moily conference
in Chicago that July
   which formed the Farmer-Labor Party!

  The F-LP was born from the long time battle
      for Progressive results in America
  It was a weaving together
  of the Labor Party of Illinois, plus labor parties in
  Connecticut, Indiana, New York, Ohio, and Utah,
    & surviving fragments of the "Bull Moose" Party

July 5
  the Democrats in San Francisco
  chose James Cox for president after many ballots
     & Franklin D. Roosevelt for vp

August 9
  Cap-slime in Britain drooled for war with Russia
  so British labor orgs
  set up a Council of Action
  to call a general strike if England
     forged slaughter in Russia

August 20
  The 19th Amendment, the right to vote for women
     was at last enacted!

September 7
  the first Miss America pageant
    in Atlantic City
     with Margaret Gorman the victress

September 16
  a bomb was placed near J. P. Morgan headquarters
    near Wall Street
     killed 30, injured 300

  Anarchists were suspected
  but no one was ever arrested

September
The "occupation of the factories"
by 500k steel and engineering workers in Italy
who announced they'll run them themselves

Prime minister Giolitti broke it up
though he forced
the owners
"to make concessions"
as they say

This was the fall that the Klan
ran a guy for governor o' Oklahoma
where the wind went whistling
through the burning cross

———————————— **John Reed** ————————————

John Reed picked up typhus
in Russia
and died there on October 19

He was buried in the Kremlin wall

October 27
the League of Nations moved to Geneva

November 2
There were several hundred in Pittsburgh
who heard the first live broadcast of presidential election returns
o'er KDKA

operated from the roof of a Westinghouse plant
In US it was a capitalism-controlled shot, the spread of radio
In England, the nation controlled it,
forming the far-famed BBC
which was a monopoly till '73

———————————— **The Harding Normalcy** ————————————

The great Eugene Debs
ran for president from the Atlanta Pen

under the exhortation
"Vote for Prisoner 9653"
& picked up 920,000 votes

Lawyer and newspaper owner, and then US Senator from Ohio
Warren G. Harding pledged a "return to normalcy"
and won by a big margin
16m to 9m for Cox

November 16
the Bolsheviks ended the civil war. They won.

───────────────── **Ponzi '20** ─────────────────

Charles Ponzi scammed Bostonians
with vows of huge profits on foreign postal coupons.
In August, investigators declared the coupons a scam.

Ponzi, the first of the pyramid schemers,
paid old clients with new clients' money

He scam'd over 20k people of over $10m
& six banks failed when the his scheme collapsed

& "Ponzi Scheme"
became an American
watch-phrase

November 20
Woodrow Wilson picked up a Nobel Peace Prize for his work
promoting the League of Nations

November 21
Another Bloody Sunday
this one in Dublin
IRA op's in Dublin killed eleven suspected British agents

then that afternoon the Black and Tans
op'd fire on people watching a football match in a Dublin stadium

with 12 dead and 60 injured

On Christmas Day
Pres-elect Harding pardoned Eugene Debs

Debs sent his five-dollar release cash to the
                    Sacco-Vanzetti Defense Committee.

        To this day no one
        really stands up for Debs
        for what those
                    repressionist creeps
                    did to him

December 29
    the French Communist party was founded
    and a new Socialist Party, headed by Léon Blum

Novum '20:
    Trojans, the tommy gun, the Baby Ruth chocolate bar,
                    and legalized abortion in the Soviet Union

    The word robot was first used, by Czech playwright Karel Capek
                    in *R.U.R.*

    The Concept of Nature A. N. Whitehead

———————————————— **Main Street** ————————————————

Sinclair Lewis' *Main Street*
                    smoked into print!
                    earning him the enmity
                    of thrift-exemptive buy-&-sell-manic
                    Babbittophiles (*Babbitt* out in '22)
                    in the towns of the Nation

    It was the same year that Edith Wharton's *The Age of Innocence*
                    presented its europhilic New Yorkers
                    staring obsessively at ancient Europa
                    while shining the light from Plymouth Rock
                                            at its mores

    The ACLU was founded the year of *Main Street*
    by Roger Baldwin, Jane Addams, Helen Keller,
                    Norman Thomas, Morris Hillquit and others
    because of cap-vom's spitting on the Constitution
                    in order to suppress so-called "Reds."

216

A critic in France, Henri Collet referred to *Les Six:*
Darius Milhaud, Francis Poulenc, Arthur Honegger,
Louis Durey, Germaine Tailleferre, and Georges Auric

Franz Kafka *The Country Doctor*

Linen:
　Thelonius Monk on October 10　Charles Bukowski　Aug 16
　　　　Federico Fellini born Jan 20
　　　　　Isaac Asimov born Jan 2
　　　　　　& Peggy Lee, Bella Abzug, Charlie Parker
　　　　　　　　　　　Dave Brubeck!

Films o' '20:
The Golem,
Dr. Jekyll and Mr. Hyde, with John Barrymore
Mauritz Stiller's *Erotikon*
The Mark of Zorro with Douglas Fairbanks

Gleam onward, O Century!

Party Years

"A whole race going hedonistic,
deciding on pleasure...."
F. Scott Fitzgerald, "The Jazz Age"

They called them the Roaring Twenties
whose presidents were Harding and Coolidge
with the initials "n.m."
for "not much," ever affixed

Andrew Mellon, one of the nation's wealthiest,
was their Secretary of the Treasury

and all Mr. Mellon could do
                was shove shove shove
                        to better his tax position

and so many others were shoving
                as if it were a sea-to-sea casting call
                        for the great novel *Babbitt*

———————————— **A Big Fine for Germany** ————————————

                January 24 till the 29th
                the Paris conference of allies
                        set up a schedule of payments
                        for Germany

        March 23 the Weimar Republic announced
                it wouldn't be able to pay the
                        600 million pounds due May 1

February 27
        Riots twixt Communists and Fascists in
                                beautiful Florence

March 1
        the inauguration of the 29th president
                        Warren G. Harding
                known for his horseshoe pitching
                & later for having shoed himself
                        with no-talent money grubbers

March 15
        Rwanda in East Africa
                was "given" to England by Belgium

———————————— **Une Génération Perdue** ————————————

        "That's what you are. That's what you all are,"
                Gertrude Stein told Ernest Hemingway
        "All of you young people who served in the war
                        you are a Lost Generation."

The Mystery of Vanguardism

March saw the release of
Lenin's New Economic Policy
  —a step back from his "War Communism."

O'er & o'er in Marxist chrono-tracks
    one sees the word *Vanguard*

Under Leninism
a Vanguard Party was needed
   but could not sprout like Spartan teeth
      from the Proletariat—

Publishing groups, militant unions, ethnic federations,
and Intense Dedication had to wheel into action
    before a V. P. could form—

Those groups that at last could fuse
   in the V.P. were called "pre-party formations"

Meanwhile, Lenin's NEP slowed down the nationalization of industry
    begun at the '17 rev

     —there was wide starvation in Russia
     Later that summer Lenin asked all the world
     to help "their starving fellows in Russia"

It allowed the Russian economy
to have some small scale private enterprise
    and manufacturing

The Communists tried to smooth things out with the peasants
by replacing "prodrazverstka," the policy of
   seizing agricultural surpluses
   with "prodnalog,"
    an agricultural tax

The 4th Comes to Columbia

On April 15 the great Albert Einstein
   described Time as the 4th Dimension
     at a Columbia University talk

April 27
The Reparations Commission set the German WWI fine at
132,000 million gold marks, or £6,650,000,000
a huge, huge sum
of which, in years to come, the Germans paid only about ⅛th
even when the amount was cut by 75% by the Young Plan of 1929

―――――――――――――― **Nativism** ――――――

Congress voted a quota bill
to restrict immigration to
150,000 a year
for Asians and Europeans

and only 3% of any nationality of that nationality's
total number already in the USA
which biased the immigration
toward northern Europeans.

We'll wall off them commies, them Eyetalian anarchists—
plus some U.S. Unions
wanted to keep out them work-cheap aliens

April 12
President Harding
said that the US could never be a part of the
League of Nations

and then on June 30
named ex-pres William Howard Taft
as Chief Justice of the Supreme Court
so that the '20s were a right wing oozathon
as the court overturned child labor laws
abolished the minimum wage for women
outlawed picketing
& upheld the yellow-dog contract

July 2
Joint resolution of Congress declared th' war with Germany concluded

July 14
Nicola Sacco and Bartolomeo Vanzetti were found guilty of robbery
and murder after a 6-week trial

& then a six-year struggle
                by the American left
                        to forestall the execution

July 29
    Hitler became president of the National Socialist Party
    Time Machine! Time Machine!

—————————————————— **Arbuckle** ——————————————————

On Labor Day
            in a 12th floor suite
                    at the St. Francis Hotel in San Francisco

                    comedy star Fatty Arbuckle
                    raped a starlet named Virginia Rappe
                            tearing her crotch with a champagne bottle
                                            & later with cubes of ice

                    so that she later died from an infected, ruptured bladder
                    It was one of the biggest scandals
                                        of the 20s

—————————————— **Polio at Campobello** ——————————————

            He'd worked for Woodrow Wilson
                    in the Navy Department from '13 to '20
            then ran for Vice President
                    with Gov. James Cox o' Ohio
            till the horseshoe man Harding's victory.

            The next summer Franklin Roosevelt
            was spending some weeks at Campobello Island
                                        in New Brunswick

            The vacations of the hyperenergetic
                                    oft lack vacation
            & so it was that August for the high energy FDR:

            tennis, sailing, baseball, jogging, partying
            & swimming in the
                    brrrr-it's-cold Bay of Fundy

till August 10 the future President took sick
& by the 12th
      was paralyzed from the neck down
              with poliomyelitis

      & faced many months of ghastly pain
      his legs in plaster casts at first
      with endless exercise for years
           to get back even partial
              use of the limbs

October 1
  a gunfight erupted, with 10 hurt,
      at a Ku Klux Klan parade in Lorena, Texas

———————————— **The Irish Free State** ————————————

    Lloyd George, the Liberal politician
      who had in '11 brought England
          its national health care system
    now was prime minister
    and helped bring about
      the Irish Free State
      of 26 Irish counties

There was a conference in London on October 21
and a treaty signed on December 6
making the Free State a self-governing "dominion"
      within the Commonwealth,
      still owing allegiance to the Crown

    the Irish Dáil ratified the treaty
          on 1-7-'22.

    The 6 northern counties
      stayed British

    and thus were set
      the battle zones for
        decades of strife

November 2
Margaret Sanger and Mary Ward Dennett formed the
    American Birth Control League

A bard named T. S. Eliot, Harvard '14
       the former editor of the imagist magazine *The Egoist*
         & toiling as a bank clerk in London

came to Paris November 21
     and showed Ezra Pound a long poem
        with the ghastly title
          "He Do the Police in Different Voices"

The bard went on to Lausanne
        for a fortnight of rest
     where he restrung the poem
     so that when he saw Pound again in Paris
     in early December
        it had the much better title "The Waste Land"

Pound liked it
& set Eliot up with a NY publisher
          as a book

Eliot left Ezra a typescript
        which EP made dark
          with the crows of emendation
        chopping it by half
   till it emerged as a Great Poem
          published in December of '22.

The month that Eliot
        came to Paris
    Canadians Frederick Banting and Charles Best
isolated insulin!

And not too many months later
        it was first used to treat diabetes

Novum sub sole 1921:
      Chanel #5 and Bandaids
      Babe Ruth smacked 59 homers for the Yankees

Duchamp's *Why not sneeze, Rose Sélavy?*
Bertrand Russell, *The Analysis of Mind*
Braque, Ernst, Klee, Léger, Matisse, Miró, Mondrian

Picasso—
wow-time in paint and shape
Sergei Prokofiev, *The Love for Three Oranges,* an opera
Edgard Varèse, *Amériques*
Anna Akhmatova, *Anno Domini MCMXI*
D. H. Lawrence, *Women in Love*
Eugene O'Neill, *Anna Christie, The Emperor Jones*
John Dos Passos *Three Soldiers*

and, somehow, "jazz outlawed on Broadway"

Goodbyes and linen:
August 2, Enrico Caruso at 48   Lightnin' Hopkins born Mar 15
Sugar Ray Robinson born May 3   Daniel Berrigan born May 9

1921 films:
Nosferatu, F W Murnau
The Sheik Rudolph Valentino
The Kid Charlie Chaplin
The Beggar Maid starring Mary Astor

Vanity Fair came up with the term "Flapper"
for a young woman
who worries not so much for "femininity" but
"dresses in a provocative manner"
puffs big c sticks
& acts like a surl-girl

January 15
William T. Cosgrave first prime minister of the Irish Free State
formed a provisional gov't
January 24
the Eskimo Pie

frozen ice cream on a thin wooden stick
                                    patented by a guy in Iowa

————————————————————— **Ulysses** —————————————————

The great Sylvia Beach published *Ulysses*
& Joyce received his first copy on February 2

Meanwhile, repressionist slime in the USA
                                    banned it

(In 1919 the US post office had seized an issue of *The Little Review*
which had printed part of *Ulysses*

the first of four seizures,
and in '21 a court had ruled it obscene

The Little Review was fined for pub'ing porn)

Then Sylvia Beach
            told them all to go fuck themselves
                                    and agreed to do the book.
It was not till '34
that the book was allowed
            in the USA and '36 in Merry England

April 1
    Strike till August 15 of coal workers

            More pay, more play, more day! o miners

April 7
    an Oiloid forked an interest free loan to Sec of Interior Albert Fall
    to lease the Teapot Dome Oil Reserve in Wyoming
                                    to the Marathon Oil Co

That was the month th'
    Communist movement in the USA
    decided to emerge
            from its isolated & persecuted time-track

    Tough luck

The Young Communist League formed secretly in Bethel, Conn
and in May
a "legal convention" was held for the new Young Workers League.

───────────────── **Big, Big Problem for Commies** ─────────────────

It was difficult
to walk down
white-picketed
       Main Street
with a banner
calling for a
"Soviet America"

May 25
Vladimir Lenin suffered a stroke that left him partially paralyzed.
(A series of strokes followed, and he died on Jan. 21, 1924, at the age
    of 53
Petrograd was renamed Leningrad)
       Trotsky, a little more eager to forge a world wide rev
      & Stalin, just a little bit less,
             were already shoving for control

May 26
Harding signed legislation
    setting up a Federal narcotics control board

May 30
the Lincoln Memorial was dedicated in D.C.

June 24
antisemitic slime in Germany
    assassinated the German foreign minister Walter Rathenau

August
Roscoe "Fatty" Arbuckle was acquitted of rape and manslaughter
               of Virginia Rappe the previous year
Nevertheless there was a huge public outcry
      over the smutty lives of stars
         & celluloid eros.
The movie companies answered
with the Motion Picture Producers & Distributors of America
    headed by former Republican National Chair
               Will Hays

Hays set voluntary standards for picture content
no sex sans marriage,
crime never pays
& the Church is always good

October 14
First mechanical telephone switchboard installed in NY

──────────────── **The March on Rome** ────────────────
October 28

The Fascists tended to overmyth this putative March.
In the summer of '22 there was violent turmoil
in Italy
& the Fascists took control of several cities

Then, just before Halloween, Mussolini insisted on a Fascist Gov't
King Victor Emmanuel III tossed out the Prime Minister
and asked Mussolini to come to Rome from Milan Oct. 30
to try to form one

Rather than march, Mussolini came by train
while 40,000 Blackshirts
trudged toward Rome
camping outside the city in fall rains
then Muss-vom took power

& formed a multiple government
of Liberals, Nationalists and Fascists,
a mix where joy was quickly tossed

from the oi _____ joy teeter totter
╱╲

November 26
Howard Carter,
taking a toke of 3k-aged Egypto-air,
peeked into Tutankhamun's tomb

eyes widening in the murky glare of gold, ebony, lapis-lazuli,
& stacks of gold-plated chariot wheels!

The creepy radio preacher Billy Sunday kept attacking her
and the Ku Klux Klan flamed with anger
                              as the dancer toured the big halls of America

It was a Sunday night, December 10
when the great bard Hart Crane

saw Isadora Duncan dance
                              in Cleveland
"It was glorious beyond words"
                              he wrote to a friend

"and sad beyond words too,
            from the rude and careless reception she got here."

She danced an all-Tchaikovksy program
                  for the 9,000 in the audience

mostly to silence
            and what Crane called "maddening cat calls."

At the end
            she came to the footlights
                              in the same red dress
                                          that had so shuddered Boston

            & suggested to the crowd they
            should read the Calamus section of *Leaves of Grass*
            (perhaps she was thinking of the poem
                              "Scented Herbage of My Breast")

"Glorious to see her there," Crane wrote
"with her right breast and nipple quite exposed,
telling the audience that the truth was not pretty,
                  that it was really indecent,

            & telling them about Beethoven,
                        Tchaikovsky & Scriabin."

December 30
      the Union of Soviet Socialists was established
      a gathering of Russia, Belarus, the Ukraine
                              and the Transcaucasian Federation

228

Novum in '22:
Waste Land
    T. S. Eliot's 433-line masterwork
               after EP's redlining & chopping by half

    Leonard Woolley
    dug up fragments of Ancient Ur!

    and brought back more of ancient Sumer

    and how a huge flood boiled across Sumeria
    (Iraq)
    about 2800 BC

    and may have provided material for the bards
    who sang flood-tales in *Gilgamesh* and the Bible

    Siddhartha
               and the first technicolor flick

    Sinclair Lewis' great *Babbitt*
    Virginia Woolf's *Jacob's Room*
    e. e. cummings *The Enormous Room*
    Eugene O'Neill *The Hairy Ape*
    Bertolt Brecht *Drums in the Night*

    Readers Digest's first issue in February in Greenwich Village
    plus *Better Homes and Gardens*
    and Emily Post's
             619-page *Etiquette in Society, in Business,*
                              in Politics and at Home

Linen & bye byes:
    Nov 15 Marcel Proust strikes side of bucket
    August 1 Alexander Graham Bell also smites bucket
    March 12 Jack Kerouac began breathing
    April 22 Charlie Mingus!
    June 10 Judy Garland!

    Ivan Bunin's "Gentleman from San Francisco."
    Ralph Vaughan Williams *A Pastoral Symphony*
    George Antheil, *Airplane Sonata*

    and for a century-long celebration of bruises, mock warfare and ouch:
    the National Football League was formed

THE POETRY LIBRARY

1923

Parlor games were big in the United States
mah-jong, crosswords, contract bridge
bowling & photography.

The populace loved Zane Grey novels
such as *Riders of the Purple Sage*
in the zooming normalcy

January 11
Germany failed to make W1 reparations payments
so a 100,000 French and Belgian soldiers surged into th' Ruhr
Germans put up passive resistance and sabotage
—Fr/Bel cut off the Rhineland from rest of Germany

(By September reparation payments had resumed
—just in time for the attempted Nazi putsch)

January 14
An uh-oh
that did not make the church socials
in Cabool, Missouri
when the Fascists formed a militia in Italy

March 4
In the Teapot Dome scandal
Albert B Fall resigned
in re Senate invest. of unlawful leasing of gov't oil reserves et al.
(6 years later, in '29 Fall was fined plus gi'en a year in the slams)

May 4
New York State Legislature
repealed the NY State Prohibition Enforcement Act
thus starting the end of prohibition

230

The Irish Civil War
1922–1923

There was war
       north & south
               in Ireland

(so much strife in the world
               between its norths & its souths!)

The IRA, under Eamon de Valera
       fought the '21 treaty
       They wanted to be a free Republic
               free from the English scepter

The Irish gov't imprisoned 1,200 & executed 77
               till de Valera called off the
                       fight in May of '23

May 23
       12 members of a theater group in New York City
       were convicted for putting on Sholem Asch's *God of Vengeance*
       under a law which prohibited "immoral" plays

July 4
       Klan barf in Indiana
       held the largest rally ever in a northern state
                       thousands
                       in robes and hoods

       with picnics &
       parade floats threatening papists and blacks

       The Klan was reforming,
               summiting in '25 with 4 million followers

       Its targets: Jews, Cath's, bootleggers, filth-sellers, and
       illegal sex

               (you could purchase an eye-holed sheet by mail order
                               for $4.00.
               By 1930 it had dried up like a slimemold on a sidewalk
                       back to around 100k supporters
                       the Klan, always there, always murking the nation's mirror)

July 6
   The USSR formally came to be, with a new constitution

August 2
   Warren Harding died in San Francisco
                  of a cerebral embolism

   VP Calvin Coolidge became president
            Coolidge had a simple view of the nation:
                  "The business of America is business."

   Calvin was a low metabolism type
   who rarely worked more than 4 hours a day
   took lots of naps
            & slept 10 a night

   The Republican Party claimed the Coolidge money-flow was
            "permanent" i.e. an endless reign of perma-cash
                  as long as you were willing to dash & clash

August 31–September 17
            another coal strike in th' USA

September 15
   Governor John Walton placed Oklahoma under martial law
                  because of terrorist Klan activities

            It makes the eyes wince to research it

───────────── **Better World Choral Societies** ─────────────

            There was a national network of affiliated choruses
            especially Jewish workers choral groups
                        singing Yiddish folk and labor
                        songs of Europe and the USA
                              in the '20s and '30s

            Where are they now
            those Better World Choral Societies?

            In 1923, for instance
                  the Freedom Singing Club
                  (Freiheit Gezangs Ferain)

a left-wing croon-group
was set up in NYC

croon through the aeons O singers!

•

September 29
    The British mandate in Palestine,
            a prize from World War I, began

November 8-9
    Hitler tried to take over the State Gov't of Bavaria
    then march on Berlin
            with a scheme of foisting Nazi rule on the nation
    It didn't work
            but it got him great ink and anti-fame

    Hitler was supported by a General named Ludendorff
    Bavarian police opened fire on 2,000 Nazis, killing 16
    Hitler was tried for treason, and given 5 years
            In prison for just 8 months,
                        he wrote *Mein Kampf*

    There was huge huge inflation in Germany
            the mark fell to 4.2 million to the dollar

December 6
    the First Labour Party victory in England
                        Yay!
    It lasted till August '24
            when the prime minister decided to grant the Soviet Gov't
            a loan & most favored nation trade status

─────────────── **Lenin Fading** ───────────────

        By the end of '23
        Lenin was fading quickly.

        Stalin allied himself with Zinoviev and Kamenev
                    to prevent Trotsky from taking over.

New in '23:
    William Butler Yeats was awarded the Nobel Prize

233

& Rainer Maria Rilke had completed *The Duino Elegies*
created o'er a vast hubbub of turmoiled months and years
first two poems in 1912 near Trieste at the Duino castle
the third in '13 in Paris
the fourth in '15 in Munich
and then in '22 he finished the Elegies
and also *The Sonnets to Orpheus*

    Americans Joseph Erlanger and Herbert Gasser
        found a way to locate the electric currents in nerves!

        and ultimately determined that the velocity of nerve signals
        varies with the thickness of the nerve fibers.

        We'll give them the Nobel Prize in '44—well deserved

Another good science tool in '23:
a Swedish guy named Theodor Svedberg
invented the ultracentrifuge
        high speed for "separating out small colloidal particles
                        and macromolecules."

Martin Buber's *I and Thou*
Buber sought a socialist binational Arab-Jewish state in Palestine

Kahlil Gibran's *The Prophet*

        Sigmund Freud found a
        cancerous growth on his jaw and palate
        but could not stop smoking

    After seven years of operations and dipping health
        he finally stopped puffing cigars

Brancusi's *Bird in Space*
Miró, Léger, Ernst, Picasso,
        now doing their greatest
and in the USA the first hillbilly recordings,
"The Old Hen Cackled and the Rooster's Going to Crow"
        among the tunes

plus Edgard Varèse *Hyperprism*

In Harlem the Cotton Club

and the Charleston was brought to NYC in the Ziegfield Follies
at the Amsterdam Theater

The Milky Way and Butterfinger,
diaphragms,
and Warner Brothers
Frank Mars created the Milky Way
Yankee Stadium opened
Time Magazine began
and in S.F. the first supermarket

The electric icebox
from Frigidaire
began its own revolution

and the "sliding closure"
was soon to be known as the Zipper
because an English writer described it as
"Zip! It's open! Zip! It's closed"

―――――――――――――― **Ahh, Bessie** ――――――――――――――

Bessie Smith's
"Down Hearted Blues" and "Gulf Coast Blues"

she was a big star for 10
then faded
died in car crash in '37
when a hick hospital
refused to treat her

Wallace Stevens *Harmonium*
Robert Frost *New Hampshire*
Shadow of a Gunman Sean O'Casey
Elmer Rice *The Adding Machine*
Aeolian Harp by Henry Cowell

and then linen and bye byes
Jan 9 Katherine Mansfield at 34
March 26 Sarah Bernhardt at 77
May 1 Joseph Heller born Sept 1 Rocky Marciano
Oct 23 Roy Lichtenstein Denise Levertov Oct 24
December 2 Maria Callas born   Harry Smith Nov 27

please do not forget the births of
Norman Mailer on Jan 31, Diane Arbus, Henry Kissinger
Hank Williams & Richard Avedon

Lift up those Charleston legs! O Nation

January 21
    When Lenin passed away
        the Congress of Soviets
        decided to preserve his body
            in a mausoleum
    & Petrograd was renamed Leningrad

January 22
    The Labour Party won in the General Election of late '23
    & the Conservatives were placed in a bye-bye mode.
    British Prime Minister Stanley Baldwin resigned on Jan 22
    and Ramsay MacDonald formed England's first Labour gov't!
        with Philip Snowden as chancellor of the exchequer.

    Ten days later Britain recognized the USSR

February 3
    Woodrow Wilson passed away

February 8
    America's first execution in the gas chamber
    a Chinese immigrant, Gee Jon
        in Carson City, Nevada

1924
    The Mongolian People's Republic

Mahatma Gandhi
  just released from 2-year prison gig
    began a 21-day fast for peace
      Indian unity and religious tolerance

--- **Bosons** ---

Rewrite the textbooks! Here come the Bosons

Albert Einstein, working with Satyenda Bose
come up with Bose-Einstein Statistics
  for "handling" the subatomic particles called bosons.
  (Bosons are elementary particles with an "integral spin." And what's
  an integral spin? Many particles seem to be spinning on an axis.
  Quantum mechanics requires that the angular momentum of
  particle spins can take on only certain values: either zero or an
  integer or half-integer multiple of the constant $h/ = 1.04 \times 10^{-27}$
  erg-seconds.
  Got it?)

April 1
  Hitler was sentenced to 5 years in prison
        but released on December 20
  These were the months he wrote his manifesto, *Mein Kampf*

April 11
  Social Democrats won the election in Denmark
      All Right!

May 4
  German elections to the Reichtag:
  Social Democrats 100
  Nationalists 95 seats
  Center Party 65
  Communists 62
  and not even a breeze for now, the Nazis at 32

June 1
  Congress set up the first Border Patrol, under the control
          of the Immigration Service

June 10
    Calvin Coolidge was renominated
                at the Republican Convention in Cleveland

June 24
    For 102 ballots at the Democratic Convention
                                in NYC
    it was New York Governor Al Smith
                                vs a guy named William McAdoo

    so that a Wall Street Attorney named J. W. Davis finally became the
        nominee
    as a compromise w/ William Jennings Bryan for VP

June 30
    Albert Fall was indicted by a Federal Grand Jury for bribery
                in th' leasing of the Teapot Dome Oil Reserve in Wyoming

───────────────── American Thrill Kill ─────────────────

        Among the unfortunate American archetypes
            of the century of gore
                        was that of angry teen-punks
                        adding knives to nihil.

            Much of the nation was attentive
            to the Leopold-Loeb trial
                        in August

        Nathan Leopold 19 & Richard Loeb 18
            rich kids who confessed to the thrill-kill of
                        14-year-old Bobbie Franks

            Th' magniloquent Clarence Darrow saved them
                                from the chair
            99 years plus life

───────────────── More Nativism ─────────────────

        In the National Origins Act of 1924
        just 5,802 could come from Italy
        while Great Britain could send over
                        66,000

238

October 1
   Jimmy Carter was born in Plains, Georgia.

October 9
   the Labour gov't fell
                  as one of the chronologies states
   "on question of prosecution of the acting editor of *Workers' Weekly,* J. R.
   Campbell, for inciting soldiers to mutiny rather than be used to
         break strikes"
   The Labour PM Mr. MacDonald was accused of secretly blocking the
                  prosecution of Mr. Campbell

October
   the *Manifeste du Surréalisme* by André Breton
   codifying what school children long had known

                  Row, row, row your Boat
                  Gently down the Stream
                  Merrily, merrily, merrily, merrily
                  Life is but a Dream

October 25
      The British Foreign Office published the "Zinoviev Letter"
                  which putatively
                  urged uprisings
                  in the army and Ireland

                  and said to be by the shudder-producing
                  chair of the Comintern head
                        one Grigory Zinoviev

                  roll, o cap-eyes, roll!   ☺ ☺☺☺

October 29
   Conservatives won the British election
   & so, on November 4
   Ramsay MacDonald resigned as prime minister
   & Stanley Baldwin formed a conservative gov't
   w/ Winston Churchill as chancellor of the exchequer
   Baldwin soon told the USSR that England would not proceed with
                        treaties neg'd by the Labour gov't.

November 4
   Calvin Coolidge glutted into another term

with 15.7m to Mr. Davis & the Democrats at 8.4m,
and Progressive Bob La Follette at 4.8m
(the Progressives were for gov't
ownership of natural resources
in the name of the people)

December 7
Another German set of elections
Soc Dem 131 seats
Center Party 69
Conservative Nationalists 103
Communists 45
Nazis fell to 14

Novum 1924:
J. Edgar Hoover was appointed acting director of the Bureau of
Investigation

& the Computing-Tabulating-Recording Company
changed its name to IBM

MGM was formed
and released Erich von Stroheim's *Greed*
mutilated & cut from its 10-hour length
& don't forget Wheaties,
Kleenex,
the Macy's Thanksgiving Day Parade

George Gershwin's *Rhapsody in Blue*
Desire Under the Elms & All God's Chillun Got Wings,
by the great Eugene O'Neill
E. M. Forster's *A Passage to India*

In France Louis de Broglie
proposed that particles can also behave as waves
opening the D to wave mechanics
Fernand Léger's film *Ballet Mécanique*
Ottorino Respighi *The Pines of Rome*
Serge Koussevitsky conducted the Boston Symphony

Robinson Jeffers' stunning book
Tamar and Other Poems
Thomas Mann *The Magic Mountain*
George Bernard Shaw *St. Joan*

& the first insecticide was developed

Linen & Minus Six:
Franz Kafka borne away on June 3
George Bush born June 12
James Baldwin born Aug 2
Joseph Conrad at 67 Aug 3
Puccini at 66 on Nov 29

the "Fonofilm" talking picture method created
                        and Columbia Pictures

the first Walt Disney cartoon, *Alice's Wonderland*

two million radios in use in the US of A

            Hello, Sucker! shouted the hostess
            in the New York Speakeasy
            to the financier
                        sneaking in for alcohol

        In general a pandemic and semisecret
        sneer at Prohibition
                        and gangster groups took hold

            Hello, 1925!

───────────────── **Josephine Baker** ─────────────────

        When she was 18 she'd starred
                    in *The Chocolate Dandies on B'way*
        & then age 19 came to France

and was an instant star
with *La Revue Nègre*

Women darkened their skins with walnut oil to emulate
Josephine Baker, the Black Venus

then she moved to the Folies Bergère
where her banana dance
naked except for a skirt of swaying bananas
brought her reddened palms of praise.

Later she risked her life
with the French Resistance

January 3
Mussolini announced assumption o' dictatorial powers, the twerp

——————————— **Trotsky in 1925** ———————————

On January 16
Leon Trotsky was tossed out
as head of the Revolutionary Military Conference

He ceased being able to help shape policy
was fully expelled from the party in 1927,
and thrown out of Russia in '29

——————————— **The Scopes Arrest** ———————————

In March
the state of Tennessee
banned the teaching of evolution

and then on May 5
crack-hicks arrested John T. Scopes
for teaching Darwin
in a public school

May 4–17
Geneva Conference on "arms traffic and use of poison gas in war"
Drool-heads in the US Senate refused to sign
the Geneva agreement for decades

July 10
    the Tass news agency in the USSR

───────────────── **The Scopes Trial** ─────────

        The trial of John Scopes in Dayton
                began in July

        Clarence Darrow was his attorney
        & the former idealist secretary of state
              now crazed fundamentalist
                  William Jennings Bryan
          was asked by the
          World Christian Fundamentals Association
          to join the the prosecution

   The wide-inked trial made many snicker
          at the simper-headed fundamentalists

  yet Scopes was found guilty
  and the conviction overturned only on
        what they call a
           "technicality"

July 25
    the great Erik Satie gone to the Big Chord
         in total poverty
            which he managed to keep hidden
       though surely his friend the wealthy Poulenc
      would have known
         & should have helped,
             even anonymously
                  but didn't

        Erik Satie
        a man of skyline melos
          such as the exquisite *Gnossienne #5*

August 8
    Speaking of drool-heads
    40,000 Klansmen in robes marched down Pennsylvania Ave in DC

September 23
    Gene Tunney beat Jack Dempsey on points
    for the heavyweight championship in Phillie

October 16
    The great state of Texas banned the teaching
    of evolutionary theory in public schools

December 3
    The boundary was confirmed 'tween Northern Ireland
                                        and th' Irish Free State

Early in December
    the fame-burdened poet named Vachel Lindsay
                            was in Washington to give a reading
    when a busboy in the hotel
    copied some poems
                and handed them to the poet
                            in the dining room

"I looked back and saw Mr. Lindsay
                        reading the poems
    as I picked up a tray of dirty dishes" the busboy later wrote

Lindsay liked the verse & told the press.
The next day
        reporters and photographers
        came to interview
                    the "negro busboy poet"
                    discovered by the author
                            of "General Booth Enters into Heaven"

    though Langston Hughes soon wearied
    of leisure class lunchers
                requesting the maître d' to
                    bring them the marvelous black bus-bard
                                        to have a look

December 6
    the John Simon Guggenheim Foundation was established

December 14
    Alban Berg's *Wozzeck*
    leading to *Lulu* of '35
    in Schoenberg's 12-tone system

Novum in 1925:
    the Pauli exclusion principle:
    that no two electrons craze-whirling about a nucleus
        can have the same set of quantum numbers

    Art Deco was born at the Exposition Internationale des Arts
                        Décoratifs et Industriels Modernes in Paris

    Harold Ross founded *The New Yorker,*
    the first volume of Pound's *Cantos*

    also Kafka's *The Trial* was
    published, against the author's '24 deathbed wish
    to have his manuscripts torched

    Hitler's *Mein Kampf,* Vol 1
                No! No!
    & F. Scott Fitzgerald's *The Great Gatsby*

    the deepfreezing process for cooked foods
    by Mr Birdseye and Mr Seabrook
           making it possible for Miriam and me to enjoy,
                  the marvels of Mrs. Paul's frozen potato pierogi!
                Thanks, o innovators!

    Al Capone took over organized crime in Chi

    Whitehead's *Science and the Modern World*
    Henri Pirenne's great *Medieval Cities*
    The first Surrealist exhibition in Paris

    & post-Lenin Commies in Russia
                moved against abstract art

    George Gershwin's *Piano Concerto*
    Prokofiev's *Symphony #2*
    Aaron Copland *Symphony #1*
    and in Chicago Louis Armstrong began the Hot Five recordings

    while December 10
                the Grand Ole Opry began radio broadcasts

    Henry Ford, hating jazz
            set up a series of folk dances

Paul Robeson gave his first concert of spirituals
The first motel, in California of course
Lux soap
        Marcel Breuer of Hungary
                came up with the tubular steel chair

Red Grange signed for $100,000
                to play for the Chicago Bears

The Mexican gov't
            nationalized its oil fields—
            with foreign ownership replaced by 50-year leases

Sherwood Anderson *Dark Laughter*
Theodore Dreiser *An American Tragedy*
e. e. cummings *XLI Poems*
F. Scott Fitzgerald *The Great Gatsby*
Ford Madox Ford *No More Parades*
The Pulitzer for Sinclair Lewis for *Arrowsmith*
Gertrude Stein's *The Making of Americans*
Virginia Woolf *Mrs Dalloway*

Sean O'Casey *Juno and the Paycock*
Noel Coward *Hay Fever*

Fritz Lang's *Metropolis*
        Eisenstein's great *Battleship Potemkin*
Charlie Chaplin in *The Gold Rush*
                with its famous boiled shoe
        Greta Garbo's *Joyless Street*

Births '25:
Feb 20 Robert Altman   March 26 Pierre Boulez
May 19 Malcolm X   May 30 Julian Beck
William Styron June 11   Sept 8 Peter Sellers
Oct 3 Gore Vidal
Oct 13 Margaret Thatcher   Same day as Maggie! Lenny Bruce
Oct 22 Robert Rauschenberg
Oct 24 Luciano Berio
Nov 20 Robert Kennedy

            Ah, that Time could have Augured Better
                for Robert Francis Kennedy!

A big Textile Strike in Passaic
                    beginning in January
and lasting a year

It involved all six of the woolen and worsted mills
and other textile places
                    in that part of NJ

Botany had proposed a 10% wage cut
                    & mass picketing followed
The workforce was mainly Slavic
but Hungarian workers at Botany had
                    organized the walkout

The Passaic strike was the first to be led by the Communist Party
                    (with the issue of dual unionism set aside)

Liberals around the nation supported it,
w/ a huge effort by recent Harvard graduate Albert Weisbord,
                    who ran the strike for th' CP

The strike succeeded in halting the 10% cut
but failed to get union recognition.

        & there were tensions 'tween commies and
                    non-commie unionists.

All hail the history of strikes!

January 14
    Finland, Norway, Sweden, Denmark
    the former Viking states
    now, after centuries,

bare sarked for peace instead of berserker for broadaxe
signed treaties for the nonBellonian settlement of disputes

February 26
Coolidge signed the Revenue Act, reducing income taxes

The money-maddened Secretary of the Treasury
Andrew Mellon
had lobbied Congress for big income and corporation tax cuts

a big boon to superwealth
and no trickle-down
as they had promised.

The mon poured into the stock market
up up up up
then Crash

March 11
Eamon de Valera quit as chief of Sinn Féin

From April to October
there were four attempts on Mussolini's life

after which
the Fascists grabbed total power

Mussolini abolished parliament
and instituted cap pun
for treason, insurrection, assassination

eager to kill & killingly eager

May 1
US Marines landed in Nicaragua
(to "preserve order"
in text-speak)
The US had been there since 1912
then finally departed in '25
only to return
The US trained a national guard
which was fought by General Augusto Sandino
who waged guerrilla warfare
till the US split again in 1933

May 9
    Two Americans, Floyd Bennett & Navy Commander
    Richard Byrd
            in a Fokker tri-motor
                    flew off from the Spitzbergen Islands
                                    north of Norway
    and seven hours later passed o'er the North Pole!

May 20
    Coolidge signed the Civil Aviation Act
                    giving government control over civil aviation

July 26
    Philippine legislature called for plebiscite for independence
    but the governor vetoed it

September 5
    Ford Motor established the 5-day week, with an 8-hour day

October 19
    In USSR Leon Trotsky was tossed from the Politburo
    Grigory Zinoviev also
            after the takeover of Joseph Stalin

───────────── **Bad News for Free Will** ─────────────

Ivan Pavlov, a Russian, published his *Conditioned Reflexes*,
the famous account of bow-wows salivating
at a bell's sound
after being "conditioned" to chow down upon a ringing bell

This would give heft to the concept that
learning and behavior, even for soul-bearing humans,
comes often out of conditioned reflexes

uh-oh.

October 31
    Escape artist Harry Houdini passed away in Detroit
    —a few weeks earlier
                    his foot was broken by
                    equipment used in his far-famed
                                    water-torture cell trick

Then in Montreal he made extravagant claims
on the strength of his stomach muscles
& a student, sans warning,
                    punched him twice
            and tore his appendix
                    so that he passed not long thereafter
                                        from poison
            at 52.

                            •

                    In the US the
Communists won the leadership of the Auto Workers Union
It was the only union in the auto industry through the early '30s

The Union had a newspaper exposing bad workplace conditions
and held shop gate meetings

Then on March 30, 1930 there was a Communist-sponsored
unemployment demonstration with more than 50k in
            the streets of Detroit, and others in other auto cities
            Flint, Toledo and Pontiac.

Novum in '26:
    a US biochemist named James Sumner
    crystallized a pure enzyme, "jack bean urease"
                    proving that enzymes are proteins
    and "can act catalytically."

The word "totalitarianism" entered th'
                    Oxford English Dictionary

                            •

The right-wing populist, Father Charles Coughlin
who mixed calls for nationalization of the banks
                    with anti-Semitic tripe
                    made his first radio broadcast in Detroit

Robert Goddard of Clark U in Mass
created a rocket powered by gasoline and liquid oxygen

The Sun Also Rises
            by the 27-year-old Ernest Hemingway

Fritz Lang's flick
        Metropolis
which he began upon returning from a '24 visit to the States.
In the movie
       rich bosses dwell richly in skyscrapers
              while the workers slave in earth's innards

John Maynard Keynes' *The End of Laissez-Faire*
          advocating gov't intervention in the marketplace

Austrian physicist Erwin Schrödinger
              fashioned wave mechanics
John Dos Passos helped found the *New Masses*
  —in '27 was arrested picketing for Sacco & Vanzetti
  & in '28 he took a trip to the Soviet Union
  U.S.A. a 1,450 page trilogy his masterwork

The year Puccini's posthumous *Turandot* premiered
& *The Desert Song* with music by Sigmund Romberg
       opened at the Casino Theater on November 30

In Italy
    the Fascists tried a "corporatist" reshuffling of industry
    13 state controlled corporations
    and the National Council of Corporations

    workers were represented by Fascist labour syndicates
       & strikes and lockouts were declared illegal

Linen, worms:
    May 21 Robert Creeley June 1 Marilyn Monroe
    June 3 Allen Ginsberg   June 27 Frank O'Hara
    August 23 Rudolph Valentino passed at 31
    Dec 5 Claude Monet at 66   December 23 Robert Bly
    December 29 Rainer Maria Rilke at 51

Novum in '26:
Book-of-the-Month Club
Charles Atlas opened a gym in NY
        for body building

NBC, Good Humors, miniature golf
      and A. A. Milne's *Winnie-the-Pooh*

The vast subatomic whirl
                    came more to confusing view as
physicists Enrico Fermi and Paul Dirac
came up with Fermi-Dirac statistics
applying to those subatomic particles, fermions,
with "half-integral spins." Protons and electrons are fermions.
(Fermions are to be distinguished from bosons, with an integral spin.
Dig?)

White Buildings, by Hart Crane
Langston Hughes, *The Weary Blues*
Kafka, posthumous *The Castle*
T. E. Lawrence, *Seven Pillars of Wisdom*
D. H. Lawrence
        the *Plumed Serpent*

Sean O'Casey *The Plough and the Stars*
Eugene O'Neill *The Great God Brown*
Religion in the Making by A. N. Whitehead
Arshile Gorky began *Artist and Mother*, which
                    took him ten years to finish
George Grosz, Miró, Giacometti, Man Ray, Georgia O'Keeffe's *Black Iris*

Béla Bartók's ballet *The Miraculous Mandarin*

            & Jelly Roll Morton's band the Red Hot Peppers
            recorded for Victor

        Go, Jelly Roll, Go!

January
    Werner Heisenberg's *Principle of Uncertainty*
                        in Copenhagen

The German physicist had come to Denmark to study
        with Niels Bohr
        and on a cold January
        strolling through a park

Heisenberg flashed on a remark from Einstein:
"It is the theory which decides what can be observed."

Later in '27 Mr. Heisenberg put forth
his paper "About the Quantum-Theoretical Reinterpretation of
Kinetic and Mechanical Relationships"
        aka the uncertainty principle

He used the uncertainty principle to show how it was impossible
to observe or determine the position of a subatomic particle
without the observation affecting the particle's velocity

Position and velocity could not be measured at the same time

If the observer was always part of the process
under observation then
objectivity was no longer a valid concept

The uncer prin troubled Einstein
who spent years trying to prove it wrong
                                but it survived

April 9
        Nicola Sacco and Bartolomeo Vanzetti were sentenced to die
                        after all their appeals were denied
                                in the Massachusetts courts

        there was a great and huge world-wide agitation for their release

The Gov of Mass one Alvan T. Fuller
chose an advisory committee
                "The Lowell Committee,"
to look into executive clemency

A human being named Lawrence Lowell,
                th' president of Harvard, was on the committee

so that it was known as the Lowell Committee
The L.C. concluded that the trial and its process had been just

"on the whole" and that clemency was not warranted

Harvard was known for a while as "hangman's house"

May 4
  Coolidge's Secretary of State was Henry Stimson
  He helped bring together factions in Nicaragua
              & then the USA was "asked" to supervise elections

  Stimson later ran the US War Department
                                    for Franklin Roosevelt

May 20
  Charles Lindbergh sailed up from Roosevelt Field at 7:54 am
  to Paris
          33.5 hours later
                    in *The Spirit of St. Louis*

  He was 25, and copped a $25k prize

June 20
  Till Aug 4
  England, USA and Japan
  met in DC to discuss naval disarmament
  but failed to agree

  Well, if they'd come up with an agreement
  then maybe Pearl Harbor fifteen years later
                              might not have hap'd

August 7
  International Peace Bridge op'd 'tween USA and Canada

August 10
  Artist Gutzon Borglum began carving Washington, Jefferson,
  Lincoln and Ted Roosevelt
                    60 feet high
                    in the Black Hills granite of Mt. Rushmore

August 23
  Nicola Sacco and Bartolomeo Vanzetti were executed for the 1920
  murder, millions around the globe
                    believing they were framed for their anarchism

  It was covered in John Dos Passos' *USA*.

In later decades there were ballistic tests
                              and books written
                                    & the case never really closed
(They were pardoned in '77 by Gov. Michael Dukakis)

September 14
    Isadora Duncan was driving
                a sports car in Nice
                    in a long flowing scarf
                which tangled in the wheel
                                    & she was strangled

                Her autobiography *My Life* came out that December
                            was very widely read & praised
                                    for its boldness & scope

September 27
    Babe Ruth smacked his 60th homer
                into the bleachers at Yankee Stadium

October 10
    Sup Ct ruled the lease on Teapot Dome was invalid
    because of fraudulent negotiations done by Interior Sec Albert Fall

November 13
    the Holland Tunnel opened
    named after its principal engineer, Mr. Clifton Holland

November 14
    Trotsky and Grigory Zinoviev were tossed from Com Party

December 27
    Show Boat by Oscar Hammerstein and Jerome Kern
    at the Ziegfeld Theater

'27 linen:
    Born were John Ashbery (July 28), Gina Lollobrigida, Olof Palme,
    Cesar Chavez, Galway Kinnell (Feb 1), Andy Warhol (Aug 6)

Novum '27:
    the year of jukeboxes, and Hostess cakes
    the Ford Model A, and the first transatlantic call
    —3 minutes for $75

The Iron Lung
      by Harvard physician Philip Drinker

and an all-mechanical cotton picker
which in the coming decades
would send African Americans north
                                for jobs
homogenized milk from Borden

George Lemaître
      a Belgian cleric
            proposed the concept of an expanding universe
            from a primal Big Bang flame-forth

Mr. Hermann Muller
discovered that x-rays and ultraviolet light
            can cause mutations or hereditary changes

Al Jolson's *The Jazz Singer*

No! No!
      Adolf Hitler
           Mein Kampf Vol. II
                      No! No!

and *Public Opinion* by Walter Lippmann
Wilhelm Reich's *The Function of the Orgasm*

Bertrand Russell *The Analysis of Matter*
Martin Heidegger *Being and Time*

Edward Hopper's *Drug Store,*
and Arnold Schoenberg's *String Quartet #1*

Isaak Babel *Jewish Tales*
Willa Cather *Death Comes for the Archbishop*
Ernest Hemingway *Men Without Women*
Hermann Hesse *Steppenwolf*
Franz Kafka *America*
Sinclair Lewis *Elmer Gantry*
Virginia Woolf *To the Lighthouse*

and Thornton Wilder's *The Bridge of San Luis Rey*

Fox Movietone News began
                    with images and soundtracks!

Abel Gance's epic *Napoleon*

CBS was formed

            Form! America, Form!

The great Thomas Hardy
                on January 1
                        down on the brass-walled farm
                        with Osiris
                        w/ a million year field of wheat
                                            to scythe
            He was 87.

It was the year o' the first of Stalin's "Five-Year Plans."
    The plan was to gain "Socialism in One Country"
                                    via 5-year plans.

Plan → Plan → Plan → Plan

January 19
    Totalitarians in the USSR announced
    that Trotsky and 29 other "oppositionists"
                        have been stomped into "internal exile."

1928
    Laughed-at-in-history U.S. customs twerps
    seized Constantin Brancusi's
    Bird in Space as an unidentified piece of bronze industrial
                                    equipment

257

March 13
   in early March on the Santa Clara River
   the St. Francis dam was oozing brown water
                              indicating vast trouble
   which was ignored by the LA water department
                  which had just enlarged the dam
   but then on the 13th
                  it blew & water 200 foot high
                              killed 450 below

May 20,
   In Germany Soc Dem's increased their number of Reichtag seats
   to 153, with Center at 62, Commies at 54, etc etc, and Nazis 12

   Now is the time
                  to send in the Time Machine
                              for Hitler removal

May 22
   Congress passed the Jones-White Act
                  with gov't subsidies for American shipping

1928
   George Papanicolaou, Greek-American pathologist,
   began to develop the eponymous Pap smear,
                  the first test for cervical cancer

May 25
   Amelia Earhart first woman to fly across the Atlantic

July 26
   Lights of New York, the first all-talking feature film,
                  opened in New York

July 30
   George Eastman first color motion pictures in Rochester

The Kellogg-Briand Pact
——————————— To End War Forever ———————————
August 27

The Kellogg-Briand Pact
                  was named after the Secretary of State Frank Kellogg

15 nations signed a paper in Paris
                that officially abolished war

It grew out of a nonaggression pact with France, to protect
France against any future German border-shoving motions.
After all had not
          H. G. Wells called WW1 the "war that will end all war"?

August 28
    Threepenny Opera opened
    by genius Marxists
                Kurt Weill and Bertolt Brecht
    a translation of John Gay's 1728 satire, *Beggar's Opera*
            to the '28 Berlin underworld
                        big hit in Berlin

September 19
    In New York
    Mickey Mouse in *Steamboat Willie*

                        •

    This was the year
    Japan frothed increasingly reactionary

    Suppressing left wing groups
                and sliding into fascism

———————————— **Charles Kerr Publishing** ————————

Charles Kerr
          aging
                thirsting to retire

    from 42 years of nonstop Socialist publishing
                            in Chicago

    sold his controlling shares in the cooperative company

    to John Keracher, known as a "gifted street speaker," tireless
            cross-country
    lecturer, author, leaflet-writer
                & head of the Proletarian Party

Keracher surged onward,
                                running it for another 42 years

                                    •

October 6
    Chiang Kai-shek was elected president of China

———————————————— **The Big Bull Market** ————————————————

        There was a Bull Market on Wall Street
        as humans and institutions
                        borrowed money to purchase stocks

        Drool o greed-heads, drool!

October 12
    the Iron Lung was used for the first time in Boston

October 27
    American Trotskyism was formed
                when James Cannon, Max Shachtman and Martin Ahern
                were stomped out of the Communist Party

            because they were critical of the Soviet Union

            Trotskyism came about in the US of A
            pretty much as in other nations
            as a reaction against the creepiness of
                                Soviet Communism

            Yet cap-eyes were to roll   ☺ ☺☺☺
            in fright at Trotskyism
                            too

October 20
    Republicans coined the phrase, "A chicken in every pot,
                                a car in every garage"
                        for Herbert Hoover's campaign

November
    Herbert Hoover was elected president over Al Smith
                21.3m to 14m

Smith was against prohibition
& a, shudder, Irish Catholic
while Hoover was the
self-made engineer millionaire

Socialist Norman Thomas tabbed in with 267,835

Novum 1928:
Lady Chatterley's Lover,
Virginia Woolf's *Orlando*,
Ben Hecht's & Charles MacArthur's *Front Page*
Ravel's *Bolero*

The acid later called Vitamin C was iso'd!
followed by Vitamin A in '33
then in the late '30s and into '40s: E, K, B_{12} *et alia*.

The great Alexander Fleming discovered penicillin
He'd left some staphylococcus bacteria exposed
in his lab
at Queen Mary's Hospital in London

Later he spotted a mold on the bacteria
and areas around the mold patches free of staph

He id'd the mold as *Penicillium notatum*
the sort that grows on stale bread
and showed that it could be used against
human disease

It was difficult to purify,
but came into lifesaving use in W2.

A physicist named Arnold Sommerfeld
proposed that electrons behave like a "degenerate gas"
in a conductor, and that only a few, high energy electrons
actually conduct the electricity

Hot Christmas read: Benito Mussolini's *My Autobiography*

George Bernard Shaw's *The Intelligent Woman's Guide to Socialism
& Capitalism*

Margaret Mead *Coming of Age in Samoa*

Paul Robeson sang "Ol' Man River" in *Showboat*
(British production)

Earliest commercial use of
important term "boogie woogie,"
                    as in "Pine Top's boogie-woogie"

Gershwin's *An American in Paris*

Vladimir Horowitz made his American debut
Jimmy Rodgers, "The Soldier's Sweetheart"

Stephen Vincent Benet *John Brown's Body*
Aldous Huxley *Point Counter Point*
Federico Garcia Lorca *Gypsy Ballads*
Eugene O'Neill *Strange Interlude*
Ez Pound *A Draft of the Cantos 17-27*

Charles Demuth *I Saw the Figure 5 in Gold*
        Brecht's *The Caucasian Chalk Circle*
Vladimir Mayakovsky *Klop/The Bedbug*
The Little Matchgirl Jean Renoir
and Luis Buñuel and Salvador Dali's 17-minute *Un Chien Andalou*

Linen and bye bye for '28:
March 12 Edward Albee
Ché Guevara born on June 14
Leoš Jánaček passes at 74 August 12
Anne Sexton Nov 2   Grace Kelly Nov 12
Dec 7 Noam Chomsky

In Britain the lance
        was officially abandoned for purposes of war
        Bye, lance

        Abandon that lance, O Universe!

January 22
    Trotsky was tossed from internal exile
              and headed for Constantinople

St. Valentine's Day Massacre
February 14

    some thugs for mobster Al Capone
    the bootleg king in Chicago
    posed as policemen
        & killed seven thugs in a beer warehouse
            working for mob rival Bugsy Moran

    There's nothing quite like thugs killing thugs
    to moil mass interest in America

The legendary Mr. Capone seemed invincible
        with his razor-slashed face
till finally in '31 the feds caught him on a tax evasion charge
& he was given 11 years in the slams
        —syph killed him in '39

The First Five-Year Plan
May

    Josef Stalin was utterly determined
    to industrialize his vast nation
        in a quick spurt of years

    & to collectivize the entirety
        of Russian agriculture

There were some who wanted to move more slowly
                                    but Stalin prevailed

and the first Five-Year Plan, 1700 pages long
                        for October '28 to October '32
                                            was voted into place
            by the Fifth All-Union Congress of Soviets

The Five-Year Plan sought to double coal production
—tripling pig iron—
& huge steel mills and tractor plants were built

The State seized the grain harvests
and organized independent peasant-owned farms
                                    into State-run collectives
in a process known as "dekulakization"
—the kulaks historically were a
                more or less prosperous part of the peasantry—
Many kulaks resisted, burned crops, killed their animals
Many were sent to Siberia
                and there was famine
(But by '32 ½ of USSR farms had been collectivized)

The human toll was vast
Roy Medvedev has estimated
    that 10,000,000 were "dispossessed" during collectivization
    and that around 2,000,000 died.

What? You Never Heard
of Dual Unionism?

This was the year for a
shift in Comintern policy, reversing the strategy of "boring from
            within" to "dual unionism"

to create separate vanguard unions
            whose goal was to challenge the
                economic system as well as to
                    make better working conditions

April 15
    After a complaint from th' Daughters of the American Revolution
    the New York City fuzz raided the
                Birth Control Clinical Research Center

May the
> first Academy Awards
>> with Paramount's *Wings* the best film

Also in May
> Georgia O'Keeffe moved to the Southwest

May 30
> In the first general election under universal adult suffrage
>> in England
> Labour won 287 seats, conservatives 260, liberals 59

Go, Labour, Go! Go!

August
> In Jerusalem
> Arabs attacked Jews, killing 133
> British soldiers assisted in stomping back the Arabs
>
> sparked by a dispute over the use of the Wailing Wall
>> & Arabs fearing a Zionist movement
>
> which wanted to make at least part of the English-run Palestine
>> a Jewish state

August 6–13
> at a Reparations Conference at the Hague
> Germany accepted what was called the Young Plan
>> named for an American banker named Owen Young
>
> It saved the Germans $
> in that they had only to repay the Allies' war debts
>> but NOT the cost of reconstruction
>>> and th' Allies agreed to depart from the Rhineland by
>>> June of '30
>
> Hitler was less than pleased.

September 19
> Stock prices had more than doubled since '25
>> & this day on Wall Street they summited
>
> Drool, o money-slaves, drool!

September 14
    In Gastonia, North Carolina
    textile union worker and ballad singer Ella May Wiggins
    was murdered by
                anti-worker sleaze
                    at the Loray Textile Mill

    five were indicted but none ever ate
                from the metal plates of jail

On October 19
    the greed-head thrill pulse to sell sell sell
             had grown to spurt level
                 & stocks began to fall

―――――――――― **The Stock Market Crashes** ――――――――
October 24–29

First there was Black Thursday October 24
when there was a wide, wide river
              of sell-orders
      & no
      buys

    'tween 11 & 12 AM
         and the "panic" had begun

The stock market closed from noon on Oct 24 till Oct 28,
           known as Black Monday,
and then Black Tuesday, Oct 29
        black ↘ black ↘ black ↘

11 greed-heads offed themselves
        in the Babbittean mal-storm of
           Black Thursday

In the next few months
banks called in loans, and foreclosed on mortgages

Conventional wisdom held that capitalism was a self-correcting
high wire act
    but investment capital dried up, companies cut back
         & millions were out of work

—thanks, o self-correcting system

WALL ST. LAYS AN EGG

November 8
    the Museum of Modern Art opened
    with exhibits by Cézanne, Gauguin, Seurat, Van Gogh
                          Yes!

November
    the John Reed Clubs were founded in NY
    by the editorial board of *New Masses*
    with a slogan, *Art is a Class Weapon*

    (the surrealists might have preferred
                Art is a Painting Class Weapon)

    The John Reed Clubs apparently reflected a Comintern
    decision to move the class war
                out upon all the nooks & crannies of culture

    By '34 there were more than 30 clubs
    then, in '34, the Comintern wanted a Popular Front
               and the JRC's were terminated

November 29
    Lt. Commander Richard E. Byrd
          with three others in a Ford trimotor
    circled the South Pole for an hour
              the first flight

———————————— **Appliances for the Masses** ————————————

    By 1929
       one home in four
          had an electric vacuum cleaner
    & one in five had a toaster!

    The electric refrigerator & washing machines
         were making a clean revolution

Over 10,000,000 households
had radios!

At night
lonely listeners
to th'

in the farm houses
on the prairie
& in the towns
after dinner
sports, news, music
& half-hour serial dramas

Novum in '29:
Edwin Hubble showed the universe to be expanding
—uh-oh—
and furthermore
that the speed of galaxies in the Outbound
is directly proportional to their distance from the observer!

—uh-oh.

Popeye the Sailor Man, 7 UP, mobile homes,
Erich Maria Remarque's *All Quiet on the Western Front*
soon to be banned by Naz-slime

Salvador Dali joined the Surrealists
& there was the 2nd Surrealist Manifesto

Max Ernst, René Magritte, Mondrian, Klee
Henry Moore
wild art!

Magic Mountain, Buddenbrooks, Death in Venice
combining to give Thomas Mann the Nobel Prize

Tunes o' '29, the great Hoagy Carmichael's great "Stardust"
plus "Happy Days are Here Again"

& when Bessie Smith
recorded a two-reel film of "St. Louis Blues"
                    it was suppressed for its "bad taste."

Laurens Hammond patented the electric Hammond Organ

Max Brand *Machinist Hopkins*
            William Faulkner *The Sound and the Fury*

Hemingway *A Farewell to Arms*
            Sinclair Lewis *Dodsworth*

Thomas Wolfe *Look Homeward, Angel*
            Virginia Woolf *A Room of One's Own*
                        Noel Coward *Bitter Sweet*
                        Elmer Rice *Street Scene*

The word "apartheid" was first used in Afrikaner text
The Vatican City State in Rome became an independent entity

                    And everywhere
                    there were Speakeasies,
                    laughing at Carrie Nation
                                & the No Nos
                    while shy people in the Ozarks
                    dangled their crocks o' homemade hootch
                                        down in their wells

Einstein's *Unitary Field Theory*

A. N. Whitehead, *Process and Reality*
and also his *The Aims of Education and Other Essays*

Edmund Husserl *Formal and Transcendental Logic*
                        you haven't read it?

Born in 1929
    Martin Luther King January 15
    Edward Dorn born on April 2
    & Claes Oldenburg on January 29, Adrienne Rich
    Beverly Sills
    Roger Bannister May 23
    Jacqueline Kennedy
    Audrey Hepburn May 1

Yasir Arafat
Anne Frank June 12
Arnold Palmer Sept 10   Ursula LeGuin October 21
        in the gnarls of the time-track

Flicks o' '29:
The Virginian, with Gary Cooper
The Phantom of the Opera, with Lon Chaney

& th' Amos 'n' Andy radio show began on NBC

In February
    Herbert Hoover sent a group to Haiti, to prepare an end of
            US occupation
    while persuading President Borno to leave office

February 18
    Amateur astronomer Clyde Tombaugh
    at Lowell Observatory in Flagstaff
                            found a new planet, Pluto

March 6
    The Communists dubbed it International Unemployment Day
    and hundreds of thousands of jobless workers
                                    marched in major cities

    The size of the demos
                    astounded even radicals
    this first evidence shown to the middle class
            of mass unemployment

    and cap-eyes no doubt rolled in fright

March 13
   Mahatma Gandhi began the Civil Disobedience in India
            with a Salt March
                  from Ahmedabad to the coast

March 14
   Movie version of O'Neill's successful play, *Anna Christie*, opened, with
   Greta Garbo starring.
                  Her first talkie. She had been a huge star of the silents,
                  The Temptress, Flesh and the Devil, and *Love.*

   The movie world awaited her voice. It floated.
                  O'Neill's tale of an American prostitute who falls for a sailor.

———————————— **The Sea Salt Disobedience** ————————————
                     April 6

      Gandhi and 30 associates
      had walked for 320 miles to the Gulf of Cambay

      Behind the march was a truckful of hand-woven cotton

      At the ocean, Gandhi broke the law by
                        extracting and tasting sea salt
      to protest India's evil salt tax
                        on the impoverished
      (There was an imperial monopoly on the making of salt)

      He served a jail term,
                  till early in 1931

June 17
   The Smoot-Hawley Act was signed by Hoover raising the tariffs
   on imported goods from 33% to 40%
   which made it almost impossible
               (as Roosevelt noted three years later when he was Pres)
                        for Cuban sugar to be imported to the US
                                          thus destabilizing Cuba
   Depression, o cap-eyes, depression!

October 14
   George and Ira Gershwin's *Girl Crazy*
                        opened in NYC

1930–34
　US period of Diego Rivera, David Alfaro Siqueiros, and
　　　José Clemente Orozco.

The American mural movement of the 1930s produced
　　　　　　　　　　some 2500 murals around the nation

September
　the Cyclotron, invented by U of C physicist Ernest Lawrence
　　　　　　　accelerated a proton to 37k miles per second!

Lawrence later was one of the leaders in building the a-bomb

September 14
　Sleazebag Nazis surged a bit in German elections:
　Soc Dems 143 seats
　Commies 77
　National Socialists 107 seats

November 5
　Sinclair Lewis won the Nobel Prize in good part for his great &
　　　　　　　tragicomic novel *Babbitt*
　　　　　　　　　the first American to win

--------------------------- **Mother Jones** ---------------------------
November 30

Mary Harris Jones
60-year union organizer
　　　all the way back to the Knights of Labor
one of the founders of the International Workers of the World
risked her life so many times
　　　　　confronting the kill-heart of mine owners
　such as the Rockefeller goons at the 1913 Ludlow Strike—
　　　　　　passed away in Maryland
　　　　　　　　　age 100

December 11
the Bank of the United States clanged shut, financial crisis

December 26
Hart Crane at last completed his 75-page *The Bridge*
w/ th' Brooklyn Bridge its symbol of the synapse of
creativity
from now back to the ancients
& characters including Columbus, Whitman, Emily D,
burlesque dancers, officers, workers, hoboes, and
Amer-Indians

"Thousands of strands have had to be searched for, sorted,
and interwoven,"
Crane had noted during its writing.
Then, the day after Christmas
Crane wrote Caresse Crosby in Paris
"I am hastily enclosing the final version of "Quaker Hill"
which ends my writing on *The Bridge.* You can now go ahead ...
I've been slow, Heaven knows,
but I know that you will forgive me ..."

He was rushing to get the letter aboard the *Mauretania*
"or else risk the delays of one of the slower steamers."

Novum o' 1930:
Scotch tape by MMM
plus flashbulbs and pinball machines

Trotsky's *The Permanent Revolution,* his autobiography

and the Farm collectivization program back in the USSR sped up

──────────── **More Uh-oh for Particles** ────────────

Physicist Paul Dirac propounds
anti-particles
identical to known particles
but with a different charge

proton has + charge
antiproton a - charge

electron a - charge
antielectron (or positron) a + charge

Antiparticles
make up what is now i.d.'d as Antimatter

Also in 1930:
J.M. Keynes *Treatise on Money*
William Empson *Seven Types of Ambiguity*
Margaret Mead *Growing Up in New Guinea*
Sigmund F *Civilization and its Discontents*
—wow, is it discontented!

Institute for Advanced Study founded at Princeton

Pope Pius XI condemned diaphragms and rubbers
as a "grave and unnatural sin"

The great Weill/Brecht opera *The Rise and Fall of the City of Mahagonny*

The works of Leon Trotsky
were banned in Boston

The Chrysler Building was completed in NYC
with its famous Art Deco ornamentation
Its beauty was partly forged by the 1916 zoning law
which facilitated the spikifying of some skyscrapers
by requiring that, at a certain height
buildings had to "retreat from the street"
in order to allow air and light to "penetrate"

Retreat it did, near its summit, w/ eagle-faced gargoyles
& tapering semicircular stackings, like a metal
cake for the wedding of Apollo & the Goddess of Chrome
a thing at which to gaze
as was the Daily News building at 42 and 3rd.

Dashiell Hammett *The Maltese Falcon*
Robert Frost *Collected Poems*
T.S. Eliot *Ash Wednesday*
John Dos Passos *42nd Parallel*
Jean Cocteau's *The Blood of a Poet*
W.H. Auden's *Poems*
Noel Coward *Private Lives*

Hitler Voms Upward

The World Wide Depression
was used by Hitler to vom upward
so that by th' end o' '30 the Nazis were the second largest party.
Rightists slime-slashed
into the public's disaffection with extant political parties
rising unemployment
scapegoating the Jews—
plus the Nazis were
much better than, say,
the American Klan
at propaganda & advertising
and big-time German capitalists
wanted to thwart leftists
whatever it took.

The Big Bang

Confounding Hitler, and all other isms
the Russian-American physicist
George Gamow
spread the theory of a
Big Bang origin of the Universe

'30 blazing births! and keening goodbyes:
Jan 23 Derek Walcott
March 23, D. H. Lawrence passed at 45
March 22 Stephen Sondheim born   March 23 Gregory Corso
May 8 Gary Snyder born   May 15 Jasper Johns
July 7 Arthur Conan Doyle passed at 71
July 15 Jacques Derrida linen
Joanne Woodward Feb. 27, Ornette Coleman,
Jean-Luc Godard Dec. 3, Neil Armstrong! August 5

Bobby Jones won four national golf championships the same year

'30 flicks: *All Quiet on the Western Front, L'Age d'Or,* by Buñuel,
& Marlene Dietrich's *Blue Angel*

Roll it, O America!

March 3
    Herbert Hoover signed a bill making "The Star-Spangled Banner"
                                    the national anthem

―――――――――――――――― **The Scottsboro Case** ―――――――――――――――

A freight train
           was moving through Alabama March 25
―freights were the Greyhound buses
                   of the poor
A fight occurred 'tween some white guys & some blacks
                            in a freight car
The whites were tossed off
               and complained to the police

When the train clacked nigh to Scottsboro
Sheriff's deputies searched the cars
       & found 9 black kids and two white girls
       ―uh-oh

Few things made the South more bonkers
than black guys alone with white girls
                and possibly balling.
The women were in a tough predicament
        especially if they were on board willingly.
        They said they'd been raped

     A short while later
         the nine black youth were brought to trial
         in groups of three
              each trial lasting a day

Doctors testified that no rape had occurred
but the all-white jury convicted them.

Outside the courthouse 10,000
                    hate-addled crackers cheered the
                            first day's verdict
                                    while a brass band played

8 of the 9 were sentenced to die in the chair.

                    There was a big international outcry
                    led by the International Labor Defense
                                    a communist group
                        & also the NAACP
                    with one of the women recanting her
                            tale of rape
                            and a new trial was scheduled for 1933.

──────────────── **Changes in Spain** ────────────────

On April 12
    Republicans did well in municipal elections in Spain
    One Niceto Alcalá Zamora demanded that King Alfonso XIII
                                    leave on the nonce

On the 14th the right-wing king departed
and Zamora assumed the presidency of a provisional gov't.

In June, on the 28th, the Spanish general election
                            gave left parties a big majority!

Suddenly schools were built, divorce legalized,
and, unfortunate
        for later history
                many churches were burnt and clergy attacked
                                    after th' king was tossed
angering the pious, including the pious impoverished.
Then, for various reasons including
                the usual ghastly leftist schism-ism
                plus lack of money
                the government could not go through
                        w/ promised land distributions
                                which "angered the left"
                                    as the textbooks say

Five years later, Civil War

———————— April Vienna Bank Bye-Bye ————————

Vienna had been the fiscal capital of the world
yet that spring Austria's premier bank, called Credit Anstalt
                                                    went bye-bye

the result was to strengthen
the right-wing nuts o' German-speaking nations
            when millions lost their life savings.
                    & the demagogues stood up pointing
                                        at you-know-who
                                                as the culprit

———————— Anger, Farms & Gambling ————————

In the USA that summer
the huge wheat crop
            led to a collapse in prices
                        and anger among farmers

while in Nevada the Depression
drove it to legalize gambling, quickie nonreligious marriages,
& divorces after six weeks,
after which
            there wasn't much more of a money problem
                        unto the century's end

———————— Howling in the Reichstag ————————
Early '30s in Germany

The poet Stephen Spender spent the early '30s in Germany,
and Christopher Isherwood,
                soon to write his *Berlin Stories*

The poet noted how there were some 29 parties
                "howling at one another in the Reichstag."

        Hatred among groups was intense
        & Hitler was already beginning
            to use "The Big Lie"

yet to many Euro-American intellectuals
Germany's wild avant-garde
in music, art, building design
was a thrilling lure

&, to quote Stephen Spender
"Germany was the harbinger"
of two possible paths:
"the hell of fascism
or the potential paradise of communism"

Both paths held their passion
—for those who hungered for Superman
another Roman Empire, a 1000-year Reich
& a godly Führerprinzip

—or for those who wanted
a tough-assed Dictatorship of the Proletariat
a mere defensive measure
forced upon the Soviet Union
by capitalist enemies

which would only last till all the world
was in the hands of the working class
after which the state and national borders
would wither

September 7–December 28
the Second Round Table Conference on India was held in London
& included Mahatma Gandhi
for the All-India Nationalist Congress

Britain offered a limited freedom
but Gandhi wanted total independence
& the great man of Ahimsa
went home to riots 'tween
"upper-caste" Hindus
& the harijan "untouchables"

September 10
the English gov't, with a deficit of 120,000,000 pounds,
decided to balance budget
through big cuts

so on September 10 there were riots in London and Glasgow
and even a naval mutiny on the 15th over pay

This was the year cap-slime inaugurated the "means test"
where those on long term unemployment
were made to prove what they possess
before more help was provided
   leading to more & more suffering
         in the English Depression

September 17
 LP records were first demo'd by RCA in NYC

September 20
 Britain abandoned the gold standard
       and Japan also on December 11

September
 Japanese invaded Manchuria

 and meanwhile Mao
 gathered a bit of strength
 with his rural radical "Marxism in the mountains."
 In November, Mao was made chair of the first
        Soviet Republic of China

 a kind of self-fulfilling prophecy
      of what was to come

October 16
 US representatives came to the League of Nations Council
     on the issue of Japanese aggression in Manchuria

 Another example of how War 2 might have been averted
     had the US joined the League back in 1919.

October 17
 Al Capone was sentenced to 11 big ones for tax evasion

October 25
 the George Washington Bridge
 'tween Jersey and NYC
   was the longest suspension bridge of its time
   its cables were 3 feet in diameter with 26,474 parallel wires.

The ghastly power-mad Stalin
cracked down on Art
     & sent out his secret police
         to enforce conformity

Intellectuals and artists were silenced
& everybody was worried about being shot
The great Vladimir Mayakovsky and Sergei Yesenin terrorized
                and driven to suicide

Anna Akhmatova was denounced as a "harlot nun"
and forbidden to publish for nearly 20 years
though she kept on writing in secret

What did Stalin want?
     Soviet Realism, or else: blam!

December 5
   I think Vachel Lindsay must have hated his bardic voice
It was one of those nights where the soul seems like an anvil
and the poet who once thrilled the public
         with his semi-sung chants
now despondent and mired in mid-life debt
       burned his vocal chords
          with a bottle of Lysol
            & passed away
             at 52

December 7
   the White House turned away hundreds of marchers
         seeking employment.
  "Let them eat laissez-faire!"
     and breadlines began to form
        around the nation

Novum in '31:
Martha Graham's *Primitive Mysteries*
     from her all-woman troupe
   daring, angular, erotic, stark
       and with a social conscience!

speaking of which Linus Pauling
that year

laid out "resonance"
        which explains, using quantum mechanics
        how organic compounds share electrons

and there was Gödel's Proof,
from U of Vienna math whiz Kurt Gödel

that no mathematical system is free of undecidable paradoxes
each system has holes and incompleteness
and always statements which can't be proven
                                or disproven
        uh-oh

                        &
Austro-Am Wolfgang Pauli
proposed a massless particle to account for th' energy missing
        in beta decay.
        Later this will be found to be
                        the intriguing neutrino

Also Novum in '31:
the electron microscope
                (two German guys, focusing a beam of electrons
                                through a vacuum chamber)
                and Clairol hair dye

In Detroit Elijah Muhammad formed the Black Muslims
Edmund Wilson *Axel's Castle*
John Dewey *Philosophy and Civilization*
Salvador Dali's great depiction of melted watch Space-Time
                                The Persistence of Memory

Rockefeller Center began
                (to be finished in '39)

Edgar Varèse *Ionization*
        Sergei Rachmaninoff's melos banned in USSR as decadent

Wallace Stevens *Harmonium*

William Faulkner *Sanctuary*
Pearl Buck *The Good Earth*
        Eugene O'Neill *Mourning Becomes Electra*

and Chevrolet brought out the first pickup
the Schick electric razor
Alka-Seltzer,
freon first used as aerosol

and the linen/life-loss synapse:
Alvin Ailey January 5   Boris Yeltsin Feb 1
James Dean Feb 8 Joanne Woodward Feb 27 (some chronicles
have Woodward linen in '30)
Mikhail Gorbachev March 2 Clint Eastwood May 31
Willie Mays May 6   Andy Warhol August 8
Barbara Walters Sept. 25   Mickey Mantle Oct 4
Desmond Tutu Oct 7
Oct 18 Thomas Edison lights out at 84

Charlie Chaplin's *City Lights*
Bela Lugosi, *Dracula*
Boris Karloff
went "sensitive"
in a portrayal of the monster in *Frankenstein*
Fritz Lang's eery-ooey *M*
Greta Garbo in *Mata Hari*
Cagney's *The Public Enemy*
"Come & get me, copper!"
and in the USA the first TV broadcasts

By '32 30% of the US workers were unemployed
& revolution was in the wind
unless ...

January 4
the Japanese army invading Manchuria
arrived at the east end of the Great Wall

That was the day
  Gandhi had returned to India from the London Conference
  the civil disobedience campaign had revived
  and he was arrested.
  The Indian National Congress was deemed illegal
      and the Indian gov't was given emergency powers for 6 months

January 7
  Chancellor Heinrich Brüning said Germany could not & would not
  continue to pay reparations for WWI

January 22,
  Congress voted to create the Reconstruction Finance Corporation
  —to lend money to banks and industries

  In July it was empowered to give moolah to states for public works

Early 1932
  Aldous Huxley's *Brave New World*

————————————— **The Lindbergh Kidnapping** —————————————
March 1

      In the night
      Anne Morrow & Charles Lindbergh's 19-month-old son
      Charles Jr.
                  was snatched from their just-completed
                  grand style house near Princeton, New Jersey

      The perp left a homemade ladder under the bedroom
      window and a ransom note in "broken English"

      There were negotiations
      and $50k was handed over to someone in a cemetery

      but no child
                  and then he was found by a road

      In '34 a human named Bruno Richard Hauptmann
      spent a 10 spot from the cemetery

      & $30,000 more turned up in his home,
                  plus lumber matching the ladder

      & he was electrocuted in '36 for the murder

The Ford Massacre

Private thug-guards and police fired March 7
on a leftist-led Hunger March
                outside the Ford Plant in Detroit
                        that killed four & wounded a hundred

March 9
        The Dáil of the Irish Free State elected Eamon de Valera
                                president of its executive council

Good News for Unions
March 23

The Federal Anti-Injunction Act
(the Norris-LaGuardia Act)
                established workers' right to strike
and prohibited management from forcing employees to sign
"Yellow Dog" contracts
                        requiring them not to join labor unions

with the result that injunctions
                could not so easily be used
                                to thwart workers getting living wages.

It made it easier to set up unions
Federal judges could not issue injunctions to stop a strike
except when there was substantial damage to an employer's
                                                property.

Evil & Good

Hit-vom surged in the April 10 elections
Paul von Hindenburg getting 19.5 million for president
Hitler 13.4m, and Thälmann (Commie) 3.7m.

while in India
Gandhi and his supporters continued their
                national civil disobedience campaign
                                        to push for selfgov't

& an end to the castes.

Stomped into the slams in Poona, Gandhi announced
                              "a perpetual fast unto death"

which would win reform for the untouchables or Harijans
        (Children of God), as
Gandhi called them.

British responded five days into his fast
        & agreed to give more "representation"
        for lower-class Hindus and—Gandhi's ultimate objective—
        promised a later electoral stage
        in which there would not be
                    high-caste & low-caste electorates

April 26
    Hart Crane jumped from a steamer
                    in the Gulf of Mexico
                              returning to the States
                from a visit to Mexico
                        on one of the first Guggenheim Fellowships

May 20
    Amelia Earhart was the first woman to fly across the Atlantic
                    sailing Newfoundland to Londonderry, Ireland!

———————————— Ancient Vengeance in Spain ————————————

The Cortes (parliament) in May, 1932, banned parochial schools,
                dissolved the Jesuits, and nationalized church property
            thus giving the right a rare chance
                    to meld the impoverished pious
                                with the drooling rich

Beware of quick vengeance
for ancient grudges

June 30
    In England the interest rate settled down to 2%
            & began a 7-year swing of "cheap money"

Roosevelt is Nominated in Chicago
July 2

Franklin Roosevelt broke the stupid tradition
of nominees not addressing the Convention

He traced in his speech
how greed-head corporations
had lowered production costs
without rewarding either the workers
                or the stockholders
then invested huge profits
                in the stock market

"The consumer was forgotten.
Very little of it went into increased wages;
the worker was forgotten ... the stockholder was forgotten.
     And ...
very little of it was taken by taxation."

The president-to-be
                ended his speech with famous words:
"I pledge you, I pledge myself, to a
                New Deal
                        for the American People.
... This is more than a political campaign; it is a call to arms.
   Give me your help, not to win votes alone,
      but to win in this crusade to restore America to its own people."

The Great Rent Strike Rebellion of '32

A strike began in the Bronx near the
                Allerton Avenue Coöps (inhabited by leftists)
—police fought groups of tenants wanting rent reductions
Women led hand-to-hand resistance against horses and cops

Though landlords got together to stomp it down
the rent strike spread to Brownsville, Williamsburg, Boro Park and
                                        other places.

287

The Concept of Artistic Monotony

In '32 the new Congress of Soviet Writers
bonked forth with the official rules on socialist realism:
"It demands of the artist a truthful, historically concrete depiction
of reality in its revolutionary development."

Stalin and the army were to be glorified

The New Soviet Man was the sole hero
(Abstraction and Experimentation were
to be conducted in Siberia)

The Congress of Soviet Writers at its first shindig trashed
Proust, Joyce and Pirandello

The Bonus March
July 28

In ghastly Depression's penury
the House passed but
the Senate rejected a bonus bill in June
to be given to WW1 vets

so there was a Bonus Expeditionary force
15,000 strong,
led by a guy named Walter Waters
from Oregon
that surged upon Washington

They kept arriving in D.C. from around the country
vowing to remain till War 1 bonuses were distributed
a few hundred $ per person

They grew more demanding
and why not?

They took over a former armory
and occupied abandoned buildings near Capitol
plus shanties by the Anacostia River

President Hoover
called in the troops led by Army Chief of Staff Douglas MacArthur

with tanks, machineguns, & cavalry
beating and teargassing and swinging sabers

'gainst protesters and spectators
two were killed

Their shantytown was in flames,
and the Bonus Army was routed
in a rightist display
that might have only been a faint flicker
of gore to come
had Roosevelt not saved the system

July 31
in the Reichstag elections Naz-vom won 230 seats
Social Democrats 133
Center 75, Coms 89
but neither Naz-slime nor Soc Dems would
join a coalition

The Nazis were Big Lie rowdy, wearing brown uniforms
and debates waxed to riot-level shouting

(In order to confront Naz-vom
the gov't ordered new elections in November '32,
and the Nazis lost 61 seats—
Hitler by then had a half million storm troopers!)

August 26
the Comptroller of Currency ordered a moratorium on foreclosure
of first mortgages during the Depression

———————————— **Rev Not Happening** ————————————

The Soviet Union noticed that
Germany was not going commie
as the Vanguard Party theory had predicted

but instead was going jack boot!
so the Sov's began to sign nonaggression pacts
with France, Poland, Finland, Estonia and Latvia

September 15
    an Agrarian Law in Spain,
            allowed the expropriation of "landed estates"
            to be overseen and administered by an Institute of
                Agrarian Reform

    All right!

September 25
    Catalonia was allowed autonomy
                with its own flag, language, parliament

October 3
    the Governor of Nevada ordered a 12-day banking holiday
                                    to save his State's banks
                        from total money suck-out

November 1
    the Highlander Folk School opened
                in a two-story house in Monteagle, Tennessee
    founded by southerners who met at the
                        Union Theological Seminary

    Highlander was one of almost 250 functioning labor colleges
                                    during those years
    started by the Socialist Party, unions, the IWW etc.
    under the theory that education is a great great tool for social change

    Among Highlander students were
                Stokely Carmichael, Fanny Lou Hamer &
                        & the epochal Rosa Parks

    Christian socialist Horton Miles was one of the founders
    Other founders were Don West, James Dombrowski,
        John Thompson—
                        You can look them up

November 6
    Another election in Germany!
    Naz-vom 192
    Soc Dems 121, Coms 100 (a gain for the Coms)

    It was a further stalemate, giving Nazi storm troopers more chance to
                        make moil & kill

290

──────── The Great Victory of Roosevelt ────────
November 8

Roosevelt won 42 states vs. Hoover's six.
Roosevelt 22.8m, Hoover 15.76m
and Socialist Norman Thomas 881,951

November 19
Hit-slime tried to form a coalition gov't but failed

──────── More on the Scottsboro Case ────────

In November the US Supreme Court ordered
                    a retrial of the Scottsboro defendants

The retrial began on March 27, 1933
and even though one of the young women
                    now repudiated her rape charge
all defendants were found guilty again

What happened? Intense protest
till an Alabama judge overturned that verdict
with a new trial in '36
and then in '37 four defendants were released, and the remaining five
                    still got big sentences, last one not freed till '50
and all were ultimately pardoned
                    for the injustice

December 28
a Resolution in Congress against the cancellation of Germany's
                                        WWI debt

──────── The Racist, Classist Tuskegee Syph Study ────────

In Macon County, Georgia
one of the poorest in the poor South
the US Public Health Service
        decided to run a study
        to see what untreated syphilis did to
                                        black males

Many crackers (including cracker doctors)

thought syph did less harm to blacks
The Health Service picked 400 black males with syph
They didn't tell them they had it
but merely that they had "bad blood."

(The Tuskegee "study" lasted 40 years, till '72
during which over a 100 died of it,
many went blind or insane
       & many had lives of continuing bad health
from syph-connected ailments)

They were discouraged from having treatment elsewhere
    & the miracle drug penicillin
when it became available after War 2
was kept from them

A whistleblower in the PHS, one Peter Buxtun,
alerted the press, and public outrage
ended the classist, pain-worshiping syph-scam

Another Famine in Russia

There was one of the periodic famines (going back to the 1890s)
in Russia though many texts have blamed the commies
& the collectivization of farms.

Novum 1932:
    Existence of neutrons was confirmed
in England by James Chadwick,
and also the American physicist Carl Anderson
detected the antielectron (predicted by Paul Dirac in '30)
in a cloud chamber at Cal Tech
& named it the positron

A Greek cat named Aristotle Onassis
bought six freight ships
the beginning of his megamoney

Erskine Caldwell's *Tobacco Road*
Reinhold Niebuhr's *Moral Man and Immoral Society*
Louis-Ferdinand Céline's *Journey to the End of the Night*

Vitamin C was iso'd and i.d.'d by Am biochemist C.G. King

Alexander Calder invented the mobile
plus the first "store mag" *Family Circle*
            given away in Piggly Wiggly supermarkets

Art! Ben Shahn, Thomas Hart Benton, Matisse, Pablo,
                                    Man Ray, Giacometti, Jean Arp

& the age-defining tune,
            Yip Harburg's "Brother Can You Spare a Dime?"
                        from the musical review *Americana*

The prevalence of evening radio shows
            The Jack Benny Show, One Man's Family, Walter Winchell

John Dos Passos *1919*
William Faulkner *Light in August*
James T Farrell *Young Lonigan*
Henri Michaux *Un Barbare en Asie*
Hemingway *Death in the Afternoon*
Damon Runyon *Guys and Dolls*
            and James Thurber "The Secret Life of Walter Mitty."

Route 66, the road of Kicks
            opened from Chi to LA

The miracle of birth!
Elizabeth Taylor, Edward Kennedy,
                        Dick Gregory
François Truffaut born Feb 6
John Updike Mar 18
Michael McClure Oct 20   Sylvia Plath Oct 27
Jacques Chirac Nov 29

            and of invention:
            Fritos, Skippy peanut butter,
                        the Zippo lighter
                        & Radio City Music Hall

127 sound films were made in '32

Dr. Jekyll and Mr Hyde,
Gary Cooper, in *A Farewell to Arms,*
I Am a Fugitive from a Chain Gang
Howard Hawks, *Scarface,*

Johnny Weismuller in *Tarzan the Ape Man*
Grand Hotel

Seethe at the Edge, My Nation

January 2
    In Spain
    the anarchists and syndicalists
                    surged upward in Barcelona

January 22
    the Second 5-year plan began in the USSR
    to build heavy industry
    and also make more consumer goods
                    in the planned economy

———————————————— **Hitler Gets It** ————————————

In Germany at the end of January
the German Chancellor, a guy named von Schleicher
was unable to bring together the center, left & right
                                    to form a government
and resigned. The fading, agéd President Hindenberg
followed the law & offered the Chancellorship
                    to the one who led the largest party
                                    in the Reichstag:

            Adolf Hitler.
            He accepted.

February 14
    the Michigan governor closed the banks for 8 days

to save two of the largest

        other states did the same

February 15
    The president-elect had come from a 12-day fishing trip
    had given a speech in Miami
    & was sitting in his car by the bandshell
    Chicago's mayor Anton Cermak unfortunately
    was standing on the running board
             when five shots were fired by one
             Giuseppe Zingara

Cermak was killed
& Zingara apparently told the police
        "I'd kill every president."

———————————————— **The Reichstag Fire** ————————

The Parliament Building in Berlin, known as the Reichstag,
             was destroyed by fire Feb. 27
A Dutch guy named van der Lubbe was arrested, tried and beheaded
The Nazis claimed it was the
             prolegomenon to commie-rev in Germany

It was long believed that the Nazis set the fire
             as an excuse to axe down the left
but some later research pointed to van der Lubbe acting on his own.

"This is a God-given signal!" shouted Hitler,
             or a signal of evil
as he used the fire to seize total control
             and to get decrees granting totalitarian powers.
He forced an Enabling Act through th' Reichstag,
             to give himself a legal basis for dictatorship

Hit-vom tossed all 81 Communist deputies out of the Reichstag.
All political parties except Nazis were banned
Civil servants had to prove they had no Jewish blood
Laws for sterilization of the defective were passed
             and for the "perfection of the Aryan race"

    & the Concentration Camps began
             Dachau, near Munich, was the first

•

March 1
Six states declared Bank Holidays to keep
people from grabbing out their money
fearing the Big Burn

———————————————— **The Inauguration** ————————————————

Roosevelt was sworn in March 4th
and gave a speech
that thrilled the desolation:

"So, first of all, let me assert my firm belief that the only thing we
have to fear is fear itself—nameless, unreasoning, unjustified terror
which paralyzes needed efforts to convert retreat into advance ..."
&
"Our greatest primary task is to put people to work....
&
"Finally, in our progress toward a resumption of work we require
two safeguards
against a return of the evils of the old order:
there must be a strict supervision of all banking
and credits and investments, so that there will be
an end to
speculation with other people's money ..."
He was going to protect America, he told the listening nation,
with or without the support of Congress:
"I am prepared under my constitutional duty
to recommend the measures that a stricken Nation
in the midst of a stricken world may require."

In the months that followed
right-wing groaners groaned words such as "fascism"
or "communism"
as the USA copied the European social democracies
with strong federal action

March 4
FDR chose Frances Perkins to be Secretary of Labor
a remarkable woman
too little sung
in the late-century Time-Track

For instance, she described social insurance as
"a fundamental part of another great forward step
in that liberation of humanity
which began with the Renaissance."

———————————— **Good Neighbor Policy** ————————————

Roosevelt mentioned in his inaugural speech that
the US would no longer intervene in the Western Hemisphere
a big big change that held, more or less,
for 28 years
till the Bay of Pigs.

The next day March 5
in a General Election in Germany
called by Hitler to increase his seats
Naz-vom won 288 in the Reichstag
Soc Dems 120
Coms 81
Center 74
uh-oh

That was the day that President Roosevelt
called Congress into special session
for what in history was known as

———————————— **The First Hundred Days** ————————————
March 9–June 16

During those hundred
Congress passed 15 major bills
to relieve human suffering
& in Roosevelt's words,
to save the "profit system"

Whatever the mix of reasons
the federal government
shoved into the I'm-okay psychopathy of the right
and began to feed, cloth & comfort
millions of anguished & impoverished Americans

──────────── **Four-Day Bank Holiday** ────────────
March 6–9

Roosevelt declared a 4-day holiday for banks
plus banned all foreign exchange transactions
                    & gold and silver exports

He was concerned that the whole US banking system
                    might dissolve & be destroyed
He was thinking of issuing scrip
                    for citizens to use for purchases
& to publish the names of those
                    hoarding huge amounts of gold

March 12
        was Roosevelt's first Fireside Chat over national radio
                to mollify the masses
                it's okay to put your cash in banks

──────────── **Rivera Completes Detroit Frescoes** ────────────
March 13

Diego Rivera had worked on his huge *Detroit Industry* frescoes
since the previous June
                on the walls and niches of the Garden Court
                        of the Detroit Museum of Art

His work was underwritten by Edsel Ford
but when the public was invited to view
                        these beautiful walls to the glory
                                of workers & engineering
right-wing nuts & tsk-tskers waxed furious
there was nudity! and possible sacreligion!
                        hints at socialism & Marxism!

Whitewash those suckers! they shrieked
Edsel Ford and thousands of Detroiters rose to defend them
                so that they're there right now—& glorious—
                        Don't miss them when you're in Detroit

March 20
        The first concentration camp in Germany,
                in Dachau, near Munich, thanks to the Nazis

298

March 23
 Hitler was given dictatorial powers till '37

———————————————— **The Oxford Pledge** ————————————————

Meanwhile some students at Oxford
scooped scads of world-wide ink
              when they pledged not to kill other humans
                            for "King and country."

By the fall many students at antiwar conferences
adopted a US version of the Oxford Pledge—
to "refuse to support the government of the United States
                            in any war it might undertake."

A national poll showed 39% of students endorsed the pledge.

———————————————— **The First New Deal** ————————————————
1933–34

a group of eco and social reforms

The first aspect of the ND was '33-'34
with the National Recovery Administration, the
Agricultural Adjustment Administration
              & the Public Works Administration

to stimulate fiscal recovery and provide employment

The New Deal soared after 12 years of laissez-faire get-the-moneyism
(A right-wing Supreme Court, as we shall see,
              tossed out the NRA in '35 and
                            the AAA in '36)

———————————— **The Civilian Conservation Corps** ————————————
March 31

The Civilian Conservation Corps—the great CCC
              was vortexed into history by Congress.

By early July
250,000 unemployed, unmarried people
                                "of good character"
                'tween 18 & 25
& willing to send home a good % of their earnings
were enrolled in 1,468
                200-person "forest & park camps"
in all the states of the USA

planting trees, working at conservation.
—The CCC lasted till '41
                under the erosive erasure of the rattling right

April 5
    Roosevelt signed a declaration banning gold-hoarding
    and requiring all humans in the USA
                to deliver all gold to banks

            Roll, o cap-eyes, roll:

April 12
    Roosevelt proposed minimum wage legislations

            Continue rolling, o cap-eyes

──────────── **The Composers Collective** ────────────

For three years, beginning in '33

the Composers Collective
                with maybe 12 composers
trained in conservatories
gathered in the time-track
                to help in the class struggle

Among its composers were Elie Siegmeister,
Marc Blitzstein, Earl Robinson, Charles Seeger,
Herb Haufrecht, and others

including an occasional visit from Aaron Copland

The Composers Collective

went forth with four-part choruses, rounds,
                                      & tunes with proletarianophilic texts
           to demonstrations, benefits
                  & picket lines

         In '34 & '35 they published two volumes
            of the *Workers Songbook*

                Never give up

May 2
     Hit-slime suppressed trade unions

May 12
     The Federal Emergency Relief Act was enacted
     to transfer money to the states for unemployed to work at
         relief projects
     The Act established the great Public Works Administration
                         which operated & built many projects

May 12
     Agricultural Adjustment Act was passed,
           restricting some crops, and paying farmers
                           for uncultivated acres
               to raise some $ for suffering farms.

         The AAA set up a vast network to allow interest groups
                        to tell their beliefs.
         Millions of American farmers, including blacks
                   voted in AAA referenda

———— **A Planned Economy in a Big Watershed** ————
                        May 18

Congress passed the Tennessee Valley Act,
                   creating the Tennessee Valley Authority

This was as close as the Roosevelt era actually got
to attempting an actual planned economy

The original vision of the law included such things as
the bringing in of small industry
the building of fertilizer facilities
the Federal construction of roadways & rural electrification

the creation of large water-retaining forests at the
                                        headwaters of streams
the building of dams & hydroelectric facilities
                                        owned by the Nation!

            Roll, o cap-eyes, roll!   ☺ ☺☺☺

May 27
        Congress passed the Federal Securities Act
                    requiring all stock issues and bonds
                                        to be registered
        & bringing the concept, in Roosevelt's words,
        of "full and fair disclosure" to investors
        "of all of the material facts relating to new security issues"

———————————— **Rivera's Rockefeller Mural** ————————————

After his great frescoes in Detroit were completed
        Diego Rivera, and his wife Frida Kahlo,
                        headed for New York City
where the director of Rockefeller Center, one Nelson Rockefeller
had commissioned him to create a 63′ x 17′ mural called
                                Man at the Crossroads
in the great hall of the 70-story RCA building

It was another grand Cycle of Life depiction
in the theme of a huge whirling four-blade propeller
                & in one of the panels, opposite a section of
                        society folk playing cards
                                was V. I. Lenin
Rockie didn't dig it
and in May ordered the covering of Rivera's mural
                even though Lenin appeared in the original sketch

They exchanged letters in the *NY Times*

May 4, "The piece is beautifully painted, but it seems to me that his
portrait, appearing in this mural, might very easily seriously offend a
great many people.... As much as I dislike to do so, I am afraid we must
ask you to substitute the face of some unknown man where Lenin's face
now appears."

May 6, Rivera replied to Nellie: "The head of Lenin was included in the

302

original sketch ... and in the drawings in line made on the wall at the beginning of my work.... I ... suggest that I could change the sector which shows society people playing bridge and dancing and put in its place, in perfect balance with the Lenin portion, a picture of some great American historical leader, such as Lincoln, who symbolizes the unification of the country and the abolition of slavery, surrounded by John Brown, Nat Turner, William Lloyd Garrison or Wendell Phillips and Harriet Beecher Stowe, and perhaps some scientific figure like McCormick, inventor of the McCormick reaper, which aided in the victory of the anti-slavery forces by providing sufficient wheat to sustain the Northern armies."

Rockefeller in effect told Rivera to fuck himself
cancelled the almost completed work
                           & kept it covered with canvas
Then a year later ordered it smashed and removed
                                 to his own effacement
                                        in the tracks of time

June 6
    When the first drive-in movie opened in Camden, New Jersey
           the hearts of millions of high school lovers experienced
                       a jolt of thrill from the Jungian Oversoul!

——————————— **Salvation from Foreclosure** ———————————
June 13

Roosevelt signed the Home Owners Loan Act
setting up a federal agency
to save those whose homes
              had been lost to cap-slime
                  since 1-1-30
          through foreclosure or forced sale
and also those who could not pay past due taxes
                       & those in current default.

The government rewrote home loans at 5%
                allowing 15 years for repayment
        with repairs to houses part of the loans

ahh bring back those five percenters!

FDIC!
June 16

Congress passed the Banking Act of 1933, which established the
Federal Deposit Insurance Corporation
(It was called the Glass-Steagall Banking Act
& guaranteed deposits under $5,000)

National Industrial Recovery Act

The same day, June 16,
Congress passed the National Industrial Recovery Act, setting
up the National Recovery Administration
appropriating $3.3 billion for public works projects

When he signed this huge bill
to organize the economy of the nation
by hiring hundreds of thousands
& commencing "a vast program of public works"
Roosevelt said: "It represents a supreme effort to stabilize for all time
the many factors which make for the prosperity of the Nation, and the
preservation of American standards. Its goal is the assurance of a
reasonable profit to industry and living wages for labor with the
elimination of the piratical methods and practices which have not only
harassed honest business but also contributed to the ills of labor."
All right!

Mid June
Foreclosures by cap-slime on homes & farms
had grown to more than 1,000 per day—
Roosevelt called for a law to prevent
small home foreclosures

Huddie Ledbetter
July

John Lomax & his son Alan that summer
went around the South for the Library of Congress
recording Negro folk music
lugging a new fangled device
weighing 315 pounds
that cut the tunes on aluminum disks

In the ghastly Angola State Pen
50 miles northwest of Baton Rouge

the man later known as Leadbelly
astonished the father-son team
with his fine guitar & repertoire

Among the tunes cut on metal
                        to Ledbetter's twelve-string guitar
were three takes of "Irene Goodnight"

July 14
    Naz-vom suppressed all other political parties

By July 28
    Roosevelt had held 37 press conferences!

July 29
    In Upper Darby, Pennsylvania
                a baby named Nira Collins was christened—
        named after the National Industrial Recovery Act!

August 5
    Roosevelt established the National Labor Board
                (with twenty regional boards)
                    to handle labor disputes
            under the planned economy of
                                the N.I.R.A.

———— **At Last Making Non-Invasion a National Policy** ————
August 12

Supported by the USA (but not with troops
                under Roosevelt's Good Neighbor policy)
Fulgencio Batista and the Cuban army
                            overthrew Pres Machedo

FDR confidante Sumner Welles was Ambassador to Cuba in '33
He supported Batista
        but when there was a counter-rev of supporters of Machedo
        some wanted the usual American invasion—
                but, to FDR's lasting glory
as William Appleton Williams pointed out in his book

Empire as a Way of Life
> FDR sent naval ships off the coast of Cuba
>> but no landing was made

August 23
> The great Gandhi was released from hospital detention in Poona
> after fasting for 8 days
>> & now weighing just 90 pounds

August 25
> Canada, USA, USSR, Australia and Argentina
>> signed a Wheat Agreement to stabilize prices

——————————— Black Mountain College ———————————

> A classics scholar named John Rice
> founded the great Black Mountain College
>> near Asheville, NC
>>> for the fall of the year

>> Back in April
>> Storm Troopers stormed the Bauhaus
>>> in Berlin

>>> and it was closed

> The Bauhaus teacher/painter Josef Albers
> had his teaching contract snuffed out by the city of Dessau
>> in a letter that sneer-listed the Bauhaus as
>>> "a germ-cell of bolshevism"

> Josef & Anni Albers came to Black Mountain
> in November
>> to teach
>>> & escape the evil

——————— A Surge to Unionize the Auto Industry ———————

> After passage of the National Industrial Recovery Act
>> the AFL began an organizational drive in the auto industry

> Key to organization on the shop floor
>> were the Communists,

a legal group protected by the
Constitution

The Communists, according to the *Encyclopedia of the American Left*
"and their allies in Detroit, Cleveland, and Toledo
        organized the AFL's most successful federal labor unions,
and spearheaded a rank-and-file movement among autoworkers
that eventually forced the AFL to charter the UAW in 1935."

October 14
        Germany withdrew from the Disarmament Conference and
                                resigned from the League of Nations

                        uh-oh

October 17
        Einstein arrived in US, fleeing the Nazi repression
        —Kandinsky, Klee and others
                        also fled the filth

November 7
        Fiorello LaGuardia was elected mayor of NYC,
                        halting 16 years of Tammany Hall control

November 10
        In a press conference
                        Roosevelt came out against capital punishment!

November 12
        The German people seemed to dig the filth
        as 92 percent of those voting (96% of the electorate)
                        thudded approval of the Nazis

November 17
        the USA recognized the USSR
                        & started trading
                & the right wing, from nut to noir,
                                waxed bonk-bonk

Spanish Right Wing Vows to Get Rid of Marxists, Masons, Separatists and Jews

On November 19
    The Spanish Confederation of Autonomous Right Wing Groups
    won the largest # of seats in the general election, 115
            radicals with 102
                    center parties 167,
                            and left 99

    Right Wing Confederation entered the Radical gov't led by
                                            Alejandro Lerroux

    & vowed to scrub-a-dub Spain free
                    of "Marxists, Masons, Separatists and Jews"

            The Spanish Republic had treated the church
            in such a manner
            that the right was united.

            Local gov'ts had restricted religion, which
            made temporary friends of
            religious peasants & their normal enemies
                            the wealthy landholders

    The coalition of socialists and liberals,
            which had controlled the Cortes (the Spanish Parliament)
            broke apart from the slow progress
                            of land reform.
    The Anarchists, as numerous as the Socialists,
    boycotted the November voting that turned over power to the nuts

    A right winger then became president
    He sent the army to uproot crops on redistributed lands and arrested
                    starving peasants for collecting acorns

    (The left would make another surge and rule once more
                    before the upcoming Civil War.)

December 5
    Ratification of the 21st Amendment
                    repealing prohibition

            So long, suckers!

308

December 6
    In a big move forward
            for personal freedom

    Judge John M. Woolsey tossed aside the ban
                    on the great *Ulysses*

December 15
    Crackermania still crackering in Tennessee
    A court released a black
            and a white mob lynched him

Novum for '33:
    Nobel Prize to American geneticist Thomas Morgan
            for showing that
                    hereditary traits are carried by chromosomes

    Gertrude Stein's autobiography,
            The Autobiography of Alice B. Toklas,

    written as if it were her lover's
                    witty and prone to flame-jobs on literati

    Miss Lonelyhearts Nathanael West
    "Stormy Weather" by Arlen and Koehler
    Ah ,Wilderness! Eugene O'Neill

    Windex, the short distance radio
                    known as the Walkie-Talkie
                Dorothy Day's *Catholic Worker*

        Monopoly, Ritz crackers
                and The Lone Ranger on radio

    Leon Trotsky's *History of the Russian Revolution* (in 3 volumes!)

    Hermann Goering formed the Geheime Staatspolizei
                        or the Gestapo

    the Arabian American Oil Co was founded in
                the new Kingdom of Saudi Arabia
                (Saudi Arabia had been controlled by the Turks
                        for 400 years, till WW I)
    by Standard Oil of California
            getting 60 year exclusive access to th' oil 'neath Arabia Petra

World Series: NY Giants o'er Washington Senators 4-2
Chicago Bears stomp NY Giants 23-21 in th' first NFL championship

André Malraux' *La Condition Humaine*
set in Shanghai in '27 when Gen. Chiang Kai-shek about-faced
              and slaughtered the Communists that had been his allies

J. M. Keynes *The Means to Prosperity*
        causing right wingers to grrr, grouse, grind their teeth in sleep,
        suffer pordobreath, lefthating nausea and eery eructions

Orwell *Down and out in Paris and London*
C. G. Jung *Modern Man in Search of a Soul*

E. Armstrong patented Frequency Modulation in radio

Hitler closed down ca 200 newspapers
              Gandhi founded a weekly, *Harijan*
              for the "untouchables"

Duck Soup, by the Marx brothers
                    banned in fascist Italy
                          perhaps they thought Karl was one of them
Ecstasy, with the nude Hedy Lamarr
42nd Street, with Busby Berkeley choreography
The Invisible Man Claude Rains
King Kong
Little Women
Mae West's *She Done Him Wrong*

The Swiss chemist Tadeus Reichstein synthesized Vitamin C
First successful operation to remove a lung
Arthur Eddington *The Expanding Universe*
Enid Starkie's great *Baudelaire*
A. N. Whitehead *Adventures of Ideas*

Béla Bartók, Piano Concerto No. 2
Olivier Messiaen *The Ascension*
Kurt Weill *The Seven Deadly Sins,* a cantata

Erskine Caldwell *God's Little Acre*
Dorothy Sayers *Murder Must Advertise*

Federico Garcia Lorca *Blood Wedding*

Linen/Bye o' 33:
Susan Sontag on either Jan 16 or 28, Willie Nelson
James Brown
Calvin Coolidge ceases at 60 on Jan 5
Philip Roth Mar 19
Peter Orlovsky July 8   Richard Rodgers July 23
Roman Polanski Aug 18
Henryk Górecki Dec 6

Eleanor Roosevelt

Racists hated Eleanor
and also social conservatives
        who spiked her with their wincy funless lip-lash.

Her husband needed the Southern Democrats
& couldn't really take a stance against the crackers
so his wife filled the void

    She was like hydrogen peroxide in the lynch-wound

    One of the signposts of real progress
    during the Roosevelt years
    was the slow slow too slow but real
    disallowing of crackers to lynch

    It was the poet Charles Olson's concept of
            "Polis is
            Eyes"
    observing and urging
            that slowly began to stop lynching

that and the marvelous invention of
two-way radios in rural police dept's
so that officers could call for help

January 14
Elections in Catalonia were won by the left
in other parts of Spain
rightists prevailed

———————————— **The Gold Reserve Act** ————————————
January 30

Gold coins were abolished
as part of the US monetary system
with no gold coins to be issued in the future

& no currency of the US would be redeemed in gold
except as directed by the Treasury sec & the President
& then only in bullion

& gold was set at $35 per ounce

January 31
the Federal Farm Mortgage Corporation was founded
to take over farm mortgages and stanch foreclosures

January
Hitler signed a nonaggression pact with Poland,
which had an army of 250,000.
Poland then waxed complacent (though confident)
while Germany secretly rearmed

———————————————— **Sandino** ————————————————
February 21

The National Guard in Nicaragua
under the command of ghastly right-wing Anastasio Somosa
killed Augusto César Sandino
on the airfield in Managua

(Sandino had called off guerrilla warfare

to end the 7-year US intervention)
General Somosa then began his 40-year dictatorship.

March 24
    the Tydings-McDuffie Act, giving independence to Philippines
        33 years after the racist slaughter
            of the Philippine war

1934 in Mexico

Lázaro Cárdenas became president &
during his six years in office
gave 44,000,000 acres to agricultural coöps
    who then gave out the land to 800,000 peasants

In 1938 his gov't nationalized the oil companies

The oiloids whined to Roosevelt to send in troops
    but, citing the "Good Neighbor" policy,
      & for the good of history
        the good president declined

Dust Storms Take the Topsoil

150,000 square miles of America's midwest
    was roiling in death dust
as huge "black roller" Dust Storms blew maybe
300 million tons of topsoil
    from farms of Texas, Ok, Ark, and Col
      that May
      & farm upon farm was abandoned

    Cattle ran in circles
      till their dust-filled lungs
        dropped them down
    Children too were sometimes smothered
        in the shriek-dirt
    or slept with towels on their heads

    As Woody Guthrie sang,
    "That old dust storm killed my baby,
    But it won't kill me, Lord.
    No, it won't kill me."

313

When cap-slime foreclosed
pickup trucks & even hand-drawn wagons piled with house stuff
    headed West
                from the shrieking howl

The howl clouds hissed as far as DC
where Roosevelt got Congress to establish the
Soil Conservation Service
and the great Civilian Conservation Corps
which planted millions of trees for windbreaks

            Finally the dust bowl shrank
                    and the rains returned in '40

────────────────── Uranium ──────────────────

Italian physicist Enrico Fermi
            uh-oh
learned about the effects of bombarding uranium atoms with
neutrons

────────────── Nye Takes on WW1 Greed Heads ──────────────

On April 12, the U.S. Senate appointed the Progressive Republican
Senator Gerald Nye of North Dakota
                    to head up a Committee to look into
                    the profiteering of arms makers in WW 1.

Profiteering was in the news (an article not long before, for instance,
                                in *Fortune Magazine*)

Within a few months the Nye Committee
had turned away from exposing the profits of armsmakers
to look at the ways
        economic interests had
        influenced America's going to war in '17

He brought the du Ponts and J. P. Morgan to testify
& the Committee concluded that bankerly greed-minds
                        had made unacceptable profits

Many Americans agreed with Nye that

international bankers of the East Coast
had brought slaughter to American youth
for reasons of greed

Nye's Committee proposed a stiff tax
on all incomes above a certain level
during war time
to stifle profiteering.

It continued its hearings into 1937
& helped set the isolationist tone
in the years leading to war

--- **Bonnie & Clyde** ---

Near Gibsland, Louisiana
a couple of hick murderers
named Bonnie Parker and Clyde Barrow
specialists in the $1,500 heist
who had killed 12
caught the public's imagination
in a 21-month run on the run

were offed on 5-23 by five sheriff's deputies and a
Texas Ranger

--- **Censorship** ---

Repressionist twerps
in the U.S. Customs Service
seized Henry Miller's *Tropic of Cancer*
and banned it

The book was not published in the U.S.A. till '61
and suffered then obscenity trials
till '64 when a Supreme Court decision freed it for freedom

June 6
Roosevelt signed the Securities Exchange Act
& the Securities & Exchange Commission was founded
to cop-eye the securities market to prevent another '29 crash
and hold down stock-scams

Joseph Kennedy was chosen as SEC Commissioner

June 18
Roosevelt signed the Indian Reorganization Act
after seeking to learn from the Indians themselves.
There were 9 regional conferences to talk directly
with Indian groups

This was part of the "Indian New Deal."
In '33 FDR had appointed activist John Collier as
commissioner of Indian affairs. For 50 years there had been
an allotment program which broke up Indian tribal lands
in order to fork them over to whites & to individual Indians.
The Indian Reorganization Act ended the allotments,
provided money for Indian tribes to buy new land,
& repealed prohibitions on speaking Native American languages,
tribal
ceremonies and traditional dress on reservations.

To Roosevelt's credit, New Deal programs such as the CCC
employed many American Indians

June 19
Roosevelt signed the Communications Act,
setting up the Federal Communications Commission

June 28
Roosevelt signed the Federal Farm Bankruptcy Act,
with a moratorium on farm mortgage foreclosures

———————— **Southern Tenant Farmers Union** ————————

An interracial protest group began among sharecroppers and
tenant farmers of eastern Arkansas
called the Southern Tenant Farmers Union

The Depression was starving the tenant farms
& New Deal crop reduction programs were
forcing big evictions from the land.

Black & white sharecroppers
worked together
aided by the Socialist Party

to lobby the feds to get some
of the crop reduction money

The Tenant Farmers Union grew
There was fierce opposition from plantation owners
though the interracial solidarity held

In 1935 it organized a cotton choppers' strike
to raise day laborer wages.

By 1936, the Southern Tenant Farmers Union
had more than 20,000 members in Mo, Ok, Tenn, Tex, and Ark.

There was planter terror, murders, arrests, beatings,
which made it impossible to run its operations "in the field"
So, after '36 it operated from Memphis.

Meanwhile the usual Socialist-Communist conflicts
brought harm to the Union

though it struggled onward
a big source of hope
for those who hungered
to bring economic justice to rural production
—you can look up their history

Bread, Circuses, Banks

John Dillinger was paroled in '33
after staring 9 years in a cell
& set up a gang
that looted Midwest banks
wearing natty clothes
& thrilling the populace
always prone to Juvenal's
listing of "panem et circenses"
—bread & circuses
as its main fascination.

Dillinger poured acid on his fingers to erase his prints
He was Public Enemy #1 &
J. Edgar Hoover and the FBI went after him
gunning him down as he left the Biograph Theater in Chi with

a hooker
apparently set up by a brothel madam
on July 24

———————————— **Fred & Ginger** ————————————

Fred Astaire and Ginger Rogers
began their dance films

Their dances were filmed
in long, flowing takes,
with full figure solos &
pas de deux

Dancing, in the days of the Hays Code,
was as close to balling
as the Nation could see

As Katharine Hepburn allegedly said, "He gave her class, and she
gave him sex"

———————— **The Night of the Long Knives** ————————
June 30

Ernst Röhm's Brown Shirts, or *Sturmabteilung,*
were demanding leadership o'er the military

Then, in an attack directed by Hermann Goering and
Heinrich Himmler
sleaze sliced sleaze:

the SS killed Röhm & 400 others
"satisfying" industrialists and generals
who were afraid that the upcoming Hitler
power-grab would get too freaky
even for the far right

President Hindenburg telegraphed Hitler:

"You have saved the German people from a great peril. He who
wishes to make history must also be able to shed blood."

Most of the Brown Shirt duties, including the running of the camps
went to the SS.

Big Strike by Organized Labor
July 16–19

There was a General Strike by organized labor in San Francisco
to support 12,000 striking longshoremen

More than 100,000 workers in SF and Alameda counties
hit the bricks

The press puked at it as commie
& there was widespread police and vigilante violence

but in labor matters
what seems like a defeat
pummels the winds
with glory wings.

The textbooks talk of the
raw class conflict of '34
which meant vigilantes, company thugs,
hired bullies, national guard, fuzz

This happened after the 1933 New Deal laws
that gave the right to organize!
engage in collective bargaining!
& hit the bricks
with law!

In San Francisco the dockworkers
liked the rebuilding of the International Longshoreman's
Association
(stomped down in the post War 1 repression)
& led now by a great union man from Australia
named Harry Bridges

President Roosevelt appointed a
National Longshoreman's Board
which helped arbitrate wage increases
and set up labor committees
in the various Pacific ports

July 20
>Himmler grabbed control of the secret police
>& the SS was made an independent org inside the Nazi party

August 2
>Hitler was declared Führer of the Third Reich
>& all officers had to take an oath of loyalty to Adolf

Ballet

Lincoln Kirstein invited George Balanchine to create the
School of American Ballet in NYC

American Ballet became the NYC Ballet in '48.

Upton Sinclair Runs for Governor

>The writer named Upton Sinclair
>>famous through the century
>>for his social novels
>>beginning with the '06 *The Jungle*
>>which singlebookédly
>>>brought standards to the stockyards
>>then *Oil!* of '27 (set in the Teapot Dome
>>crook-clique)
>>& *Boston* of '28 on the Sacco & Vanzetti case
>>>changed his registration from
>>>Socialist to Democrat in 1933

>That year he wrote *I, GOVERNOR OF CALIFORNIA,*
>>*And How I Ended Poverty:*
>>—*a True Story of the Future*

>He founded a group called End Poverty in California (EPIC)
>and announced his candidacy for Governor

320

On August 28, 1934
he won the Democratic primary
and began a huge campaign
    on the principles of End Poverty in California

    He was running against Republican Gov. Frank Merriam
    & it seemed as if Sinclair would win big

A newspaper *EPIC News* came close to 2 million in circulation
as the campaign surged

The core of EPIC's plan was
            "production *for use*"

setting up "land colonies" & coöps
    increasing inheritance tax
    more taxes on public utilities and banks
    & an old age pension of $50 a month

Sinclair pointed out that there were 500,000 unemployed in
    California:
"There is no solution to this problem except to put these
unemployed at productive labor, to make them self-sustaining, to
let them produce what they are going to consume ..."

    He proposed utilizing several thousand idle factories
    and the rest that "are working less than half time."

    The state would rent and run the factories
    "The workers will turn out goods," he said, "and they will
    own what they have produced."

    Farmers would be encouraged to bring their produce to state
    warehouses, they would be paid receipts with which they
    could pay their back taxes

    Food would be shipped to cities, "and made available to the
    factory workers in exchange for the products of their labors."

    EPIC called for "land colonies" around cities and towns where
    land held by speculators would be used by the unemployed.
    "The state can furnish machinery, and the unemployed can
    go to work and grow their own food, making gardens where
    now are patches of weeds."

When Fiorello La Guardia sought info on EPIC, Sinclair told him
"You should try it in New York.... Take over some idle factories in
the city and exchange shoes and clothing for farm produce from
upstate...."

The establishment was vehemently opposed. Why? Sinclair:
"The answer is because they are afraid of the precedent. They are
afraid the plan will succeed, and show the unemployed how to
produce *for use* instead of *for profit*. It will put into the minds of the
unemployed the idea of getting access to land and machinery by
the political method, by the use of their ballots. And once they get
access to good land and modern machinery they will produce so
much, they will make such comfort and plenty for themselves,
that they will never again be content to support the parasites of
Wall Street."

      The right wing went into a seething & productive rage
      using all the mass-marketing techniques of
                        the Hollywood era
      to kill Sinclair's campaign

      Sinclair shuddered the moguls
      with an announcement that the movie biz
          should contribute more to California
                      in the form of taxes
      and that California itself should make flicks
      "and show them in our own theaters
                with our own orchestras"

      mal-minded movie producer
      Louis P. Mayer (& others) led a vicious media campaign
          in an early American use of Big Lie political tactics
         so efficacious
            too
           13 years later in the Red Scare

    Staged newsreels showed bums voting for Sinclair
      while proper upstanding citizens were seen
                voting Republican
    The Big Lie moguls showed fake newsreels
        in moviehouses
        of migrants rushing to California
    to suck up the largess from Sinclair's EPIC program
              as if it were hard news

The big studios forced their employees, writers, stars
to donate to the anti-Sinclair campaign
It was called the "Merriam tax"

Even though the right wing spread
a fake endorsement of Sinclair by the commies
The Communist Party USA viciously opposed Sinclair's candidacy
The SP also, since Sinclair had become a Democrat

It worked &
Sinclair lost "narrowly," as they say
on November 7

—————————————————— **Pretty Boy Floyd** ——————————
October 22

He was a hero in Oklahoma
helping the oppressed by
stealing from the eye-rollers
& now and then giving to the poor

He hated bankers
and finally he was killed by FBI agents on 10-22
&
Woody Guthrie wrote a song about him
with those great lines:

> *Yes, as through this world I ramble,*
> *I see lots of funny men,*
> *Some will rob you with a 6-gun,*
> *and some will rob you with a pen.*
> *But as through your life you'll travel,*
> *wherever you may roam,*
> *You won't never see an outlaw drive*
> *a family from their home*

(which Joan Baez so beautifully sang on her album
Joan Baez in Concert)

You can find him in Steinbeck's *Grapes of Wrath*

The Long March
1934–'35

After grim defeats by Chiang Kai-shek's army
Mao and about 100,000 began
                   the famous Long March in October
to escape the encirclement of 750,000 Nationalist soldiers.
For 8,000 miles they walked in decimating terrain
        along edges of Tibet's mountains
                 and through the steppes of central Asia

It took a year
—he lost ¾ of his troops.
        till the Red Army
        arrived in the northwest of China
        in a place called Yenan on the Yellow River
        where they lived in caves in the hill clay
                 to build the Chinese Soviet

        In October of '35
        after the Long March,
           Mao wrote a poem,
           with the quatrain:

                On the peak of Liupan Mountain
                red flags ripple in the west wind
                Today the long rope is in our hands:
                when shall we tie up the Gray Dragon?

Democratic Landslide in Off-Year Elections

Cap-slime used stockholder money
                 to yell like hell in ads & p.r.
                     'gainst the New Deal
but the New Deal won in a gush
with 69 Democrats in Senate to 25 Republicans
& 322 Democrats in House to 102 Republicans

The Killing of Kirov
December 1

A man named Leonid Nikolayev
waited by an office at Commie headquarters in Leningrad

to kill a party leader Sergei Kirov
who dared to argue with Stalin

Stalin soon implicated his rivals
in rounds of show trials,
executions, & pressured confessions

for the Great Purge
when all of a nation was afraid
of the knock
the secret police
the bullshit trial
the blindfold
& lead to the head

Novum in '34:
DuPont worker-scientists created nylon
Disney Donald Duck,
& others the laundromat

There were some great American melodies, "Blue Moon,"
& "I Only Have Eyes for You,"

Lillian Hellman's *The Children's Hour*
Luigi Pirandello won the Nobel Prize

The Mass Psychology of Fascism by Wilhelm Reich
Ruth Benedict *Patterns of Culture*
D. T. Suzuki *An Introduction to Zen Buddhism*
Abbé Breuil *L'Evolution de l'Art Pariétal dans les Cavernes*
et Abris Ornées de France

Virgil Thomson *Four Saints in Three Acts*
Belgian jazz guitarist Django Reinhardt
and violinist Stéphane Grappelli
formed the Quintette du Hot Club de France, Paris

Pianist Fats Waller emerged

James M. Cain *The Postman Always Rings Twice*
Henry Miller *Tropic of Cancer*
Robert Graves *I, Claudius*
Fitzgerald *Tender Is the Night*
William C. Williams *Collected Poems, 1922–1931*

Robert Sherwood *The Petrified Forest*

Alcatraz in SF bay was bought for a prison

Births & Byes: bard John Wieners born on Jan 6
    Ralph Nader Feb 27, Gloria Steinem March 25,
    Diane DiPrima on Aug 6   Sophia Loren Sept 20
    Amiri Baraka on October 7 Roberto Clemente
    Plus Marilyn Horne, Van Cliburn, Kate Millett
                Edward Elgar passed Feb 23 at 76

Flicks: *The Thin Man*
       The Scarlet Pimpernel

Clark Gable and Claudette Colbert in Frank Capra's
It Happened One Night, with the famous Walls of Jericho blanket
      on a rope
           to split up their shared motel room

January 11
    Amelia Earhart flew solo from California to Hawaii

January 15-17
    Grigory Zinoviev, Lev Kamenev, and 17 other former big league
        Commies
    were tried and imprisoned for "moral responsibility"
        for Sergei Kirov's murder in '34.

        Thousands more were arrested in the USSR

They called '35 the Second New Deal
                with a continuing focus on making things better
                for working people & small farmers

                Beginning this year
                there was much conflict between the New Deal
                & the US Supreme Court right wing majority
                            whose hatred of regular folk
                                    was marked by their hatred
                                            of social legislation

──────── **Roosevelt Asks Congress for Social Security** ────────
                        January 17

The president asked Congress to pass legislation
for unemployment compensation,
old-age benefits
& Federal aid to dependent children
        "for the support of existing mothers' pension systems
        & for services for the protection and care of homeless, neglected,
        dependent, and crippled children."

"I am not at this time" wrote the president, "recommending the
adoption of so-called 'health insurance,' although groups
representing the medical profession are cooperating with the Federal
Government in the further study of the subject and definite progress
is being made."
                        (If only he had *insisted*
                                    on National Healthcare!)

March 16
        Germany revoked the disarmament clauses of the
                        World War I Versailles Treaty
                                    & brought back the draft

Late April
        Much froth at the annual meeting of the U.S.
                                    Chamber of Commerce
        as delegates howled like a dust storm at Roosevelt
        that he was seeking to "Sovietize America."

May 1
Resettlement Administration was set up by Franklin R
"to help owners and tenants move to better land"

---------------------------- **All Hail the WPA!** ----------------------------
May 6

The Works Progress Administration
superceded the Public Works Administration
under the leadership of Harry L. Hopkins

The great WPA built 8,000 parks, 1,600 schools, 800 airports
3,300 storage dams, 78,000 bridges
650,000 miles of roads

at its high point the WPA employed 3.2m
before the job-glutted years of War 2 came
& the WPA was ended (1943)

Part of the WPA
was the Federal Art Project
which hired 1,000s of artists for public art works
including Ben Shahn, Jackson Pollock and Arshile Gorky

artists paid from national money

All right!

The WPA also sponsored the Federal Theater Project
the Federal Writers' Project and the National Youth Administration
to provide youngsters with part-time employment.

The right hated the WPA
because the pain of others is ever its drug
(and moan-droning that it was the tool of Democratic political
machines)

---------------------------- **The President of Electricity** ----------------------------
May 11

He was an electricity man.
Back when he was Governor of New York
he supported non-profit electric cooperatives

& towns like Skaneateles & Tupper Lake
　　　　　　　　built electric systems owned by the people!

The Rural Electrification Act was passed the 11th of May
& Roosevelt set up the Rural Electrification Administration
to build power lines to rural areas
　　　—where 9 out of 10 farms had no power
　　　　　　　　　　because cap-slime wouldn't do it

Within 15 years 9 of 10 farms were electric

───────────── **Right-Wing Supreme Court** ─────────────

On May 6 the right-wing majority on the Supreme Court
struck down the provision in the Railroad Retirement Act
　　　　that required interstate railroads to create a pooled fund
　　　　　　　　for the paying of pensions
　　　　　　　　　　　　to retired railway workers

The rightists snuffed it on the grounds
　　　　　pensions have no "reasonable" relation to interstate
　　　　　　　　　　　　　　　transportation

The same right-wing Court majority on May 27
　　　　　held that the National Industrial Recovery Act
　　　　was unconstitutional
　　　　　　　in *Schechter Poultry Corp vs. US*

declaring that it transferred legislative powers to the executive
& overstretched the reach of the commerce clause of the Constitution
　　　　(The US had charged, in Roosevelt's words, that the poultry
　　　　company "had violated the provisions of the code which fixed
　　　　minimum wages and maximum hours and which set up
　　　　certain trade practices to prevent unfair competition."

Roosevelt was enraged at the nut squad
　　　　　　& proposed increasing the number of Justices—heh heh—
　　　　　so that he could add some liberal minds.

Chief Justice Charles Evans Hughes
　　　　　successfully fought the expansion
　　　　　but as a swing vote Hughes

                    caught the drift of history
                          & later on helped uphold the
National Labor Relations Act and the Social Security Act
                                    as the Court slowly desleazed

June 18
    a German-British naval accord
    Germany agreed that its navy would not be larger in tonnage
            than ⅓ of Britain's Royal Navy.

            Insert here the boing-boing sound
                          of Pinocchio's suddenly lengthening nose

June 26
    the date the National Youth Administration set forth
            to provide money & work
                      for persons between the ages of 16 & 25.

July 5,
    Roosevelt signed the National Labor Relations Act
            (maneuvered through Congress by the great Senator
                              Robert Wagner of New York)
            which prevented employers from
            interfering or restraining employees
                  from the right to bargain collectively.

            It created the National Labor Relations Board
                      to prevent unfair labor practices
                      & to certify union representation

July 13
    USA-USSR trade pact

————————— **The Popular Front Against Fascism** —————————
                    July 25–August 20

        At the 7th Congress of the 3rd Comintern
                            held in Moscow
        Communists in democratic countries were urged
        to support their governments against Fascist states
        by forming alliances with bourgeois parties—

    This was the famous Popular Front
            which tossed slow knuckle balls floating like asteroids

into the minds of Am-Com's
trained as they were
for the all-out struggle against capitalism

The Line now was that a
bourgeois democratic regime was substantially different
from a bourgeois fascist regime.

Am-coms were accustomed to referring to FDR as
a demagogue
whose politics gave force to fascism.

The Comintern Secretary, a Mr. Dimitrov
opined it would be a sign—oh no!—of "schematism"
to conclude that the New Deal
was an evolution of the bourgeoisie toward fascism

Rather, it was the reactionary slime-grovels of monopoly capital
ranting at Roosevelt
who were giving power to fascism

Trotsky Not Digging It

Trotsky kept his vision of worldwide rev
& said that the '35 gathering'd
"pass into history as the liquidation congress
of the Comintern."

The Comintern in fact lost fore'er its rev-zeal
and was dissolved in 1943

August 9
Roosevelt signed the Motor Carrier Act
which set up an Interstate Commerce Commission to have jurisdiction
over interstate bus and truck traffic

Social Security!
August 14

The great & great great Social Security Act
was signed by a great President

and made possible by great senators such as Robert Wagner of NY
& David Lewis of Maryland
            —look up their life-tracks & exult!

But many others chipped at the system
                        to make it as weak & withered as they could
Those who weakened the Social Security legislation
are phantoms now
                but somewhere their lifeprints lurk
                                    for the scorn of eyes.

At least it was a beginning—
it gave pensions to those over '65
and help for disabled and blind

        The Social Security Act, wrote Franklin Roosevelt,
        "is the foundation upon which we hope in America to provide
        a real form of financial security for workers, so that the
        spectre of unemployment and old-age destitution may be
                        banished
                        from the
                        American
                        home and
                        farm."

            Yes!!!!!!!!!!!!!!

August 26
    Roosevelt signed the Public Utilities Act, requiring public utilities
                to register with the Security & Exchange Commission

——————————— **The Federal Theater Project!** ———————————

    Hallie Flanagan was the national director
                        of the Federal Theater Project
    which, to the eructional distress of right-wing nulls,
    encouraged political awareness & action
    Though it specialized in
    Shakespeare, O'Neill, Bernard Shaw, and others
    The FTP constantly had to defend itself against
                        those right-wing nulls

    The Living Newspaper

The Negro theater
the Dance Project
these three Federal Theater projects
picked up the greatest shouts from the right

The Dies and Woodrum committees of Congress
blasted FTP as communist
& after June 1939
it was defunded by Congress

•

The howling black dust clouds
continued to lift away the Midwest soil
and the migration of totally broke, skimp-carted
hungry Americans
continued to the West

——————————————— **Will Rogers** ———————————————

His vestiges in America
faded fairly quickly
but when his plane crashed on August 15
the nation was stunned and mournful

Will Rogers was an enormously famous actor, humorist and columnist,
with a tough & straight-bantering cowpoke persona
whose radio shows were heard by all the American factions

(His Sunset Boulevard swimming pool
shaped like the State of California
was 32 years later used for fun & thrills
by the Manson family & rock star Dennis Wilson
a tale for Volume II of
America, A History in Verse)

August 30
Congress passed a Revenue Act,
increasing taxes on inheritances and gifts

---------------------------------- **The Kingfish** ----------------------------------

They called Huey Long the Kingfish
He was more or less the dictator of Louisiana
        a former governor, now Senator
                controlling a vast system of patronage

He was one of those Southern populists
quick with words and long on riffraff-riling rants
When he was governor the state gave free textbooks to children
                & knocked out the evil poll tax
Later, in the US Senate
        he promised a guaranteed income
                & high taxes on the rich

He hated the New Deal, accusing FDR of failing his promise of
"breaking down the big fortunes to give enough to the masses
to end poverty."

The Republicans were counting on him
to run, third party, for president

but September 8 he was shot in the stomach
by the son-in-law of a political enemy
                & passed two days later

---------------------------------- **The Nüremberg Laws** ----------------------------------
September 15

The first law stripped citizenship from German Jews
who were now without rights, barred from public office
                & not allowed to teach.

Then there was a second law, for the
        "Protection of German Blood and German Honor"
banning marriage 'tween Jews and Germans
& Germans were prevented from employing Jewish servants
                under the age of 45

After Hit-vom signed the law
        the anti-Semitic blasts on radio, newspapers,
                textbooks, and speeches
                    burbled forth

Jews began to disappear in the middle of the day or night
                        & the Swastika became Germany's official flag
& Leni Riefenstahl's soul-song to Hitler
                  Triumph of the Will
               tracking the '34 Nazi convention in Nuremberg
                                    premiered in Germany

―――――――――――― **Fascists into Ethiopia** ――――――――――――
October 2

Mussolini invaded Ethiopia
                     on the Red Sea
                           where his troops fired poison gas!
What about *that*, Ezra Pound!?
Though Roosevelt & Congress banned
                 arms sales to both countries
they left some greedhead loopholes:
                 oil companies were allowed
                        to sell huge amounts to fuel the Fascists

and a few days later the ineffectual
                     League of Nations set "sanctions" on Italy
              but never really did anything
              & the result was to
                    erase the League
                        in the streaks of time

October 10
    a folk opera called *Porgy and Bess,*
            with music by George Gershwin,
            & libretto by Ira Gershwin (with DuBose Heyward)
            about dwellers on Catfish Row
            a black pov street in Charleston, SC

       ran a few weeks, faded,
             but became known as a masterwork

―――――――――――――― **The CIO!** ――――――――――――――

The man with the startling eyebrows, Mr. John L. Lewis
                           of the United Mine Workers

with eight other unions who wanted a

network of industry-based unions
created the Committee for Industrial Organization on November 9
breaking with the AFofL

December
Radar began in England
to track airplanes
& guard the North Sea

December 30
Eleanor Roosevelt commenced her six-day-a-week column, "My Day"

December 31
Monopoly was patented by Parker Brothers
A good game
to flex the mind
in the wanna-haves

Novum Sub Sole '35:
In Akron, Ohio
the founding of Alcoholics Anonymous
and its 12-Step program
bringing humility, persistence
& the Deity
into recovery.

The Richter Scale for measuring earthquakes
35 mm Kodachrome film
Cortisone was iso'd from the adrenal cortex
by biochemist E. C. Kendall

Henry Cowell *Mosaic Quartet*
the Gibson electro-acoustic guitar
Artie Shaw's first band

"Happy Birthday to You" was published,
apparently from a tune titled "Good Morning to All"
with words by Patty Smith Hill, music by Mildred Hill.
Did you know that every time you've sung it
you owe performance royalties?

T. S. Eliot's *Burnt Norton*
also his *Murder in the Cathedral*
John Steinbeck *Tortilla Flat*

Clifford Odets *Waiting for Lefty*

Linen/Exit:
Elvis Presley born Jan 8
T. E. Lawrence, passed away, May 19 at 46
Christo June 13
Woody Allen Dec 1
Alban Berg passed at 50 Dec 24
Eldridge Cleaver, Ken Kesey on Sept 17, Loretta Lynne,
                              Richard Brautigan, Terry Riley

and don't forget:
         Roller Derbies, bra cup sizes, the Gallup poll
         parking meters

Nelson Eddy and Jeannette MacDonald crooning in
Naughty Marietta
              then 7 more sugary croonathons

Hartford Accident and Indemnity Company executive
                         Wallace Stevens' "breakthrough" book
                         Ideas of Order
                         He was 56

          In Portugal th'
          neurologist Antonio Egas Moniz
          started doing prefrontal lobotomies
          putatively to relieve bonk bonk
          by
          drilling hole in skull to sever th' nerves 'tween
          the two frontal lobes of the noggin
                         No! No! No!

Margaret Mead's *Sex and Temperament*
          —genderistic social expectations in three cultures

Persia became Iran
Fox merged with 20th Century to become 20th Century–Fox

Cyrano de Bergerac
The Bride of Frankenstein, with Boris Karloff
Top Hat with Fred Astaire and Ginger Rogers
Hopalong Cassidy (the first of 66)
Mutiny on the Bounty
A Night at the Opera

Right-Wing Supreme Court Strikes Again
January 6

The Court maced down the Agricultural Adjustment Act
—a law designed to raise farm income, control surpluses,
and it had things like
a tax on the processing of farm commodities
then paying those taxes to farmers
who lowered their surpluses
(Justices Stone, Brandeis and Cardozo dissented)

January 15
Japan abandoned the London Naval Conference
because other nations refused to accept its demand for
a uniform upper limit on naval might

Japan apparently wanted all countries
to have the same sized navy

February 6
Chaplin's new film *Modern Times* opened in NYC
5,000 fans gathered outside the Rivoli Theater
to see Gloria Swanson, Ginger Rogers &
Eddie Cantor
Inside 1,000 viewers waited to hear Chaplin's voice
on screen for the first time

would it be tinny, whiny, or dreary?

Chaplin sang a song
and whew!
his voice was fine

338

The Spanish Republic
February 16

In new elections in Spain
  the right was again stomped out
    by a coalition of leftists and liberals

The Popular Front coalition of Left parties with 238 seats,
       and 163 for the right, 52 for Center

There were street fights 'tween
     socialist/communist youth and Falangist youth

Churches were burned, peasants took over estates,
    anarchists occupied factories
    It looked like a new Spain was going to emerge

   Ancient revenges
   Ancient hatreds
   Ancient injustice
    anciently flaming
till conservative generals made their move
     —a tale we'll limn-trace soon

Meanwhile in Japan

  In Japan the military
  kept getting more power

  In February it killed
  a bunch of cabinet members
  but failed to seize the gov't

  Then there was martial law
  as the military sucked up more and more
  of the budget

February 26
  Hitler oped the first Volkswagen factory

Hitler Seizes the Rhineland
March

Hitler sent soldiers to grab the Rhineland
a 30-mile demilitarized zone to the east of the Rhine River,
        which ambles down through eastern Germany
   —created by the Treaty of Versailles—
accusing the French of planning to encircle Germany

No one, not France, not England
        did anything about it.

Twerponomy
March 1

To get around the Supreme Court's twerponomy
      in tossing out the Agricultural Adjustment Administration
Congress passed, and Roosevelt signed
      the Soil Conservation & Domestic Allotment Act
which sought to deal with the howling shriek-clouds
        of soil erosion that
      were killing the fertility of the Midwest
by putting more land into soil-improving/soil-saving crops
and to protect rivers & harbors against the soil of such erosion
plus seeking to establish again, in Roosevelt's words, "the ratio
    between the
purchasing power of the net income per person on farms
and that of the net income per person not on farms"
        of the years 1909–1914.

    How? Central planning, ceaseless consultation with
    average people, and payments from the Nation's treasury.
    Take that, Supreme Court.

March 29
99% of the German electorate voted for Nazi candidates

The CCC's Third!
April 17

By the third anniversary of the
    Civilian Conservation Corps

7,436,321 acres of trees had been added to
America's national forests
& 199,214 acres to the National Parks

Roosevelt recommended the CCC be made
permanent
but the Congress only continued it
for three more years

Dumb, Congress, Dumb

June 12,
The 40-hour work week was initiated as state policy in France!
All right! First 40, then 35, then 30!

(meanwhile, that same spring
the right-wing majority on the Supreme Court voted
5-4 against the New York State minimum wage!)

———————— **Popular Front Gov't in France** ————————
June, 1936–June, 1937

The Popular Front in France won big on May 3
Socialists 147, Radicals 106, Commies 72
& parties of the right 232

so that June 4 Socialist Léon Blum
formed a Popular Front ministry in France—
a Coalition of left-wing and centrist parties opposing fascism.

The Popular Front Gov't sought extensive social reform
while suppressing fascist groups.

(There was also a Popular Front gov't in Spain under Manuel
Azana, Largo Caballero and Juan Negrin from Feb '36 to March '39,
against whom Franco fought the Spanish Civil War)

Léon Blum was France's first Socialist prime minister
and the first Jewish p.m.

The left had long held a majority in parliament
but the Commies and Socialists had refused to share power
but, the threat of fascism now oozed them into the same phonebooth

341

Blum pushed through a large packet of social legislation
the 40-hour week, paid vacations, collective bargaining!
arms factories and the Bank of France were nationalized!

but Blum dumbly, as it turned out,
                    refused to intervene in the Spanish Civil War.

June 19,
        Joe Louis lost to Max Schmeling in the 12th round
                    of a non-title bout at Yankee Stadium
                            & the Nazis suffered an aryan-gasm

———————————— **The Spanish Civil War Begins** ————————————
                            July 18

Four right wing generals
                    supported by the Germans and Italians
attacked the legally elected Spanish gov't

They were led by General Francisco Franco
                            who invaded from Morocco

Franco's generals drove toward Madrid
                            in four columns
& Franco bragged he had a "fifth column"
                    inside the city
                            that would help him.

This gave birth to the concept of the "fifth column"
which the U.S. right later used
                    in fake-quakes
                    to justify attacks on American radicals.

Meanwhile Franco
took first the south then the west of Spain around July of '36
                    assisted by Hit-vom and Muss-vom
                    (troops, ammunition and aircraft)

The Russians sent arms and advisers to the Republic,
but other govt's (including the USA) would not help.

At first France sent the Republicans 300 planes, then, at Britain's
noble urging, declared neutrality.

There was an international force that formed
        from 52 nations,
                including George Orwell and André Malraux.

By early '37, skirting the US gov't
                the Abraham Lincoln Brigade
                        composed of US citizens
                                battled the Spanish fascists

August 4
        Franco's army seized Badajoz in the southwest so that his forces
                                in the north and south could combine

August 7
        to its detriment
                as the century spun forward
        US declared neutrality in the Spanish Civil War

                The neutrality law that the student peace movement
                had endorsed earlier in the '30s
                was used by Roosevelt
                        to embargo the
                                Spanish Republic
                which would allow the triumph of the fascist right

───────────── **The Berlin Olympics** ─────────────
August 1–16

Jesse Owens from Ohio State
                won four golds

                100 meters 10.3
                broad jump 26' 5½"
                400 meter relay team 39.8
                200 meters 20.7

Hitler refused to offer congratulations
                and left the stadium in a fury

Back at home Owens had a tough time
He ran races against dogs and horses
traveled with the Harlem Globetrotters
                        then worked as a janitor

though later he was "director of Negro personnel for Ford Motor
   Company"

──────────────────────── **Lorca** ────────────────────────
                    August 18

The author of *Gypsy Ballads* o' '28
                          & Blood Wedding '33
the great Federico Garcia Lorca had come to Granada
                    for a vacation at his family's summer home

It was a few hours before Franco vommed in from Morocco

He'd just completed his play *The House of Bernarda Alba*

The Nationalists grabbed the town
                    & rounded up the mayor to kill him

Lorca hid in a Conservative's house
          but the Conservative's brother turned him over
                                   on August 16
Two days later he was shot in government headquarters
                          and tossed into a mass grave

August
   Roosevelt requested a "survey" of Communist and fascist
   organizations

   By the fall of 1938 J. Edgar Hoover had re-established the
               General Intelligence Section
               dormant since the 1924 reforms
                    (after the tearing of the Constitution
                              during the War 1 repression)

   Hoovie-men began reading Left wing publications
                    and making an index of individuals and orgs

──────────────────── **Moscow Purge Trials** ────────────────────
                    August 1936–'38

      The entire remaining Bolshevik leadership from th'
      October '17 rev
            was charged

with secret treasonous dealings with Hitler
                & Japan to dismember the Soviet Union

Stalin had an "Off with their heads!" type of mind
intermixed with his utter determination
                to forge a planned economy

In a three-year period
Stalin apparently arrested 5 million citizens
Millions were killed
and many were sent to the evil gulag labor camps

The first trial was August '36:
                Lev Kamenev and Grigory Zinoviev
Stalin's partners in the ruling triumvirate when Lenin passed
and 14 other leading old commies were
charged with membership in a secret Trotskyist conspiracy
planning to snuff Sov U's top leaders
           beginning with Sergei Kirov back in '34—
                All confessed and were sentenced to death
              though later it was shown
                  they were coerced.
There were more than a few in the USA
                that burned in their souls
                  for a planned economy
so you can imagine how Stalin's purge trials
caused huge controversies in the Western Left

where Commies had been accustomed to calling
           Social Democrats "social fascists"
           but then were ordered to form a popular front.

        The rapid industrialization
              of Stalin's two five-year plans
        when contrasted with millions of unemployed in America

        seemed to tip history to the Russians
                in many minds

Trotskyites called for a commission to investigate
the treason charges Stalin had thrown against him

There was an international commission of inquiry headed
by John Dewey, with Max Eastman, James T. Farrell, Sidney

Hook, Mary McCarthy, Norman Thomas, and Edmund Wilson.

Meanwhile liberal fellow-travelers issued an
"Open Letter to American Liberals"

urging them to have nothing to do with the Trotsky defense
committee—fingering it as tampering with internal
Russian affairs
plus aiding fascism

There were 88 signers, including Malcolm Cowley, Theodore Dreiser,
Lillian Hellman, Rockwell Kent, Max Lerner, Corliss Lamont,
Dorothy Parker, Nathanael West, *et al.*

•

September 9–17
In London, at a conference on the Spanish Civil War
'27 countries joined a nonintervention committee to prevent
the sending of war supplies and intervention of foreign forces in
the war.

•

Then General Franco was proclaimed
"Chief of the Spanish State."
on October 1

Franco controlled Cadiz, Saragossa, Seville and Burgos.
Republicans controlled Madrid, Barcelona, Bilbao and Valencia.

——————— **The Presidential Campaign Opens** ———————
September 29

Roosevelt began his campaign for reelection on 9-29
vilified by the right

& facing the fact that 85% of America's newspapers
supported the Republicans!

October 6
the British Labour Party rejected affiliation with th' Communist Party

In a campaign speech in Chicago, the President said,
"America is an economic unit. New means & methods
of transportation and communications have made us
economically as well as politically a single Nation."

October 28
    In the Republican portion of Spain
    the unions collectivized agriculture & industry
                    plus erred in banning Christian worship

—————————— **Roosevelt Says Hi to Hatred** ——————————
Madison Square Garden
October 31

The right was
gnawing like a hen-door weasel
to refoment the plunder.

A week before the vote he gave a wonderful speech,
with this inside it:

"For nearly four years you have had an Administration which
instead of twirling its thumbs has rolled up its sleeves. We will
keep our sleeves rolled up.

"We had to struggle with the old enemies of peace—business and
financial monopoly, speculation, reckless banking, class antagonism,
sectionalism, war profiteering.

"They had begun to consider the Government of the United States
as a mere appendage to their own affairs. We know now that
Government by organized money is just as dangerous as
Government by organized mob.

"Never before in all our history have these forces been so united
against one candidate as they stand today. They are unanimous
in their hate for me—and I welcome their hatred.

"I should like to have it said of my first Administration that in it the
forces of selfishness and of lust for power met their match. I should

like to have it said of my second Administration that in it
these forces met their master."

German-Italian Axis
November 1

Mussolini gave a speech in Milan with the sentence
"This Berlin-Rome line
            is not a diaphragm but rather an axis."

In May, Italy had taken over Ethiopia, but alienated France
                    and Britain by the grab

            Germany had recognized Austrian sovereignty
            back in July (and Austria had
                    agreed to be a "German state.")

Then Germany and Italy
forged an entente
with common policies toward Spain,
the Danubian countries, the Sov Un & the League of N's

In *Mein Kampf* Hit-vom had written of the need for
                                        "Lebensraum"

living space
and so had begun his thrillkill lunge
                    to seize Czechoslovakia

Roosevelt Wins Again!
November 3

Confounding all those newspapers and
                    rightists who hated his guts
FDR won every state except Maine & Vermont
                            over Alf Landon

and it had been predicted by a pollster!

(George Gallup had founded in '35
The American Institute of Public Opinion
        and correctly predicted, through sampling,
                        the trouncing of Alf)

Roose 27.7m Landon 16.67m
and William Lemke of the National Union for Social Justice 882,479

November 6
     the Siege of Madrid began
     Republican defenders were joined by
                         fighters from around the world
                                   belonging to the International Brigade.
     The Spanish gov't moved to Valencia
                         on the coast southwest of Madrid

———————————— **Edward & Wallis** ————————————
November 16

King Edward VIII notified the English establishment
that he was going to marry an American divorcée
                                   named Wallis Simpson
                    & Prime Minister Baldwin notified Ed that
                    the hitch-up would offend public opinion
                    and damage the throne's prestige.

          Newspapers broke the story on December 3
          & then on December 11
                              King Edward VIII
                              tossed off the crown
                              in a radio speech
          and was succeeded by his brother the Duke of York

          There was a giant world-wide ink & radio storm
                                             of interest

December 5
     A new constitution for the USSR,
                    with a supreme council and a two-chamber parliament

———————————— **The United Auto Workers** ————————————

Beginning December 30
there was a crest of strikes in the US auto industry
including a 44-day sitdown strike against General Motors
               which lasted till February 11

when General Motors recognized the
United Auto Workers.
Workers "sat down," i.e. shut down the factories
instead of hitting the bricks
in picket lines

There was a united front among leftists and nonleftists
(for a change)
The UAW soon succeeded in org'ing most of the industry, except
for Ford.

Cap-sludge could no longer use goons
against the legitimate rights of workers
thanks to Roosevelt
& the New Deal labor laws

Hooray! to
the U.A.W. in the Time-Fount

The Great Fallingwater

Frank Lloyd Wright's ah!-producing house
called "Fallingwater"
was finished in the Allegheny Mountains of Pennsylvania
for Edgar Kaufman

with beige concrete terraces   stone walls
& layers of cantilevered terraces
thrill-jutting above a waterfall
the most beautiful thing I'd ever seen
I thought, when I saw pictures o' it as a kid in Missouri

Novum for '36:
the Hoover Dam opened on the Colo R border of Ariz and Nev
for hydroelectricity
and Lake Mead would become the largest artificial lake in the USA

Trotsky's tome, *The Revolution Betrayed*
and after you had finished with Trotsky's
you could have read
Dale Carnegie's *How to Win Friends and Influence People*

The National Wildlife Federation formed
At MOMA two exhibitions: Cubism and Abstract Art
                      & Fantastic Art, Dada, and Surrealism

The Cradle Will Rock
Marc Blitzstein's musical about a CIO union struggle in Steeltown,
     USA.

Djuna Barnes *Nightwood*
John Dos Passos *The Big Money* (completing the trilogy *USA*)
Faulkner *Absalom, Absalom!*

Robert Frost *A Further Range*
Dylan Thomas *Twenty-Five Poems*
George Orwell *Keep the Aspidistra Flying*

The *Partisan Review* was reborn as an anti-Stalinist
        journal of the left.
        It had begun in '34 sponsored by the NY John Reed Club
        but, with the Popular Front,
        it began walking the path of the independent left
        publishing some of the best of American writing
                             till the War

Allen Lane in England founded Penguin Books,
        & what they called the Paperback Revolution began

Olivier Messiaen *Poèmes pour Mi*
Edgard Varèse *Density 21.5*

Sergei Prokofiev *Peter and the Wolf*

"Pennies from Heaven" by Arthur Johnston

The swing era began, with
band leader and broadcaster Benny Goodman labelled the
     King of Swing

Chaplin's great *Modern Times*
—a satire on the machine age
His character the Tramp was a demoralized assembly line slave
        with its famous ending:
        the Tramp and his girlfriend, the Gamine
        their backs turned to the cruel machinery
                    head down the road

It was a movie that hinted at socialism, yet made money
                              & anger on the right that rarely forgets

Linen and oi in '36!
Carol Burnett, Wilt Chamberlain, Mary Tyler Moore,
Frank Stella, Bill Wyman, Charlie Watts

Maxim Gorky passed at 68 on June 18
and Rudyard Kipling at 70 on Jan 18
and Václav Havel born Oct 5
and Dec 10 Luigi Pirandello passed at 60

Then there were
tampons, trampolines, polaroid glasses and
                              the Waring blender

Sandburg's *The People, Yes*
        and Margaret Mitchell's *Gone with the Wind*

plus John Maynard Keynes'
        The General Theory of Employment, Interest and Money
        advocating gov't intervention in the economy
                and deficit spending as recession buster

        Roll, o cap-eyes, roll!

Frank Capra's *Mr. Deeds Goes to Town*
Buster Crabbe in *Flash Gordon*
Jean Renoir's *A Day in the Country*

        A Thirty-Five Hour Week, o America!

January 8
    Congress tightened the Neutrality Act
                    to forbid arms shipments to Civil strife zones
    Roosevelt signed it
                & thus Americans could not send arms to
                             the Spanish Republic

    Ah, Franklin! Why, Franklin?

    Rightwingers in the State Department
    had banned travel to Spain,
    yet Americans were stealthily crossing the Pyrenees to
                          battle the hate

    The Young Communist League made up 60 percent of those
                in the Abraham Lincoln Brigade
                  though also Wobblies and Socialists joined

    The Socialists, for instance, had a Debs Column
                     that battled in Spain

    though open recruitment
                  caused government suppression

            Why, Franklin, why?

                yet

    rightwingers could not prevent
            vocalist Billie Holiday and tenor saxman Lester Young
            with the Teddy Wilson Ensemble
            from recording "This Year's Kisses"
                  in NYC

Holiday had had a grim servitudinous childhood
                                    had even worked as a hooker
then began recording in '33 with Benny Goodman
joined Count Basie's band in '35
                        and now was genius-voicing her
                                            great American legacy

January 9
    Leon Trotsky arrived in Mexico
    after sojourns in Turkey and Paris

    American Trotskyites
                provided secretaries, guards, funds, etc.

──────────────── **More Show Trials** ────────────────
January 23–30

    Trials of Karl Radek and 16 other commie leaders
    in USSR for putatively conspiring with Trotsky, Germany and Japan

    Radek and three were jailed, the others shot.

January 30
    At his second inaugural
    Roosevelt said "I see one-third of a Nation
                        ill-housed, ill-clad, ill-nourished"
            and he was going to do something about it.

Jan–Feb
    Big floods in Midwest
    Mississippi Missouri Allegheny Rivers
                            1 million homeless

February 8
    Italian Fascist troops
    helped Franco take Malaga in the South of Spain

──────── **Pressure on Right Wing Supreme Court** ────────
March 1

    The Supreme Court Retirement Act was passed
    allowing judges on the Supreme C to retire at 70 with full pay

Roosevelt proposed also that if judges over 70
            refused to get out of there
                    the pres could appoint extra judges
but Congress' opposition
made Roosevelt withdraw the plan
                        in July '37.

So ghastly was the right-wing debasement of the Constitution
in the U.S. Supreme Court
that Roosevelt felt they might rule against
                    Social Security legislation and the Wagner Act
                    (which guaranteed collective bargaining for workers)
that he proposed adding maybe 6 new Justices
to the court

Congress would not approve the proposal
but the Supremies nevertheless upheld both Soc Sec and
                                    Collective Bargaining

                    The threat of rev
                    & the anger of the people
                    brittled the right-wing court
            so that '37 was the year it
            reversed its view of New Deal legislation
            in *National Labor Board v. Jones and Laughlin Steel Corp*
            and *West Coast Hotel Co. v. Parrish*
            when it allowed union organization
                        and minimum wages as part of the
                        "constitutional revolution" of 1937

March 2
    Nationalization of oil in Mexico
        with a National Petroleum Corporation to administer oil lands

March 18
    Italian Fascist sleazetroops were defeated at Brihuega, and thus
    Franco's threat on Madrid was checked, for now

April 1
    Franco-vom launched a big attack in the North of Spain
    He asked both Germany & Italy for help
                        and both complied

            Why, Franklin, why?

April 19
    Right-wing Spanish Parties
    The Falange and the Traditionalists
    merged as the Falange Española Tradicionalista

———————————————————— **Guernica** ————————————————————

Planes from the German Condor Legion
                bombed four hours for Franco
                        destroying the ancient Basque city of Guernica

            in Northern Spain
                on 4-28

            the vomit vomits in the vomit

When Picasso was asked to do a work for the Spanish
                pavilion in the Paris World's Fair
                        he painted his startling "Guernica"

            the kind of work in which
            the totality of the pain
                can be either kept at bay
                    or brought full fray
                        in the eye-scan

May 6
    The long, swastika-emblazoned dirigible *Hindenberg*
                was sliding to dock
                        at the U.S. Naval base at Lakehurst, N.J.

        when it exploded
                and 36 of 97 were dead

———————————— **Farm Security Administration** ————————————

Another glory of the Roosevelt era
            the Farm Security Administration
                which helped people buy their
                own farms with gov't-backed
                        LOW INTEREST loans

    Th' FSA hired photographers

to document the rural Depression
such as Walker Evans, Dorothea Lange, John Collier, Jack Delano,
Theo Jung, Russell Lee, Cary Mydans, Arthur Rothstein, Ben Shahn,
and Marion Post Walcott

1937
Pierce Arrow went out of biz
—wish you had one?

1937
Jean Renoir's great film *Grand Illusion*
was banned in Germany, Italy and Austria

―――――――――――― **Memorial Day Massacre** ――――――――――
in South Chicago

That spring the CIO's
Steel Workers Organizing Committee
was finishing a national campaign

There was a strike in Chicago
and during its first week
there'd been fights at Republic Steel plants
'tween police & strikebreakers with guns
and union pickets.

Then on May Day, the international set of hours
to honor the betterment of workers
the Republic Local of SWOC
held a gathering near a tavern
that served as strike headquarters

2,000 strikers and families sang "Solidarity Forever"
and listened to speeches

Then there was an impromptu parade toward
the Republic Steel factory

4 platoons of Chicago police
with guns and clubs at the ready
met the marchers

The police fired & tossed tear gas

then ran after the fleeing marchers
truncheoning them
dragging men and women to vans

Ten union men died
from police fire

Chicago Police Commissioner James Allman
claimed his police had halted
a commie parade walking under
"instructions from Moscow."

In this case famous American justice
lay befouled
& the strike was lost as th' steel companies held out
till World War II
when they were pressured to sign a union contract

●

May
Conservative Neville Chamberlain
became British prime minister

May 27
the Golden Gate Bridge opened

——————————— **The Cradle Will Rock** ———————————
June 16

Marc Blitzstein's left-wing musical drama
The Cradle Will Rock
was performed at the Venice Theater in NYC

—protests had made cancellation of original perfs
scheduled for elsewhere.

June
In the USSR some big time generals were tried, convicted, shot
for "collaboration with Germany"
then there was a purge of the armed forces

June 19
   Franco-vom grabbed Bilbao, Basque capital in the northeast of Spain

June 21
   Socialist Léon Blum's request for emergency fiscal powers was denied
                              by the French Senate, so he resigned.

June 23
   Germany and Italy quit the Nonintervention Committee,
                        which had barred involvement in Spain.

July 7
   Japan attacked China

   the military had long hungered to stomp into China

   and fought for the rest of the year

   with ghastly atrocities, rapes and
                     other Homeric devices of carnage

            For a while the Communist forces of Mao
            joined the Nationalists of Chiang Kai-shek
                              to fight the invader

July 18
   they called off the search for Amelia Earheart
                        in the Pacific
                              after she had prayed then lifted up
            from New Guinea
                     on her way around the world
                              then vanished

———————————————— **Degenerate Art** ————————————————

   In Munich an exhibition of Degenerate Art
                        occurred on July 19
   Hitler had seized 5,000 examples of modern art
   & placed them alongside
            the Naz-vom-approved "Great German Art Exhibition"

            Many many more went to the Degen
            than to Great Germ

July 22
    American farmers by the more and more were losing their farms
    to the ineluctable flow of cap-grab
    so congress passed the
    Bankhead-Jones Farm Tenant Act,
            which loaned out money at 3% interest!
            Dance, o Dante, dance!
    so that tenant farmers and sharecroppers could own their own farms

        Roll, o cap-eyes, roll!

September 2
    Roosevelt signed the National Housing Act
    creating a National Housing Authority

        This was the Wagner-Steagall Act
        to help create affordable housing

        something else to make the cap-eyes roll:

————————————————— **The Two Voms** —————————————

Muss-vom paid a visit to Hit-vom on 9-25
and there was a big parade in Munich

plus visits to the Krupp kill-works in Essen

Big crowds adoring the two voms

————————————————— **Bessie Smith** —————————————

        The day after Hitler & Mussolini
                met in Munich
        the great great singer Bessie Smith
        was turned away by the
            whites-only hospital
                at Coahome, Mississippi
        and bled to death

October 1
    Franco assumed leadership of right wing forces
    and began to prepare to govern

On the 21st the right took Gijón, the last major town in the north

and on the 28th the Spanish gov't moved from Valencia to Barcelona

———————————— **A Federal Tax on Grass** ————————————
October 1

Indian hemp was not indigenous to the USA
but the Colonials grew it
         as fiber for homespun cloth
                & it was spread thereafter
                         all around the nation.

After a long campaign (led by Henry Anslinger & the
yellowy lies of Hearst) the Marijuana Tax Act of 1937 was passed
         "to impose an occupational excise tax upon certain dealers
in marihuana, to impose a transfer tax upon
certain dealings in marihuana, and to safeguard the
revenue therefrom by registry and recording."
         (the tax was $100 an oz. for leaves & flowers)

And what did a joint cost in the bistros of
Greenwich Village in 1937?
                5 or 10¢!

Reefer madness spread
         with reports of teenage girls
                hanging out, shudder shudder, in
                         "marijuana dens"
& pot-maddened players performing what the Hearst papers
         termed "voodoo-satanic" music, otherwise known as jazz.

•

November 28
     Franco began a naval blockade of the Spanish coast

December 4
     Spanish Republicans began an offensive in Aragon, lasting till
         January

December 29
     the New Irish Constitution was in force
         The Irish Free State became Eire

Novum '37:
blood banks, antihistamines, the drive-in bank, and the
shopping cart

plus Calder's *Mercury Fountain* mobile
                    at the Paris World's Fair.

Two Italian doctors
inaugurated electric shock therapy for schiz-relief
        ——a treatment used till the psyche-moilcalm drugs of the '50s

a British engineer constructed the first jet engine
zinc protamine insulin used for diabetes
                    nylon invented by Du Pont

Paul Mellon endowed the National Gallery of Art

Alban Berg's posthumous, unfinished opera, *Lulu*
Carl Orff *Carmina Burana*
Benjamin Britten's *Variations on a Theme by Frank Bridge*

Bing Crosby's "Sweet Leilani"
                    was a big seller

& US spinach growers
            erected a salutory statue to Popeye
                        for promoting spinach-choffing

John Steinbeck *Of Mice and Men*
Wallace Stevens *The Man with the Blue Guitar*
The History of the Russian Revolution by Leon Trotsky
            trans. by Max Eastman, published by
                        Simon & Schuster
and the Mercury Theater, formed by O. Welles and John Houseman

births/byes for '37:
Vanessa Redgrave on Jan 30
Jan 31 Philip Glass
April 22 Jack Nicholson
Bobby Seale Dustin Hoffman August 8
Saddam Hussein
Jean Harlow passed on June 7 at 26, George Gershwin July 11 at 38
May 23, John D Rockefeller kaks, at 97

July 2, Amelia Earhart passes at 38
Aug 3 Diane Wakoski born   Aug 11 Edith Wharton passes at 75
Aug 18 Robert Redford born
Dec 28 Maurice Ravel at 62

Flicks: *Camille,* Garbo
                        Lost Horizon, Frank Capra
                                    The Prisoner of Zenda
Disney's *Snow White and the Seven Dwarfs*
A Star Is Born, with Janet Gaynor and Frederic March

                    'Seven Wasn't Heaven

January 9
        The Republicans took Teruel, in Eastern Spain, from Franco-vom
                but Franco reseized it on the 22nd
                                and drove onward to the Mediterranean
        There was a lot of fighting along
                the River Ebro throughout '38.

        German psychopaths swarmed the sky
                        perfecting dive-bombing techniques
                        they later put to use in WWII

        Franco had also use of 50,000 Italian "volunteers."

─────────────── **Ludlow Amendment Fails** ───────────────
                    January 10

        Back in 1935 a Democratic Congressman from Indiana
        named Louis Ludlow

had proposed a Constitutional Amendment
to keep America "out of the slaughter pens in Foreign countries."

The Ludlow Amendment would have barred Congress from
declaring war without the prior approval of a majority
                                        of U.S. voters
(except in the case of attack)
Finally on 1-10-'38 enough Congressmen had signed the
petition for the Amendment
                        to bring it before the House.
Roosevelt argued strongly against it
and the Amendment resolution
                        fell by a 209 to 188 vote!
                        Whew! thought Roosevelt

January
    Benny Goodman's
    famous jazz concert at Carnegie Hall

February 16
    the Second Agricultural Adjustment Act was passed
    replacing the one of '33
    struck down in '36 by the Supreme Court

March 2–14
    Former big league Commie Nikolai Bukharin and other leaders
    were on show trial in the USSR,
                        Bukharin was shot on March 14

———————— **Ghastly German-Austrian Anschluss** ————————
                        March 12

The Nazis marched into Austria
The crowds were ecstatic
            and anti-Nazi activists were forced
                        to scrub Vienna's sidewalks

Freud hit the road, and as many Jews as could escape the camps.

Almost 100% in an April plebiscite approved the *Anschluss*
                        —the union of A with G.

After this, Hit-vom went after Czechoslovakia

promising that all he wanted was the Sudetenland

March 18
   Mexico nationalized US oil property

April 15
   Franco forces took Vinaroz on the Mediterranean
                  thus dividing Republicans in Catalonia from SE Spain

May 3-9
   Hitler visited Mussolini in Rome
                  each one thinking
                        "I am eternity"

May 26
   the House Committee on Unamerican Activities
                  was established

   It later turned out that the Congressman, Samuel Dickstein, who
   pushed hard to found it
                  was a communist spy!

   He wanted to use the Committee to attack fascists
   but it of course backfired
   when the right wing said, yes! let's attack leftists instead!
   A right-wing Congressman from Texas named Martin Dies
   became the HUAC head
                  & foam-moaned for years against Roosevelt

———————————— **A National Minimum Wage!** ————————————
June 14

            For the first time in America's history
            a national minimum wage!

            It was Armageddon time for cap-eyes!

   It took three sessions of Congress
   & ceaseless work by the brain trust
                  The first year it was 25¢
                  the second was 30¢
                        & after seven years it was to be 40¢

44 hrs was set as the work week before time-&-a-half began
and 40 hours after the second year

June 23
Congress passed the Civil Aeronautics Act, and the
Civil Aeronautics Authority was thereby created

──────────────── The Japs into South China ────────────────

The Japanese were threatening Southern China
in June

Chiang Kai-shek dynamited the dikes in the Yellow River
& floods killed thousands
in Chiang's attempt to slow down
the Japanese invasion into the South

And the Nationalists began the Burma Road
a 715-mile single track road from Mandalay in Burma
up into the mountains of Kunming
a supply link with the world
completed in December '38.

July 10–14
Howard Hughes in the plane, *New York World Fair,*
flew around the world in 3 days 19 hours

July 30
Henry Ford received the Grand Cross of the German Eagle
and Charles Lindbergh on October 18 picked up a "lower German
order."

──────────────── Chamberlain Visits Hitler ────────────────
September 15

Prime Minister Neville Chamberlain
saw Hitler at Berchtesgaden

Hitler was determined to annex the Czech Sudetenland
on the grounds that the people desired it

On September 22–24 Chamberlain again saw Hitler

at Bad Godenberg

He wanted th' Sudetenland immediately

Chamberlain returned to London
& tried to get British, French and Czech "acquiescence."

The 4th International

Followers of Trotsky from eleven nations
voted the vision of
The 4th International on September 3

called *The Death Agony of Capitalism
and the Tasks of the 4th International*
whose chief author was Leon Trotsky himself.

The Soviet Union was described by the 4th International
as a "degenerated worker-state"

The American Socialist Workers Party, a small entity hounded
for decades by the FBI & the secret police
played a key role in the 4th I

•

September 28
Roosevelt was at the Bonneville Dam
east of Portland
He was always a friend of the spread of
electricity
& Woody Guthrie had written some songs
for the opening

The Munich Conference
September 29

Four nations met in Munich
Neville Chamberlain for England, Edouard Daladier for France
with Adolf Hitler and Benito Mussolini

and signed off on an immediate German swarm-job

onto the predominantly German-language Sudetenland
in western Czechoslovakia.

(The Sudetenland was a piece of territory along the northern and
western borders of the Czech Republic,
named for the Sudeten Mountains)

Neither Czechoslovakia nor its ally Russia were
invited to the Munich conference

Poland and Hungary
also wanted a taste of Czechoslovakia

Czech land is mine!
No it's mine!
No, mine!

Arriving in London, the conservative Mr. Chamberlain
said he was bringing "peace with honor. I believe
it is peace in our time."

Many in the signatory countries believed it at the time
mistaking Hitler's drool on Europe's borders
for satisfaction

October 2
Then Japan split from the League of Nations
(The League had accused it as aggressor in Jap-Chi war on Sept 27)

October 6
An entity with the ghastly name of "Grand Fascist Council"
voted an anti-Semitic law:
Jews were excluded from Italian journalism + public activities
and must fork over property to the glorious Fascist State

October 22
In Astoria, NYC the first xerographic image was created
(derived from the Greek "dry" & "writing")

------------------------------ **War of the Worlds** ------------------------------
Weirdo-Entities Slithering in New Jersey

Orson Welles was 23
his troupe, the Mercury Theater

performed Howard Koch's adaptation of H. G. Wells' novel
The War of the Worlds
on CBS radio October 30

It was done as a news broadcast

There was an announcement at the beginning
that it was fiction

but the young genius Welles
knew how to make it real—
very real
At least a million listeners were terrified
Thousands prayed,
some got out their rifles
as the radio spoke of snakesque weirdo-entities slithering
out of a spaceship in a field in New Jersey:

"The eyes are black and gleam like a serpent. The mouth is V-
shaped with saliva dripping from its rimless lips that seem to quiver
and pulsate. The monster or whatever it is can hardly move ..."

The snake-blobs started eye-lasering and burning
up anyone in their path—

The broadcast verified several key aspects of psy-war:
people will believe anything, provided it's believable &
faith in the goodness of the universe
is not very deep

•

Midterm elections on November 8
Dems 261 to 168 in the House
Dems 69 to 23 Reps in the Senate

──────────────── **Kristallnacht** ────────────────

November 9 & 10
were the nights of the Broken Glass

Hitler & his death-dopes
had gone to Munich to celebrate
the 15th anniversary of

when they learned of a shooting in Paris of a German diplomat
by a young man upset over
the forced relocation of his Jewish parents.

It gave naz-vom all the excuse they needed.
Propaganda minister Joseph Goebbels
                        instructed the SS and SA to begin
                        violence against Jews

During the next 24 hours 100 Jews were killed,
many hurt, & 30,000+ were arrested
and sent to Dachau, Buchenwald and Sachsenhausen

7,500 shops and businesses were destroyed
250 synagogues burned

Many Jews were rounded up and taken to burned synagogues
                where they were beaten & forced to recite from
                                                Mein Kampf

The German people
                met the Kristall night with too much silence
rather than jubilation
so the Nazis began to hide their plans
for the total evil of what was known as
                                "die Endlösung der Judenfrage"

·

December 12
    The Japanese airforce
            sank the U.S. gunboat *Panay*
                    in China on the Yangtse River

    The *Panay* was assisting in the evacuation of
            the US Embassy
                    during the Japanese war on China

December 23
    Franco-vom offensive in Catalonia
                    to try to seize Barcelona

Rolled onto the linen,
                        & oi'd to the w.f.:
Jerry Brown, Ishmael Reed on Feb 22, Joyce Carol Oates June 16
Thomas Wolfe passed away at 37 on Sept 15

Novum in '38:
Uncle Tom's Children by Richard Wright
Jean-Paul Sartre's *Nausea*
the full *U.S.A.* by John Dos Passos
Billy the Kid Aaron Copland's ballet
Kol Nidre by Arnold Schoenberg

Our Town by Thornton Wilder
The Culture of Cities by Lewis Mumford
On the radio, *The Green Hornet*
and Kate Smith sang Irving Berlin's "God Bless America"
                        for the first time on Armistice Day

S. Beckett's great *Murphy*
Graham Greene *Brighton Rock*
Lawrence Durrell *The Black Book*
e. e. cummings *Collected Poems*
Antonin Artaud in *Le Théâtre et son Double*
            posits the "theater of cruelty"

And, from the minds of inventors:
instant coffee, fiberglass, the steam iron, the ballpoint pen
                        and Superman

Augustus John's portrait of Dylan Thomas
Jackson Pollock's *Man with a Knife*

Frank Lloyd Wright, Taliesin West in Phoenix
Sergei Prokofiev, *Romeo and Juliet*
Artie Shaw, "Begin the Beguine"

Glenn Miller formed his 2nd band,
                        and had a hit with "Moonlight Serenade."

'38 flicks:
Angels with Dirty Faces, Cagney
Alexander Nevsky by Eisenstein
Jezebel with Bette Davis
Leni Riefenstahl's *Olympiad.*

                So long, O war-drum year!
                Steeped in a crystal tear!

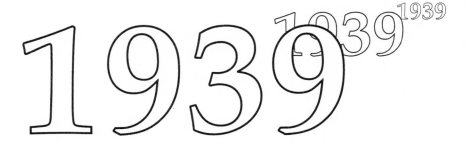

January 20
 Thirty years after he had started composing it
    Charles Ives saw his *Second Piano Sonata*
      known as the *Concord*
      in four movements,
    Emerson, Hawthorne, The Alcotts, and Thoreau

    performed at last! by John Kirkpatrick
    (it took him two years to learn it)
      at New York City's Town Hall

——————— **A Proposal for National Health Care** ———————

On January 23 President Roosevelt urged Congress
  to create a national "comprehensive health program ...
  as an essential link in our national defenses against
  individual and social insecurity."

  The great Senator Robert Wagner of New York
  introduced the National Health Act of 1939.

  The right-wing American Medical Association
  opposed it vehemently
    on the grounds it was "Socialized Medicine"

  so that this great idea failed in Congress

January 26
 The anarchist section of Barcelona fell to the right wing

February 27
    Britain and France recognized Franco's gov't
                                USA also on April 1

Feb–March
    2 million Americans were
                employed by the WPA

On March 15
    Emil Hacha, right-wing leader of Czechoslovakia
    was headed for Berlin to plead
            to Hitler not to keep stirring up trouble in Czechoslovakia
        when he was told
            we're invading you right at this
                                very instant!
        —that's the month Czechoslovakia was dismembered

    Then, March 21 Germany demanded the Free City of Danzig
            and routes "through the Polish Corridor."

            Poland said no

March 20
    further derightwingnutting of the Supreme Court as
    FDR appointed the great William O. Douglas to the Court
    This followed the January 5 appointment of
                                Felix Frankfurter

March 28
    All of Barcelona fell to right-slime
    & Francisco Franco led his
                troops into Madrid

    —The previous summer a Republican attack along the Ebro
    had failed to free Catalonia

        and the Russians pulled support, the rats,

        and soon the Spanish Republic was to fall
                                (for a few decades)

Marian at the Lincoln
March

Racist froth-heads in the Daughters of the American Revolution
refused to let the great contralto Marian Anderson
                         sing in D.C.'s Constitution Hall

Eleanor Roosevelt resigned from the DAR
and arranged for a concert on the steps
                 of the Lincoln Memorial
                    before an integrated audience of 75,000.

& ⅔ of a national Gallup poll approved Ms. Roosevelt's
                              resignation from the racists

The New York World's Fair

The NY World's Fair
            opened in Queens April 30
                    & ran through the year
       on the streamlined theme of
           "Building the World for Tomorrow"

                The World's Fair was famous for
                         its shapes & surfaces
              & the ease technology would bring
                       to the toils of the species

April 7
    Mussolini invaded Albania
    and on the 16th the Italians made it a province

    The same day Spain joined Germany, Italy and Japan
                             in the Anti-Comintern Pact.

April 14
    Roosevelt sent a telegram to Hitler & a copy to Mussolini
    asking for guarantees Germany
                would not attack a list of 31 nations

    Hitler read the list, with comments, to the Reichstag
    Herman Goering began to giggle
    and others too
            fliggle-giggling & heeze-harfing

May 23
    Th' British parliament signed off on a plan
         for an independent Palestine by '49
             Many Jews and Arabs in Palestine were not happy.

June 6
    Ghastly US bureaucrats, acting in Havana
    turned back 907 German Jewish refugees on the SS *St Louis*
        whose hearts raced wildly
             when they could see the lights of Miami
        & wept to be taken back to the insolence.
    European countries eventually took them in
        but many were captured by the Nazis in '40

    The British, to the calumny of Time,
        cut back Jewish immigration to Palestine

        & there was an assistant secretary of state
              named Breckinridge Long
        formerly an ambassador to Italy
           & friendly to fascism

    who makes me angry as I type this
    'cause I know of his insolent work in preventing
        our nation from welcoming Jews
           during Hitler's evil

    You were a disgrace, Breckinridge Long!

               •

June 28
    Pan Am began the first regular transatlantic service

June 30
    Congress, under the razory rail of the right
            abolished the great WPA Federal Theater Project

———————————— **The Black Hole & the Bomb** ————————————

J. Robert Oppenheimer
            proposed that a star larger than
            3.2 solar masses will collapse
            into a single point
                    because of its own weight
            —a thing that will later be termed a Black Hole

Also that year the American physicist, born in Hungary, Leo Szilard
observed that nuclear fission can produce a nuclear chain reaction
                        usable in a bomb

                    but, *Uh-Oh*

    German physicists Otto Hahn and F Strassman
    demonstrated nuclear fission through
                    bombarding uranium with neutrons

———————————————— **Lou Gehrig** ————————————————

For 15 seasons with the Yankees
            the great first baseman Lou Gehrig never missed a game
2,130 he played
but his health faltered in the spring

He went to the Mayo Clinic
& was diagnosed with amyotrophic lateral sclerosis
                    later called Lou Gehrig's disease

On July 4 there was a
        big celebration at Yankee Stadium to say goodbye

        in which the humbled hero
                spoke memorably, ending:
    "When everybody down to the groundskeepers and those boys in
    white coats remember you with trophies, that's something. When
    you have a father and mother who work all their lives so that you

376

can have an education and build your body, it's a blessing. When
you have a wife who has been a tower of strength and shows
more courage than you dreamed existed, that's the finest I know.
So I close in saying that I might have had a bad break, but I have
an awful lot to live for."
         —useful words for those who feel
                  the crush of an anvil in their souls.
Gehrig passed two years later

————————————— **The Letter to Roosevelt** —————————————
                          August 2

Albert Einstein dictated a letter in German
which physicist Leo Szilard
used as a source for a letter to
                    President Roosevelt
                    which Einstein signed

Einstein had a staggering renown
        & presence in the world of science.

In the letter, Einstein said,
"In the course of the last four months
it has been made probable—through the work of
Fermi and Szilard in America—that it may become
possible to set up nuclear chain reactions in a large
mass of uranium, by which
               vast amounts of power
                  … would be generated.

… It is conceivable—though much less certain—
that extremely powerful bombs of a new type
may thus be constructed."

The great physicist pointed out that
        a single uranium bomb
                might blow up a whole port.

On October 11 the letter was brought to Roosevelt
with a memo from Szilard.

It was read aloud, then Roosevelt told his secretary
General Edwin Watson,

"This requires action."

Later Albert Einstein told the great Linus Pauling,
"I made one great mistake in my life—when I signed
the letter to President Roosevelt recommending that
                                        atom bombs be made."

—————————————————— **The Hatch Act** ——————————————————
August 2

The same day that Einstein signed his letter
Roosevelt signed the so-called Hatch Act
named after Senator Carl Hatch of New Mexico

to restrict political activities by civil servants.
The law grew out of the foams of right wingers
                    against the work of the
                    Works Progress Administration

The right wanted to substitute the dole
                        for the Federal jobs of the WPA
& Roosevelt no doubt wanting to save the WPA that year
suggested Congress pass a law on political activities
                                        of Federal employees.
It did. The law proscribed any bribing or intimidation
                                by Federal officials
& now most U.S. government employees
                    could not participate in electoral politics.

A 1940 amendment prevents campaign contributions from federal
employees and extends the act to cover state and local employees in
departments receiving federal aid.

——————— **The German-Russian Nonaggression Pact** ———————

On August 23 the famous nonaggression pact
was signed by Molotov and Ribbentrop.
            It was a ten-year treaty, with a number of secret clauses

When the time came
the Germans and Soviets were to divvy up Eastern Europe,
w/ the partition of Poland and the USSR free to

wheel into the Balkan States,
Finland and Bessarabia.

The Naz-Comm deal shocked the American Left
for it augured a ghastly line-shift.
From the mid '30s onward
the CP in the USA had spent great time and energy
confronting pro-Nazi orgs such as
the Silver Shirts, the followers of Father Coughlin
& the Ku Klux Klan.

Most US Communists
reluctantly supported the line-shift
that it was necessary for the
survival of the Soviet Union

The Soviets had been unable to form alliances
for a collective defense against Naz-slime.
Plus, for instance, the Sov's were afraid
that the ruling elite in England
might actually support a Nazi
attack on Russia

Isaak Babel

Stalin-vom arrested the great Isaak Babel
author of *Red Cavalry* and *Odessa Tales*
He was taken to a labor camp where he died in '41

Thanks, Stalin.

The Invasion of Poland
August 26

That afternoon Hitler met with the English
& then the French ambassadors
in his office,
after which he walked out to an orderly and said
"Case White"

It was the signal for the invasion of Poland.
The same day he ordered the murder of all terminally ill patients

                                    to make room for wounded soldiers

There followed a few more days
                    of what they sometimes call "intense" diplomacy
while in England, children in big cities
                         began to be evacuated

Poland was certain it could stomp Germany
                              into the muck of time
even though it intended to do so
                    with the help of horses.

The invasion began with a ruse
Hit-vom staged a fake Polish raid on a German radio station
                                        on the border
It murdered some prisoners, and dressed them in Polish uniforms
            & announced on the air that Poland had invaded

A call came to Roosevelt in the middle of the night
                         telling of the attack
"It's come at last," said the President, "God help us all."

White-gloved Polish soldiers on horses
            according to a possibly spurious account
            charged the oncoming German tanks
                         for the mow-down of the millennium—
Of Poland's 1 million soldiers, the Germans captured 700k

Warsaw held out for three weeks
its radio playing Chopin's *Polonaise in A-Flat* around
the clock,
        till, nearing the end,
                it played his *Death March*.

September 3
    France declared war on Germany
    & the British Empire and Commonwealth nations
    India, Canada, New Zealand, Australia
                         declared war also

    The Conservative Neville Chamberlain formed a war cabinet
                    with Winston Churchill first lord of the admiralty

September 17
    The USSR invaded Poland from the east
                and the Polish gov't escaped into exile

The Germans handed to Stalin ⅔ of Poland
                    as per the pact of August

And then the Germans reintroduced ghettos
                              first in Łódź

October 3
    the US declared neutrality in the Euro-war

October 10
    Naz-slime began deportation
                  of Polish Jews to the Lublin reserve

October 18
    Roosevelt ordered US ports closed to subs of belligerent nations

November 4
    Roosevelt signed legislation
            for Britain and France to buy US arms
        on a "cash and carry" basis
                (amending the Neutrality Act of May 1937)

            —pay cash and carry them away
                            in your own boats

────────── **Antidote for Popculturemania** ──────────

Clement Greenberg's essay
        "Avant-garde and Kitsch"
                came out in the *Partisan Review* that fall

        in which he almost chants his disrespect for
        Kitsch "the epitome of all that is spurious
                    in the life of our times"
        Kitsch which "changes according to style but
                            remains all the same"
        Kitsch which lies to the minds of artists
                    so that they will bend under Kitsch's
                                    profit-batty pressure
        (not to mention Stalin's official Kitsch
                    which ate the soul of mad Odessa's paintbrush)
        Go read it.

The USSR invaded Finland
  which made the American non-Com left
              shudder in revulsion

Stalin had wanted to place troops in southeast Finland
        to halt any German lightning-lunge
                across the isthmus
                    to nearby Leningrad

Finland said no
  The Sovs made ghastly air strikes
          on Helsinki

    The Finns fought with cross-country ski teams
            at night
              to battle the half million Russians

On March 12, 1940 Finland signed a peace treaty forking over
              $^1/_{10}$ of its land to the Soviet Union

Novum '39:
  microfilm, little league baseball, the automatic dishwasher
      auto air conditioning
  and nylon stockings began to come to the masses

  Dichlorodiphenyltrichloroethane (DDT) was invented
      by a Swiss chemist

It was used profusely in W2
              to fumigate bedding and clothing

Coleman Hawkins' sax on "Body and Soul."

James Agee and Walker Evans, *Let Us Now Praise Famous Men*

─────────── **More Social Security!** ───────────

There were amendments to th' Soc Sec Act
w/ more workers eligible for pensions and sickness insurance
—the first payments were set for 1940 instead of '42

and some family members were now eligible for benefits

Soar, O Social Democracy, Soar!

•

More Novum '39:
   the first Food Stamps program in Rochester, NY
                        administered by the US Dept of Agriculture
   These Are Our Lives, autobiographies produced under the WPA

Linus Pauling fashioned the theory of the chemical bond

Sandburg's six volume *Abraham Lincoln* was completed
& Isaiah Berlin's *Karl Marx*

The Guggenheim Museum of Non-Objective Painting oped in NYC

Grandma Moses aka Anna Robertson
               famous immediately
                        in the "Unknown American Painters" exhibition

Béla Bartók's *String Quartet #6*
Roy Harris, *Symphony #5*

Ray Chandler's *The Big Sleep*
T.S. Eliot, *The Family Reunion* &
               Ole Possum's Book of Practical Cats
Lillian Hellman, *The Little Foxes*

and, hurray! after 17 years,
               Finnegans Wake by Joyce!
Henry Miller *Tropic of Capricorn*
John Steinbeck *The Grapes of Wrath*
Dorothy Parker *Here Lies*
James Thurber *The Secret Life of Walter Mitty*
J.R.R. Tolkien *The Hobbit*

Linen time:
   Germaine Greer January 21
         Francis Ford Coppola April 7
               Edward Sanders on August 17
                     Margaret Atwood November 18
                           Ted Koppel

Lily Tomlin
Seamus Heaney

and sad goodbyes:
Jan 28 Yeats dies at 73
June 26 Ford Madox Ford passes at 66
Sept 23 Freud
          the final *Totem and Taboo!* at 83

A bounty of movies:
*Wuthering Heights, Gone with the Wind, Mr. Chips Goes to
Washington, Of Mice and Men, Stagecoach, The Wizard of Oz*

          Yeats & Freud gone down to Dante!

And so ends Volume I of
America, A History in Verse

with Europe on fire in 1939
& the pelting to begin

in a roll of months that saw evil Kristallnacht,
the voice of the great Marian at the Lincoln,
Einstein's letter to Roosevelt on a strange new explosive,
the continuing genius of the WPA
          & its planned economy promise,
Sandburg's 6-volume study of the man in front of whom
                              the contralto sang,
the ghastly Soviet-Nazi pact & its secret dealings,
Joyce's final river at *Finnegans Wake,*
The scene of the Polish cavalry
          confronting the robot tanks,

Roosevelt wondering if the West Coast plane plants
                    could build enough fighters ...

To the many who came and went
                    on their dailies
the two big oceans would keep
                    the war-fire safely thence

but to those who paused and

added it up
it had the quality of Turgenev's *On the Eve*

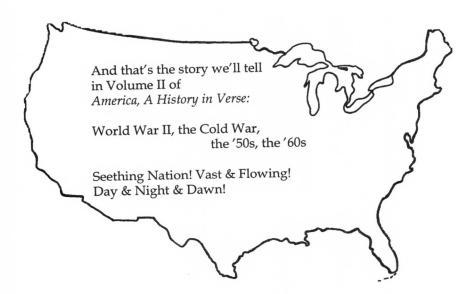

And that's the story we'll tell
in Volume II of
America, A History in Verse:

World War II, the Cold War,
                    the '50s, the '60s

Seething Nation! Vast & Flowing!
Day & Night & Dawn!

Printed February 2000 in Santa Barbara &
Ann Arbor for the Black Sparrow Press by
Mackintosh Typography & Edwards Brothers Inc.
Text set in Book Antiqua by Words Worth.
Design by Barbara Martin.
This first edition is published in paper wrappers;
there are 300 hardcover trade copies;
125 hardcover copies have been numbered & signed
by the author; & 26 copies handbound in boards
by Earle Gray are lettered & signed by the author.

PHOTO: Miriam Sanders

EDWARD SANDERS was born in Kansas City, Missouri in 1939. He studied Greek and Latin at New York University, graduating in 1964. He was associated with the underground mimeograph press movement of the 1960s, and was the founder and leader of the Fugs, a folk-rock poetry satire group that has issued many albums and CDs in their 34-year history. He ran the Peace Eye Bookstore in New York's Lower East Side from 1964 till 1970.

Sanders' 1971 book, *The Family*, the story of the Charles Manson group, remains in print in a number of countries. An updated edition appeared in 1990. Out of his researches writing *The Family* came the ideas which led to his manifesto, *Investigative Poetry*, published in 1976.

His two-volume *Tales of Beatnik Glory*, a series of interconnected stories set in the late 1950s and 1960s, was published in 1990. Volume 3 of *Tales of Beatnik Glory* has been completed, and he is at work on the 4th and final volume. A book-length celebration of Allen Ginsberg, *The Poetry & Life of Allen Ginsberg*, will be published in 2000.

Beginning in the 1990s, Sanders began bringing the concepts of *Investigative Poetry* to extended works, first to several lengthy poems, such as "Melville's Father," in the 1993 *Hymn to the Rebel Cafe*, then to the 1995 book-length biography in verse of Anton Chekhov, as well as to *1968, a History in Verse*, all published by Black Sparrow Press. *America, a History in Verse* is a further progression toward realizing the fundamental idea in *Investigative Poetry*, that poets should write history.

Sanders has received a number of awards and fellowships, including a Guggenheim Fellowship in poetry and a National Endowment for the Arts Fellowship in Poetry. His *Thirsting for Peace in a Raging Century, Selected Poems 1961–1985*, won an American Book Award. He was awarded a poetry fellowship for 1997–1998 by the Foundation for Contemporary Performing Arts, Inc. in New York City.

In the public recitals of his poetry throughout the United States and Europe, Sanders brings a mix of chanted, spoken and sung works, sometimes utilizing musical instruments of his own invention, including the Talking Tie, the Pulse Lyre, the Light Lyre, the Microlyre and the Mona Lisa Lyre.

Sanders' musical cantatas and dramas include *Star Peace* (1987), *The Karen Silkwood Cantata* (1980), and *Cassandra* (1993), all of which received theatrical productions.

He has written journalism for many publications, including *The New York Times, The Village Voice,* and *The Kansas City Star,* and is the founder and editor of the *Woodstock Journal,* a biweekly newspaper published in Woodstock, New York, where he has lived for over 25 years with his wife, the artist and writer Miriam Sanders, raising their daughter Deirdre, now an attorney.